In Beyond Aftershocks, *MavaJoyce sends a powerful message to survivors living in secrecy. She articulates the fears, shame, frustrations, and challenges experienced by many from childhood sexual assault, dispelling the myth that silence and secrecy are the best way to deal with abuse and trauma. In her triumph over adversity, she speaks for countless who have not yet found their voice. Her words and book are a gift to survivors and their loved ones.*

—Marilyn Van Derbur
Miss America By Day

Absolutely brilliant! Aftershocks *is THE book to read to comprehend our body's astounding ability to hold overwhelming trauma until the time is right to gradually release our truth to us through the magical healing power of flashbacks. We are indeed built to heal, and MavaJoyce exquisitely teaches this generic process of first surviving and then later healing trauma to return home to our true self in a way that is riveting to read. An encouraging book for all therapists and trauma survivors.*

—Sandra Felt, LCSW
Beyond the Good-Girl Jail

beyond aftershocks

Reclaiming *self* after Sexual Trauma

MavaJoyce

FOR
*the hundreds of survivors of childhood incest
who have shared this journey with me.*

Beyond Aftershocks
Reclaiming Self after Sexual Trauma
© 2020 by MavaJoyce. All rights reserved.

No part of this book may be reproduced in any written, electronic, recording, or photocopying without written permission of the publisher or author. The exception would be in the case of brief quotations where permission is specifically granted by the publisher or author.

DISCLAIMER:
This is my story, my best recollection of events that I experienced. There is no way to prove or disprove the accuracy of experiences in the distant past. Every precaution has been taken to verify the accuracy of the information contained herein; the author and publisher assume no responsibility for any errors or omissions and no liability is assumed for damage that may result from the use of the information contained within. I have changed some details and names to protect the privacy of others. I tell my story in the hope that it will be of benefit to other trauma survivors.

Book Shepherd: Judith Briles, The Book Shepherd
Editor: Peggie Ireland, Barb Wilson
Cover and Interior Design: Rebecca Finkel, F+P Graphic Design

Publisher: Golden Buckle Publishing

Library of Congress Control Number: 2019909417
ISBN trade paper: 978-1-7332098-0-9
ISBN eBook: 978-1-7332098-1-6
ISBN audio book: 978-1-7332098-2-3

Sexual Abuse | Child Abuse | Self-Help | Memoir

Printed in the USA

Contents

Author's Notes vii

CHAPTER 1   Guilt-Ridden 1

CHAPTER 2   Grief-Stricken 5

CHAPTER 3   Despondent 19

CHAPTER 4   Medicine and Myth 31

CHAPTER 5   Foreplay 41

CHAPTER 6   Breakthrough 61

CHAPTER 7   Home Sweet Home 77

CHAPTER 8   Community Encounters ... 97

CHAPTER 9   Sister Survivors 111

CHAPTER 10   Inner Child 131

CHAPTER 11   Flashes of Insight 141

CHAPTER 12   Healing Partners 151

CHAPTER 13   Family Talk 163

CHAPTER 14   Family Repercussions 183

CHAPTER 15   Relative Echoes 203

CHAPTER 16 Sparks 221

CHAPTER 17 Overload 233

CHAPTER 18 Surrender 245

CHAPTER 19 Why Am I? 263

CHAPTER 20 A Beginning 277

CHAPTER 21 Who Am I? 287

CHAPTER 22 Who Are We? 295

CHAPTER 23 Who Do I Serve? 297

CHAPTER 24 How Do I Evolve? 307

CHAPTER 25 Final Word 313

How to Work with MavaJoyce 317

Recommended Reading 319

Resources on the Web 323

Acknowledgments 328

A Story to Tell

I have a story to tell; don't know how to do it well.
> I'd like to lift my voice and shout, but don't know if it's safe to let it out.

The sordid things I've done and the dark places I've been.
> Maybe, you think acknowledging incest is a sin.

But I've faced my demons and came out stronger;
> My body doesn't ache and weep any longer.

My perps can hate me and call me crazy;
> But I will NOT be silent, isolated or lazy.

I'll speak my truth right out loud.
> I'll heal my wounds and make Little Joyce proud!

For I know, there's life to be celebrated, joy to be shared;
> My abusers will cringe when they learn that I dared;

To be all I could be, to stand up tall;
> To walk in the light and enjoy it all.

My kinfolk are mired in hate, anger and greed;

    Why would I follow their lead?

I'll sing in the sunshine and dance in the rain;

    Be grateful for love and friendships that keep me sane.

I'll not be silenced by pain and fear;

    Doesn't matter birth family, if you are far away or near.

Little Joyce and I have healed so much;

    We've heard the angels whisper and felt their touch.

Now we are one, and a new mission we've begun.

    This work is our passion, though not for fame or glory;

But for the joy we get from empowering other survivors

    To break the silence and tell their story.

—MavaJoyce

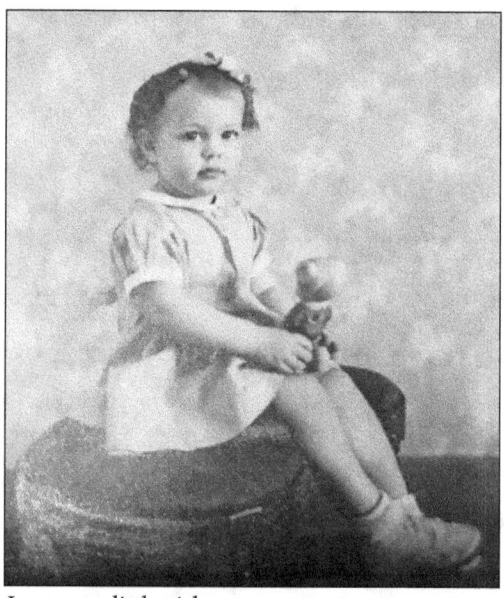

Joyce as a little girl.

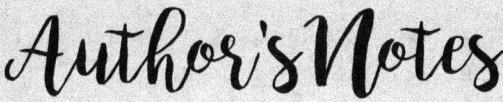

Author's Notes

*The demons in my mind and body
had become overwhelming.*

You are invited to travel on a midlife journey into my SELF—a path from people-pleasing submission to self-direction, a healing adventure from incest victim to mentor, and a spiritual walk from beliefs based on cultural expectations to an inner-directed path. In this story, you will move with me through trauma that spawned a loss of Self and a recovery that heralds a reclaimed Self.

I, MavaJoyce Kohl, entered the world in the center of the US, molded in the patriarchal culture of the Kansas breadbasket during the mid-twentieth century. From these pages, you will discover a coming-of-age story that occurred midlife rather than during teenage years. Witnessing my evolution of Self, you will grasp the dissemination of feminism and gender equality as it emerged through lived experience.

Considering my sewing history, it was logical to take the patchwork of my healing journey and stitch it into a cohesive narrative, but the pieces don't always join seamlessly.

During the five years that epitomize my healing journey and this story, I traveled thousands of miles between Kansas and Colorado. There were days when I drove four hours in the morning, had a couple of different kinds of therapy, and drove home the same day. There were times when I worked a full day at my store, Joyce's Fabric in Colby, Kansas, before driving the four hours to Colorado Springs. Sometimes I was home a week; more often, I was only home a few days. It was a time of frantically dizzying activity.

In order to avoid the whiplash of frequent back-and-forth trips, my journey reveals my path into Self as it evolved through changing relationships. Interactions with immediate family, birth family, in-laws and extended family, friends, coworkers, healers, and sister survivors would never be the same.

My therapy in Colorado was disruptive to my family and my business, as well as confusing to my Kansas friends and customers. Still, I felt compelled to continue my out-of-state therapies in order to avoid succumbing to the demons in my mind and body that had become overwhelming.

Picture a successful store owner, wife, mother, and daughter— who sees herself as responsible even though her aging parents lived at the other end of the state. A capsule view of my normal life included retail store owner, wife of a farmer (Andy Meier), and mother of teenage sons (Sam and Ben).

Through a wider lens, you would see my in-laws (Anthony and Vera Meier) who lived an hour north and my parents (Charlie and Hulda Kohl) who lived four hours east. My brothers Gene and Roger married local girls and remained near my parents. As real to me as the folks walking this earth was my Guardian Angel Elizabeth, whom I credit with guiding me through intuition.

Most holidays, Andy and I would pack up our boys and hit the road to share dinner with the Kohls. Those gatherings consisted of the women cooking, while the men watched sports on television. Still, I felt it was important for me to do everything I could to keep the family ties unbroken.

My parents traveled to our place each summer to be a part of the cherry-picking ritual. My sons Sam and Ben, with their Grandpa Charlie, picked the fruit. I manned the cherry pitter, my mother, known as Grandma Hulda, packed the cherries into bags, and Andy deposited the fruit in the freezer.

Sweltering in the Western Kansas sun, we reminisced about shared moments. Andy recalled our Canadian camping trip when my mom tried in vain to photograph a full-grown grizzly bear. The boys laughed about escapades as toddlers, when Grandpa Charlie let them drive the little Ford tractor on his farm. Hikes to the pond in Grandpa's pasture led to fishing stories where fiction mingled with fact. Happy times traveling and celebrating holidays stirred up poignant memories as surely as the White Mountain freezer churned up maple-nut ice cream.

That is one story.

In your hands, is a different story.

This … is my story.

1

Guilt-Ridden

*An icy chill crawled up my legs,
over my back and stuck in my heart.*

Before and after thinking is as natural as inhale and exhale. It's as ancient as identifying history with BC or AD and it's as current as today. Our minds position experience as it relates to some significant event. Over a lifetime, the defining moment is a moving target and eventually those targets chart the trajectory of our life path.

The conundrum for me was what to choose as my defining moment. In younger years, they were occasions—graduations, weddings, and career changes. That was before my fifties when a trio of tragedies converged to topple my world. The first of these three misfortunes left me guilt-ridden, the second grief-stricken and the third despondent.

It was an ordinary day in 1989. The sun had settled in the west and I looked forward to an evening sewing in the downstairs family room. Assembling a quilt was respite from the tensions of managing my fabric shop. I sat at the sewing machine surveying stacks of quilt squares. Layering a soft azure print against navy starbursts, I began stitching blocks into a Trip Around the World pattern. The hum of the sewing machine dulled the dialogue coming from the television.

Thirteen-year-old Ben lounged in a beanbag, intent on the action of *Miami Vice*. The music escalated—punctuated by squealing tires, blaring sirens and people screaming. I jabbed my finger with a pin intended for fabric; I hated loud noises, high drama, and fast action programs.

Abruptly, the noise stopped, and I heard, "What! What the fuck?"

> **The F-bomb circled through my head—like the repetitive whistle of a night train.**

My composure unraveled. I hurled a quilt book toward the beanbag that cradled my son. Vaulting out of my chair, which spun on its pedestal behind me, I lunged toward Ben and grabbed his hair. He jumped up and pushed me away. I drew back my hand and aimed for his face. He caught my arm, deflecting the slap. I kicked with blind abandon and scraped my fingernails down his arm, leaving red tracks.

Ben pulled down on my arms, forcing me to my knees. My breath came in spurts. Tears burned my cheeks. Foggy awareness morphed into shock.

"Mom, what's wrong with you? You act like you're scared to death!"

When he released my arms, I pulled my legs to my chest, feeling small and condemned. Ben bound up the stairs two at a time. The thud of the back door confirmed his exit.

I'd never fought anyone like that before! I wailed—childish, hopeless cries. Flailing at the beanbag like a two-year old in tantrum mode, I kicked until my toes ached. Exhausted, my rage turned to shame.

I struggled with recall. Ben said I had acted scared. My gut felt strangled; my knees were shaky. The F-bomb circled through my head—like the repetitive whistle of a night train. Could that have been what set me off? The crude F-word had always angered me but had never enraged me before. Only a lunatic would attack her son the way I had, fighting like a frantic little kid. What must this son I love be thinking of me now?

> **A timid voice within seemed to plead *listen ... to ... me.***

Desperate, I scanned the room for something to relieve my anguish. My gaze settled on a mirrored shadow box. Like my thoughts, the image in the mirror was blurred. A timid voice within seemed to plead "*listen ... to ... me,*" luring me toward an elusive part of myself crouched beneath dark shadows. An icy chill crawled up my legs, over my back and stuck in my heart.

In a split second, an ordinary day had been transformed into a crisis sandwiched between fear and shame—spread with a thick layer of confusion. That was my first invitation to take a serious look at the ageless question:

Who am I?

An unexamined life isn't worth living.
—SOCRATES

2
Grief-Stricken

I sucked in air; my belly stiffened.
My brother never phoned me.

Ben's question, "What's wrong with you?" repeated in my mind as days and weeks flew by. What kind of monster had invaded me in that moment? It seemed that Ben had forgotten about it; maybe I should, too. Forgetting would be in line with my mother's mantra: *We only remember the good.* For nearly fifty years, I'd been pushing through life, caught up in work, sometimes sucked into crisis, with little time or patience for ruminating.

Nearing the end of 1989, I looked forward to the holidays when our family of four would spend quiet times together. Ben would have a two-week break from middle school; Sam, our older son, would be home from university. And hubby Andy, wouldn't be needed at the farm.

Once into January of 1990, I breathed a sigh of relief that the holidays were over and store inventory had been completed. I looked forward to fewer demands on my time at the store I'd owned and managed for decades. Glancing out my store window while I was working on a fabric display, I saw my tall and lanky husband striding toward me.

"Hi, Honey. I expected you back on Friday. This is Wednesday. I'm confused."

"Yes, that was the plan." Andy said. "But I finished work at the farm early, so I've come home to service your sewing machines—maybe even prepare for your big birthday celebration."

After enjoying lunch together, we settled into tasks in the repair room. He began to dismantle a sewing machine and I inventoried ones still needing attention.

When the phone rang, I gave my standard greeting: "Joyce's Fabric, how may I help?"

"Joyce, this is Roger."

I sucked in air; my belly stiffened. My brother never phoned me. We were separated by more than 200 miles and by vastly differing opinions.

"Are you … alone?" Roger asked.

Something in his voice sounded different. My fingers curled firmer around the receiver. "No. I have clerks working the sales floor."

"Is Andy there?"

Now I understood. He wanted to talk to my husband about our parents' land in Western Kansas. Although Dad believed in me enough to appoint me trustee, my brothers considered me inept. They preferred to speak with Andy when they had concerns about the trust.

"Yes. I'll call him." I motioned to Andy.

I heard Roger sigh, and then say, "Joyce, it's Dad. About two this afternoon he collapsed at the courthouse, buying car tags. A massive heart attack … he's … we're at the hospital. But Dad isn't conscious."

I dropped the receiver and heard it bang against the metal shelves as my knees buckled and my body slid to the floor.

Andy grabbed the phone and spoke briefly with Roger. Then he knelt over me, brushing my hair from my eyes. "Roger says we shouldn't come tonight. Charlie isn't going to come out of this."

Desperate to block out reality, my hands flew to my face. "Why? Why my dad?"

"All four of our folks are old. We've been expecting this." He spoke softly.

"But why was Dad first?" Arms circling my knees, I began to rock, soothing the twist in my gut, and the tourniquet that squeezed against my heart.

Andy, ever practical, said, "What has to be done before we leave? Do you have a work schedule for the help? Roger said there's no chance he will live the four hours it would take us to drive there tonight. We'll leave in the morning."

"I'm not going."

"Of course, you are; you have to go."

I shook my head. "No. Don't make me go."

Andy stood and pulled me to my feet. "Don't do this, Joyce. It's your dad. You have to be there." Andy leaned against the repair bench and glared at me.

"I'm not going."

"Be reasonable, for Christ's sake. You have to go to your father's funeral." He spoke with authority—authority underscored by his six-foot stature.

"No. I don't." Grabbing my coat, I pushed through the front door, welcoming the biting wind.

Once home, I dropped onto the sofa and just stared—seeing nothing. Then I heard the garage door.

Andy called from the kitchen, "Have you talked to Ben?"

"No," I said, relieved my husband was home.

A few minutes later, Ben and Andy came into the living room. Ben gazed down at me—furrows above his blue eyes.

Andy spoke first. "I'll set out some leftovers for supper."

Ben slipped in beside me and snuggled his head onto my shoulder. "I'm so sorry, Mom."

"Thanks, Ben. Go eat with your dad. Then you can pack. I don't need to pack; I'm not going."

Ben squeezed my hand. "Grandpa would want you there, Mom. You know you're his favorite. You always could talk him into things he wouldn't do for anybody else."

About midnight, I woke up on the sofa, feeling disoriented. Remembering Roger's telephone call with his surreal message, my resolve weakened. I would go to my father's funeral. Gathering a few essentials, I threw my bag into the car before crawling into bed. Andy didn't stir.

On the road that morning, Ben chatted about school with Andy. Sitting sideways in the back with my feet up on the seat, I watched rolling hills and bare winter fields speed by and thought of all the years Dad had tilled the land homesteaded by our ancestors. Memories of the century old, two-story farmhouse where I grew up came to mind. I pictured the house dwarfed by the tall red barn behind the twirling windmill. But we wouldn't be gathering at the farm. A few years earlier, my parents left the farm that had been handed down through the family for generations and moved to the small town of Prairie Center. In 1882, my ancestors acquired a quarter section of land from the Union Pacific Railroad and joined their pioneering neighbors to settle a community where they lived out the American dream. They worked sunup to sundown, grateful that they could. Frugal living and the Protestant work ethic were integral elements of my heritage.

Surely the calculator in my head had misfired.

The four-hour trip passed quickly. Andy and Ben insisted that I cross the threshold first. Conversation stopped. A profusion of condolences broke the awkward silence. Mother stepped in from the kitchen, her lips pursed, lower on the left, in that familiar expression I recognized as determined, resigned, and non-negotiable.

Her voice steady, she said, "This is going to be hard for you, Joyce."

I managed to whisper, "And for you, too."

I thought my brothers acted like robots performing on the command of an invisible joystick. Roger spewed out the schedule. He'd agreed to a 1:30 p.m. appointment at the funeral home. The minister would meet us at the house an hour later.

"Mizpah Church has been reserved," Roger said. "All the arrangements have been made for a service at ten tomorrow."

"Tomorrow morning? Only a day and a half after …" I stopped. Surely the calculator in my head had misfired.

Roger leaned toward me and explained, "I know it's soon, Sis." But it's the best day for the service. All the grandkids can be here."

"All? Don't know about that. Our eldest son hasn't been notified."

Andy headed toward the kitchen telephone. "I'll call Sam. He'll need to drive in from Manhattan, Kansas, tonight."

Roger's wife came into the room carrying a decorated coffee cup. Faye, as slim as Roger was heavy, bore a firm countenance that mirrored her husband's. She thrust the token toward me.

The cup felt as heavy as cast iron. Curled blue and yellow ribbons spilled over the rim. Opposite the handle was a spattering of bright yellow daisies framing the words "Fabulous Fifty."

"Happy fiftieth birthday, Joyce. Sorry it has to be this way." Faye's smile faded.

A coffee cup was supposed to make this okay? In fifty years, I'd never finished a cup of coffee. Hadn't anyone noticed I drank tea? I couldn't feign I wanted the cup any more than I could pretend to like the day they chose for Dad's funeral. I sank into a chair next to a floral spray of blue and white carnations, draped with gold metallic ribbon bearing the words *Charlie's Family*.

My brother Gene moved toward the door, beckoning me to follow. "It's time to go to the funeral home, or we'll be late getting back to meet the minister."

Eight years my senior, Gene was accustomed to family members complying with his wishes. Farmer Gene wore his vocation on his back, his uniform a blue plaid shirt under gray-striped bib overalls. Outdoors or inside the house, he wore a seed company hat on his bald head.

"You boys choose the casket. I'll stay here."

"But we waited for you. You have to come," Gene said.

I sensed a tinge of tenderness in Gene's urging and acquiesced. We hurried through the rows of caskets at the mortuary, settling on a gray one lined with tufts of blue silk. I excused myself from negotiating for the steel vault, the most insane aspect of the burial process for me. I believed in dust to dust.

Upon returning, we found Mother already visiting with the minister. After introductions, she slipped away. Gene gave a nod and Roger took charge. Though Gene's gaze was solemn, there was softness in his sky-blue eyes. He looked so much like my beloved father, the father I would never see again, that I couldn't hold back tears.

The minister finished reviewing the homily and asked about music. Looking directly at me, Roger said, "There won't be any solos, just congregation hymns. You choose those, Joyce." I was stunned. A decade earlier when my parents celebrated their fiftieth anniversary, Dad had asked Sam to sing at their celebration. Dad and Mom had often traveled to our home in Colby to attend Sam's and Ben's vocal concerts. Although I believed Dad would have wanted my sons to sing at his service, I didn't have the stomach to argue. I selected "Blest Be the Tie That Binds," "How Great Thou Art" and "Sweet Hour of Prayer."

Neighbor ladies set up a buffet as soon as the minister left. Pitiful glances in my direction made me cringe. Clearly, my grieving embarrassed others, so I excused myself. Andy followed.

Faye appeared close behind Andy, her voice stern. "Get ahold of yourself, Joyce. You can't let your mother see you like this. She's held up great. Don't you get her started!"

Gulping air, I said, "You can't tell me when to cry, Faye. This isn't about holding up. This is about an empty chair."

"Well, I never …" She stomped into the hall.

Andy held me. "It's okay to cry, honey. I know you and your dad had a special bond. Our boys loved him, too. All of us will miss Charlie."

During respect calls at the mortuary that evening, Mother chose a chair near the front of the room to receive condolences. Standing nearby, Gene and Roger greeted guests. I grieved alone in a secluded chair near the ladies' room. When the ritual was over, my brothers left for their homes. Andy drove Mother, Ben, and me to her house. Waiting for Sam to arrive, Andy and I sat at the kitchen table trying to make sense of the day's events.

Andy asked, "Why haven't we heard what your mother wants? She seems to defer to Roger for everything. What's that about?"

"I have no idea. And why is the service on Friday morning, less than forty-eight hours after Dad's death? If held on Saturday, more folks could attend."

"Those decisions must have been made last night. Nothing appears negotiable now. Looks like you have to live with saying goodbye to your dad on your birthday."

We awoke to a howling wind on Friday morning. A crippling winter storm had settled in during the night. Dense fog cloaked the funeral procession as family members and friends drove the twelve miles from Prairie Center to the rural church. A thick haze blurred the hedges bordering the road. Shimmering black ice reflected off the pavement, mirroring the melancholy that united us. I sat like a mannequin beside Andy. Sam and Ben rode silently in the back seat, all of us drawn into an ominous alliance by storm and grief.

Mizpah, the little one-room church where I'd worshiped as a child, still stood at the top of the hill, but the setting had changed. The cedar hedge that once bordered the parking lot to break the Kansas wind was gone. The steeple and bell had been removed from the roof and placed near the front entry, standing like a towering tombstone. With stucco crumbling to sand at its base, the century-old building looked bare and wanting.

The undertaker directed the protocol for the service. He ushered Sam and Ben to the front row reserved for pallbearers. Mother sat between my brothers with their wives; Andy and I sat at the far end of the pew. Andy held the hymnal and sang. His eyes pleaded with me to sing the songs he knew I loved. I couldn't. I sat erect, ignoring tears too profuse to catch.

After the service, we walked through brutal wind to the adjacent cemetery—men gripping their hats and women clutching their coats. My left leg was numb from sitting through the service. Andy put his strong arm under mine and supported me on the short walk to the ceremonial tent beside the open grave. For the burial ritual, I sat weeping beside my dry-eyed mother. Bitter-cold sleet whipped through the tent's open sides. Wind gusts tore apart the floral arrangement on the casket, scattering rose petals and wheat heads into the mist. The minister hurried through the dust-to-dust homily.

Relieved to have the graveside ceremony over, we gathered in the church basement for more rituals—clasping paper plates with cardboard sandwiches and lime Jell-O. The mortician, a high school classmate of mine, took my hand in both of his. Gently rocking my hand side to side, he said, "It's okay to grieve. It will get easier with time. I promise."

My head split off in a spin, mimicking the sway of my hands. I locked my knees, determined not to let the dizzies land me on the floor.

Folks mingled after lunch. I felt as if marionettes were hovering all around me, playing a game I didn't understand. High-pitched nervous chatter was softened by guarded chuckles and punctuated by an occasional throaty roar. Shoestring relatives introduced themselves. Some folks snapped photos. Dad's neighbors, strangers to me now, filed by, shaking hands and uttering condolences. All the while, I resisted giving voice to my thought: *I just want out of here.*

> **"It's okay to grieve. It will get easier with time. I promise."**

Driving back to Prairie Center, Andy said, "The little church hasn't changed much since we were married there twenty-nine years ago."

"It seemed different to me … the piano, the altar, even the steeple standing on the ground instead of on the roof. What did you think about the service?"

"Your mother came through it really well."

"Do you think she'll feel something later? How could she go through the entire day so serene and composed?"

"From what I've seen, that's what's expected of her. Remember, Faye told you last night not to get her started crying. What I don't understand is why she stayed in the background, leaving all decision-making to Roger and Gene. Was she drugged up?"

"I'm pretty certain she didn't take any meds," I said.

Sam said, "As I remember, Grandma Hulda usually let her opinions be known."

Ben leaned forward. "We don't know what took place Wednesday night. Maybe she voiced her opinions then."

I shook my head. "What's hard for me to admit is that her steps are spryer than mine and her spirits are better, too."

"Oh, Mom," Ben said, giving my shoulder a gentle squeeze, "this has been an awful way for you to spend your fiftieth birthday."

I nodded in agreement.

As we approached Mother's house, Sam said, "I'll step inside and bid my farewells. I need to get back to campus."

Secretly, I wanted to leave, too. As other folks left Mom's house and only siblings remained, Roger asked Mom if she'd thought about when she wanted to go to the Social Security Office.

Mom answered quickly. "I was hoping Joyce could stay and help with that. There's other chores we'll need to do: write thank-you notes, take Charlie's clothes to charity, all those things."

Andy spoke before I could think. "Ben and I will go home tomorrow, and I'll come back later to get Joyce."

Instead of protesting that I really didn't want to stay, I went to bed resigned. The time for mourning was over. Tomorrow we'd get to work.

We awoke to sun streaming through the window on Saturday. In vivid contrast to Friday's storm, Saturday was a balmy winter day. Toward evening Andy and I walked around the neighborhood.

Gazing at the setting sun, I asked, "Do you think The Man Upstairs is telling us that this would have been a better day for Dad's funeral?"

Andy nodded.

"This has been a strange experience for me. I shouldn't feel like an outsider, but I do."

"You have to realize that your brothers have lived in this community their entire lives. They married local girls, so they have friends and relatives close by to support them."

"I don't understand how they can be so calm and unflappable. I feel like I've lost my best friend," I said.

"Remember, Joyce, your support system is in Colby, not here." Andy said.

"I feel like I'm on an island watching the masses mingle on the mainland."

Andy slowed his step. "I saw some folks reaching out to you at the church."

I shook my head. "Maybe so, but even when natives offered condolences, I felt estranged. It's as though a barrier cropped up between me and this place I used to call home."

> **No one ever told me that grief felt so like fear.**
> —C. S. LEWIS

3

Despondent

Joyce, I know you are tired, and I understand you are in pain. And when you are finally sick and tired of being sick and tired, you'll do something about what's making you sick and tired.

Andy came for me after I spent a week helping Mother. Returning home, our first social event was to join friends who'd postponed my birthday celebration. Even cocooned in a corner of the Country Club with close friends, I dabbed silent tears.

Dad was my rock, my guide, my guardian. It wasn't just that he taught me to drive a tricycle, a horse, and a car. And it wasn't merely that he taught me to love words by the way he recited Longfellow, Robert Frost, and Edgar A. Guest. It was more that he pulled me out of the mud when my overshoes got stuck. And he gently lowered me to the ground when I climbed up the windmill and became frightened by the height.

Mom regularly took me to church, but Dad led me into the practice of faith when he said: *Any man can plant a crop, but only God can make it grow.* Mom sent me to piano lessons until I could play hymns to accompany her when she sang. Dad taught me to sing while we went about our farm chores. Three songs were my favs: "Me and My Shadow," "I Want a Girl," and "My Blue Heaven." Mom instructed me that *women must do what men want.* Dad made me want to do anything that would please him.

> My attachment to my father was so great that his passing impacted my life daily—confounding everyone around me.

My attachment to my father was so great that his passing impacted my life daily—confounding everyone around me. I began to lose interest in running Joyce's Fabric, the business that had monopolized my life for decades. Tears poured out without warning or explanation. I found excuses to isolate myself in the office or to go home and escape from interacting with customers.

To understand the profound impact of my instability, it's important to know a little about how I handled life prior to my dad's death. In addition to supervising staff and sales at my store, I oversaw promotions and advertising. Weekly I wrote and presented ads for radio and TV and recorded public service radio programs. Additionally, I was the go-to salesperson for sewing machines. In a town of 5,000, we outsold dealers in the biggest Kansas towns, earning several trips to the factory in Husqvarna, Sweden. My new owner sewing machine classes supported our machine sales and garnered sales of accessories and fabrics. All buying decisions were my responsibility. The store was open seven days a week and one evening—with some classes outside regular hours. Rarely was the store open unless I was there.

That all changed after Dad's passing.

As for family relationships, my husband spent a great deal of time at the farm seventy miles away where we maintained a second residence. He was heavily involved in family farming operations with his brother and parents. Andy returned home on weekends to attend church and participate in Monday evening school board meetings. At the store, he oversaw sewing machine repair. His commitment to farming left me in charge of household operations and parenting fourteen-year-old Ben. Sam was entrenched in university life at Manhattan, Kansas, rapidly shedding parental influence.

On reviewing our travel plans for our February biannual buying trip to New York, I realized that I had scheduled a four-day trip, instead of the usual seven-day one that allowed time for museums and plays. I couldn't remember any reason why I had planned a shorter trip. Premonition or luck? My usual enthusiasm for shopping suppliers waned, but we got the job done. On the plane returning from New York, I scribbled notes for a newsletter. Glancing around the cabin, I saw idle people staring into space looking bored, reading books, or napping. How did folks have time to take up space and do nothing? My time was filled with frenzied planning or rehashing the past so I could improve on it.

My life—where I lived and worked and defined my existence—seemed dismal after Dad's exit. I operated like a displaced person. Not only did his absence invade my thoughts, but my self-control mutated in ways I didn't understand. It wasn't a subtle change, and I grew weary of hearing "time heals."

Ben's confirmation in April was the first family festivity without my dad. Confirmation, due to Andy's Lutheran roots, was a major event that required an extended family gathering. Seeking to involve Ben's artistic skills, I asked him to design a banner to be hung in the sanctuary. Creating with Ben was like basking in the sunshine after rain. Everything else—daily pressures of work, recurring pain and lingering grief—shrunk from importance. I was relieved that Ben seemed to have forgotten my attack on him a few months earlier. White and gold metallic accents on a red satin banner provided a stunning backdrop for confirmation photographs. My mother and all the Meiers came for the traditional church ceremony and family feast.

Much to Andy's disgust, my grief didn't abate. Most days I went to the fabric store, but my hours were shorter. As summer approached, I started doing more management tasks from home. Throughout the spring, I fought recurring bladder infections, with pain that caused me to curl up into a ball. Dr. Ted finally insisted I consult with a visiting ob-gyn. After a scope revealed no kidney abnormalities, the specialist recommended a daily antibiotic as a preventative with biannual scopes to monitor the elusive ailment.

Andy and I helped with three summer wedding receptions, tallying to fifteen the number of festivities we'd hosted since we started Joyce's Fabric. Table linens, silver service, and leading the wedding march were all part of the amenities we provided.

The rest of the summer we resumed normal routines with Andy at the farm, Ben at tennis and swim camps, and Sam at summer school. Because of my diminished stamina, we sharply curtailed the number of county fair booths where we sold sewing machines. Our record high was seven fairs in two weeks in 1987; our record low was two fairs in summer of 1990.

I phoned Mom weekly, worried about her first year as a widow. She seemed especially melancholy in August. She regretted not being able to travel as a widow. Feeling responsible for her happiness, I offered to take her on an excursion at least once a year. We sandwiched my trip with Mother between an August New York buying trip and a September Viking sewing machine convention. Mother was an able tourist; she just needed me to navigate airports.

Upon returning home, my District Representative convinced me to enter a contest for Viking Sewing Machine dealers. Winner would receive a $5,000 sewing machine. Distracted by pain and numbness in my left leg, I wasn't confident I could do a credible demonstration, but our Viking Rep disagreed. "Come on, Joyce, give it a try. A few years ago, the company got great reviews when you traveled the country teaching new dealers how to sell."

With little enthusiasm, I agreed to let the Viking Rep make the video. Andy seemed pleased when I came in second in the country, receiving a $500 check.

"Your award will boost the store coffers," Andy said. "Our bottom line has dropped with all of your health problems. You need to spend more time at the store, demonstrating machines and teaching classes."

I hated being reminded of the profits or lack thereof, but I was aware that Andy kept a keen eye on profits. Although I wished I could have spent my $500 on something personal, I didn't protest.

A variety of new physical symptoms had crept into my daily life—draining my energy, my effectiveness, and my enthusiasm. After decades of never seeing a physician, I was plagued with anemia, hypoglycemia, urinary tract infections (UTIs), swollen lymph glands, and relentless leg/hip pain.

On a visit to our family physician, Dr. Ted was particularly adamant that I needed to slow down. "Now don't be doing anything stupid these next few days. I don't want to hear that you've fallen off a ladder again."

"I don't think that will happen. We've finished painting the house."

"What? You know damn well you don't have any business painting the outside of your house. If your husband doesn't have time for that job, hire a frickin' painter!"

I was silent. Ted didn't understand that all Meiers—me included—were do-it-yourselfers.

Dr. Ted sat on a stool facing me with a penetrating gaze that defied discussion, and said, "Joyce, I know you are tired, and I understand you are in pain. And when you are finally sick and tired of being sick and tired, you'll do something about what's making you sick and tired."

> **I so wanted my pain to go away that I lied to others and myself.**

CHAPTER THREE: Despondent   25

As the months passed, Dr. Ted referred me to several specialists for my elusive illnesses. In our little town, we only had primary care physicians. Specialists came monthly from Denver or Colorado Springs. Each minor discomfort that appeared in my body seemed to develop into a major impediment. I felt like a hypochondriac as I grappled with symptoms the doctors couldn't diagnose.

We traveled to Denver twice to consult with orthopedic specialists about my leg numbness. Andy was distraught and I was disappointed when the radiologist reported that the MRI scan suggested "discogenic disease but no clear nerve root entrapment." I didn't understand his lingo, however, I acquiesced when he recommended an epidural steroid injection.

I wished I hadn't, it wasn't effective. I so wanted my pain to go away that I lied to others and myself. My practiced smile faded, but it surfaced enough to convince friends and family that I was doing better. Sitting was more painful after the epidural. Someone else drove on long trips and I knelt or stood to teach classes.

January of 1991, when the steroid injection failed to bring relief, I gave in to the urging of my in-laws to consult a local chiropractor. Initially, manipulation of my bones was weird. I felt better about that decision when I learned that some chiropractic treatments included ultrasound and hot/cold packs, like physical therapy (PT). Naming my aches and pains to new providers was humiliating. After the third chiropractor failed to relieve my pain, I gave up on them and returned to the therapies that had kept me moving the past two years: PT and water aerobics.

Undeniable fatigue appeared as another disturbing symptom in the spring of 1991. An obscure magnetism kept pulling me downward into a progressive paralysis of body and spirit. I couldn't figure out how to halt that spiral—sometimes crawling, sometimes spinning —always descending.

Andy was increasingly frustrated with my problems. "Sometimes I think Ted is sending you to visit specialists just to keep them busy."

"Oh please, Andy. The last thing I want is to be pegged a hypochondriac, like my mom."

I was determined to never become an eternal complainer. All my life, I'd listened to Mother bemoan her sad plight. You couldn't accuse her of being a whiner. She declared her victimhood with steadfast resolve that defied argument.

Andy wasn't ready to let the issue rest. "You've scheduled an upper GI test, a D&C and a Denver trip to the orthopedic clinic in June. We could be in wheat harvest and you're needed here."

Andy relented after I explained that each procedure was outpatient and I wouldn't miss much work. Sam would be coming home to help after his June graduation. That presented another frustration. Andy was distraught that Sam hadn't found employment before he graduated.

Sam drove me to Denver to see the physician who had ordered the steroid injection six months earlier. The doctor looked perplexed when I reported my pain was worse. "I'm sorry to hear that. At this time, I don't believe there is anything else I can do for you."

He picked up a cane and lowered his gaze. "I suggest you go home and get yourself one of these. A cane can prevent a fall when your left leg is not reliable support."

I clamped my fist around the crook of the cane and took a step. Synchronizing the swing of the cane with my stride felt as awkward as walking on black ice. And at that moment, I feared my fate was to be forever crippled.

As I slowly walked into the waiting room, Sam asked, "What's going on?"

Stiffening my stance and trying to appear resolute, I repeated the doctor's instructions.

"That's no way to treat a patient. I'll give that jerk a piece of my mind." Sam headed toward the treatment room.

I stopped Sam with assurance that a cane could prove helpful. Afterward, I had second thoughts. Had I discounted my son's need to intervene? At what point is it appropriate to let our children step in and speak for us? Was my health and my judgment that impaired?

I gradually depended on the cane for support and eventually welcomed it as my sturdy companion.

At one of Ben's swim competitions in June of '91, a former sewing student urged me to consult a chiropractor in Colorado Springs. Her husband had recovered from auto accident injuries with Dr. Carter's work. When I talked with Andy about this prospect, he reminded me that Dr. Ted was concerned about lumps on my neck and had recommended a biopsy if they didn't disappear in a month.

At my July appointment, Dr. Ted reexamined my neck with more than usual concern. The seven swollen lumps, all much larger than the three in June, were too large for him to lance in the office. I would need to see a surgeon.

"You aren't going to fart around with this. I've scheduled you with the hospital surgeon tomorrow at 5:00 a.m. I don't want to hear that you're too damn busy."

Ted didn't sugarcoat anything. His brusque manner and four-letter words were typical farmer talk to me. At a young age, I learned to extrapolate messages shrouded in expletives.

After I agreed, Ted asked about Sam and Ben. His affable side surfaced when he inquired about our boys.

"Don't worry about Sam," Ted said. "He's a sharp kid; he'll get a job."

Driving home, I realized the message from my doctor was bigger than his words. I mulled over Ted's reaction to the lumps. My complaints of pain and numbness had never aroused such immediate action. I believed the nodes on my neck were minor compared to my pain malaise.

The biopsy took only minutes, and unlike the epidural injection last December, there was no pain. An eerie calmness settled over me during the procedure—as if I were watching someone else under a scalpel. In the silence, I felt a presence and sensed a phantom whispering reassurance. My mind drifted to other times I'd felt that presence. I called it my Guardian Angel Elizabeth. It had been years since I had heard from her, but her presence was palpable now and her message reassuring.

Andy had breakfast ready when I returned home. The concern clouding his blue eyes and the tenderness of his embrace surprised me. I didn't try to explain why I was calm; I had no valid reason to be confident.

The lab results arrived in a couple weeks. The report stated that there was no evidence of malignancy, but the growth was so irregular as to prevent a benign diagnosis. So, my tissues were sent to another lab for further study. Five weeks later, the clinic phoned to schedule an appointment where I would learn the results of the second lab report.

Dr. Ted waved papers as he entered the exam room. "Good news. The cells were benign."

"That's great," I said. "I have to admit, I'm not surprised."

"Maybe you aren't, but I am." Uncharacteristically solemn, Doc looked down at the floor, then back up at me. "I've had three patients with nodes like yours in the past six months. You are the only one still breathing."

Intuition is our emotional GPS.
—OPRAH

4

Medicine and Myth

You appear to be surviving on sheer willpower.

The ever-present Western Kansas wind whistled gently through the elm trees as I left the clinic. At home, Andy looked up from reading the *Colby Free Press*. "Looks like you have good news."

"Yes, the cells were benign."

"You knew your body. Now you can schedule the Colorado Springs doctor."

"Since we already have reservations to shop New York in August, I could go to the Springs after our buying trip."

Before we went to New York, we sent Sam off to Las Vegas for his new job as an electrical engineer. Ben traveled with us to NYC.

We added sightseeing to the buying trip—cruised the harbor, went to Les Misérables on Broadway, visited the Met, and binged on cheesecake.

A week in New York lifted our spirits, replenished our store shelves, and lightened our bank account. After that trip, Andy and Ben returned to Kansas and I settled into the travel trailer we'd moved to Woodland Park, Colorado, a short drive west of Colorado Springs.

In addition to business resources, I'd packed a book on pain management given to me by my RN friend who had assured me the book, written by a UCLA pain clinic physician, contained credible information. The first day in the trailer I skimmed the book jacket, not convinced it was worth reading. I hadn't read a book in years, though I used to devour novels. During my teaching career, I used to read far into the night finishing a book the day I started it. Now, I only read business resources and news releases from suppliers.

Andy phoned often, wondering what I was doing—if I was lonely. I couldn't understand why he asked. I was never lonely or bored. When he asked about the pain book, I told him it was more a self-help manual than the anatomy primer I'd expected—even admitted that I didn't see how writing about my pain could alleviate it. Andy changed the subject to how much progress I'd made on writing a store newsletter and detailing a sewing machine promotion.

I saw Michael Carter, Doctor of Chiropractic (DC), in the Springs. He was soft spoken and very tall—taller than my 6'2" husband. Intent on his work, he rarely smiled. His touch was gentle, and he explained in advance what he intended to do and why. This chiropractor worked vastly different from the Kansas ones I'd seen. He didn't rush right in with a snap, crackle, and pop. Although his first treatment left me light-headed, I scheduled two more appointments that week, hoping a quick series would alleviate my pain.

Dr. Carter explained, "You have so many shorted-out circuits, you can't have any energy left for working. You appear to be surviving on sheer willpower. Energy that should be available for working is being used up in the short circuits. Any effort you put forth comes from dogged determination, not from a normal energy supply."

Mulling over just what "shorted-out circuits" meant, I happened to attend a Sunday sermon entitled "What are you running on?" at the Lutheran church in Woodland Park. That coincidence of two short circuit messages served as a catalyst for me to search deeper for the source of my pain.

I decided to look for answers by delving into the regimen recommended in the pain book. Between doctor visits, I read Dr. David Bressler's book, *Free Yourself from Pain*, and was fascinated by his unique approach to managing pain. Soon I was treating it like a Bible and studying the text. I kept a food and comfort journal and taped scripts for "progressive relaxation" on the recorder I'd brought with me for taping PBS radio programs. Following instructions to relax felt awkward. Still, I heeded the inner voice that compelled me to follow the advice in the book. Although the assignments seemed quirky, I wrote letters to and from my discomfort and drew a picture of my pain at its worst.

> **Any effort you put forth comes from dogged determination, not from a normal energy supply.**

After marginal relief from the first week with Dr. Carter, Andy agreed I could continue the treatments through the end of the year, so I scheduled a series of appointments with breaks that allowed me to return home to supervise store employees and teach sewing machine classes. After my first week in Colorado, I returned to Colby. My first day home, I worked at the store and then saw Dr. Ted. I was disappointed to learn I still tested anemic. Three months of iron supplements hadn't been enough.

After my doctor visit, we drove 230 miles east to celebrate Mother's eightieth birthday. The next morning, we stripped her stained wallpaper and painted the basement walls a soft blue with the help of my brother Gene and his wife Carrie. After setting up the redecorated room to be Mother's sewing area, we discovered boxes of home-canned treasures—jars of fruit, fermented and rank. The smelly fruit had seeped through the rims and touching the jars felt creepy—as if they were a harbinger of something ominous. We managed to slip the spoiled fruit into the outdoor trash can without embarrassing Mother, who prided herself in cleanliness and frugal living.

Whatever the barrier was that isolated me six months ago at my father's funeral hovered over Mother's birthday celebration. Again, I felt isolated.

Returning home after the Saturday noon meal was a relief. I could ice my aching left leg and not have to pretend that all was well. Instead of resting after church on Sunday, I did intake of the merchandise we'd ordered on our New York trip. Lifting dozens of fabric bolts was a mistake, intensifying the muscle spasms on my left side. Instead of relishing time at the store and enthusiastically interacting with customers, I questioned the frantic pace of my life. Driving back to Colorado on Monday morning, I felt like I'd been liberated from chaos.

Alone in the trailer, I fought guilt for leaving Andy as I sifted through store work I'd brought with me. One sunny day, armed with fashion forecasts and merchandise invoices, I drove west on Highway 24 and set up a lawn chair. Composing a newsletter seemed easier at the base of Pikes Peak where a dusting of fresh white snow sparkled on the pine trees. That evening, I wrote copy for TV ads and Andy called to let me know that Mother had phoned, wanting to come visit us. He told her it wasn't a good time.

I asked if she was upset or sounded weepy. At the same time the muscles in my leg drew taut. I breathed shallow and quick into a chest that refused to expand.

Andy assured me that Mother was okay. And right now, I needed to take care of myself.

Dr. Carter seemed confused at my next appointment when adjustments he'd made did not hold. He referred me to a massage therapist, hoping my muscles would relax and his adjustments would last longer. When that didn't help, he referred me to a lady chiropractor, new to the area and trained in different techniques. At his insistence, I went to her.

Although I yearned for a simple solution for my elusive maladies, I hated meeting yet another new doctor. I'd carefully followed instructions of doctors and physical therapists for years with minimal results. If my pain would disappear, maybe my gloomy outlook would, too. I wanted someone to identify what had a hold on me and tell me how to escape its grip. I kept praying for grace to endure and wisdom to understand.

Andy phoned to let me know I'd failed to include the foot control when I sold a new sewing machine. He said, "We can't run a successful business when you make stupid mistakes."

The guilt I felt after that call added to my discomfort. Studying the pain book helped. Solitude, relentless introspection, and writing gave me fresh perspectives. Struggle had always been central to my existence, but what exactly was I struggling for? My best efforts failed to keep me in the most important two roles: being with my family and running the fabric shop. I vowed to forge a path through the chaos, one that gave me more control over my health and the pace of my life.

Kelly Smith was the new chiropractor that Dr. Carter sent me to. She was a mere five feet tall with a halo of light red hair framing her youthful face. She worked with a strength and confidence that surprised me. In addition to muscle testing before adjustments, she used a process called Neuro-Emotional Technique (NET) to identify emotional components related to body pain. Dr. Kelly's candid and direct manner reminded me of Dr. Ted in Colby, minus the swear words. She laid out her opinions clearly, simply, with no apologies.

> **Looks like you have some mother issues to work on.**

After that first visit, she said: "Looks like you have some mother issues to work on."

Mother issues? What did that mean? Was this chiropractor some kind of freaky psychic? Nothing else she said sounded weird, so I ignored the mother reference.

Dr. Kelly was equally blunt at my next appointment. "My expertise is skeletal; I think your pain issues are with soft tissue. There are other practitioners better trained to heal muscles and soft tissue. You've already had massage therapy, but there is a more directed process called Rolfing. I would like to refer you to a local Rolfer whom I have seen."

Was she serious? Only two weeks ago I had come to her and she was ready to pass me on? Why did every professional want to hand me over to someone else? I felt like the water pail in a fire-fighting bucket brigade. But the fire I was fighting was unrelenting pain.

"He's a fine Christian man, Joyce; you can trust him. And I will continue to treat you, if you wish."

What made her think "Christian" mattered to me? Just last week my husband had said I might need psychotherapy and if anyone was going to mess with my mind, he wanted that individual to be a Christian. I didn't know enough about Rolfers to know if they "messed with your mind," but it seemed to me that all healers shared philosophical beliefs as they applied their expertise. Reluctantly I agreed to the referral, knowing I could cancel if I changed my mind.

For weeks, I'd avoided the suggestion in the pain book to write a myth. I didn't know how to define myth, much less write one. Still, the idea haunted me. Warm fall days in Colorado were intoxicating. The intense sunshine warmed the gentle breeze and golden aspens were stunning. A morning in late October I drove to a tranquil lake—Rampart Reservoir—high above Woodland Park. Captivated by panoramic mountain vistas along the way, I stopped to stretch and take photos.

With a cane to support me, I hobbled to a granite boulder the proper height to stand and write. The sun soothed my aching muscles, and nature provided the only sounds. Birds called as they flitted through the forest and water lapped against the rocky shore. I didn't know what the purpose was of trying to write a myth. Still, it felt safe to step into the unknown in this pristine setting. The pain book said to write "once upon a time" and let the pen do the rest. With "once upon a time" in mind, my hand and pen wrote:

My Myth

Once upon a time a little fish—who loved to swim freely and recklessly, ran into a brick wall

because the little fish couldn't see as well as other fish.

All the others laughed and mocked the clumsy fish,

even though earlier the fish had done the best flips of any fish in the pond.

One time, a brother fish purposely tripped the fish and made her look foolish. Another time, he dug his fins into her and shamed her.

As time went on the little fish won many awards
as a beautiful swimmer,

but she never really felt successful.

She always believed she didn't measure up

to the expectations of the fish around her.

Writing the myth was an emotional experience for me. Tears streamed onto the paper when I wrote /30/ at the end—a habit I learned in high school journalism. I judged the myth to be too short to be meaningful, but the pen wouldn't write another word. I placed it in a notebook with other exercises from the pain book. Maybe later I would write a real myth.

Magic is at the core of myth.
—COLLIN FARRELL

5

Foreplay

*That position is a fear reaction.
It's safe here. You don't need to fear me.
I'm here to help you.*

Shuttling between two states, I struggled to manage the fabric store in Kansas and my healing in Colorado. Though I used to relish contributing to community through Chamber, church and other organizations, I no longer had that inner drive. Declining health, without a diagnosis and little hope for a solution, magnified the grief I felt over my dad's passing and the guilt I felt for attacking my younger son. Acknowledging the impact of that trio of events triggered despondency I'd never known before. I'd been accustomed to being the upbeat partner in our marriage and the affable store-owner who inspired customers to drive more than a hundred miles to shop at Joyce's Fabric.

Relentless searching for the source of my pain and numbness in my leg took me from medical doctors to alternative healers.

Initially distrustful of chiropractors, I now found myself accepting referrals to fringe healing techniques. The reality was that I'd made little progress during years of working with allopathic physicians and physical therapy.

Dr. Kelly finished a treatment session in November of '91. "Remember, when you return for Rolfing, there are ten sessions in the basic series. Be aware that you'll be asked to strip down to your bra and panties so the Rolfer can evaluate your structure."

Returning home, I kept up with teaching classes three days a week. In December of 1991, I guided my Buick LaSabre west for my first Rolfing session. Nearing Colorado Springs, I realized I had no address, so I stopped at a Mobile station to phone the Rolfer. Don Marley—his voice deep, gentle, and calm—directed me to his office. The compassion in his voice didn't sound like any man I knew. Ten minutes later, I arrived at the two-story shuttered Victorian under a stately oak tree. He greeted me and explained that Rolfing involves soft tissue manipulation, gestured toward the treatment room, and told me to stand in front of a full-length mirror, in my undies.

Waiting for the Rolfer to enter, my composure collapsed. I felt small and fragile. The mirror reflected heavy breasts I detested—bulging out of a too-small bra. Narrow straps cut tracks on my shoulders and frayed elastic held the waist of my briefs. I had a new understanding of naked vulnerability. I, who never revealed the slightest bit of cleavage in public, was exposing myself to a stranger. I closed my eyes and prayed to be open to this new way of healing.

CHAPTER FIVE: Foreplay

The Rolfer sketched as he commented on the rotation of my hips, knees, shoulders and toes. He asked about headaches and upper back discomfort. I assured him that I'd never had a headache. I was there seeking help for numbness in my left leg and hip.

"It's all connected," he remarked. "The first session we'll address the whole body, and after that each treatment will be more localized. You can expect flu-like symptoms after today."

Rolfing felt like a full-body massage but with more intense pressure. When I flinched, the Rolfer said, "Pain is resistance. Did you know that? Breathe into the area that hurts and the muscles will relax."

Huh? I'd never heard of breathing anywhere but into one's chest. After the treatment, he suggested I walk around the block before I tried to drive.

At the second Rolfing session, Mr. Marley asked that I call him Don and explained that this session focused on the legs. "I'll work on the left leg first, and then let you stand up and feel the difference."

He stretched my left leg and began to knead the calf tissues. My leg jerked under his knuckles, the skin burning as if touched by a branding iron.

"Let me show you how much pressure I'm using." Don slid his knuckles down my forearm,

"That can't be the same. I hardly feel that."

"Oh, but it is the same. There's lots of tension in your legs. Try to relax. Breathe into the pain."

A few minutes later he paused again.

"Why do you pull your knees up that way? Do you realize your body is spring-loaded to return to a fetal position? Is that modesty or fear?"

"I'd never thought of that as a fetal position. That's how I usually sleep."

"Consider changing your sleeping position; it may be contributing to your pain. That position is a fear reaction. It's safe here. You don't need to fear me. I'm here to help you."

My mind said I was safe; apparently my body disagreed. No amount of self-talk stopped the knee-jerk reaction.

Repeatedly, he noted a lot of fear in my body. I thought that strange because I was sure I exuded confidence.

On my drive back home, I recognized that my life was increasingly filled with guilt. At home I didn't keep up with exercises and journaling; in Colorado I felt guilty about being away from the store, as well as abandoning Andy and Ben. Throughout it all, I hated my body for giving me pain.

> **I wonder what twisted truth in my life still needs to unravel.**

As we approached January, I hoped for better health in '92. I had cautious optimism for relief from Rolfing, as well as from Dr. Spradley—a highly recommended internist I'd waited months to see.

While lost in a void during a Rolfing session, I saw the image of a tightly coiled cable that grew larger and heavier as I followed it behind closed eyes. At first, I watched the cable silently and felt the tension in my body intensify. When I finally told Don about the cable, he acknowledged my vision and kept working. Soon the cable began to soften and untwist, until it completely disintegrated. The tension in my body relaxed proportionately as the cable softened and disappeared.

I opened my eyes and spoke, more to myself than to Don. "I wonder what twisted truth in my life still needs to unravel."

After the session, I mentioned how I prayed for grace to accept whatever came my way and wisdom to learn the lessons. Don asked if I had ever meditated. He found meditation more comforting because the goal was to be silent and listen whereas he needed to know what to ask for when he prayed. I learned of a free "Orientation to Transcendental Meditation™ in Colorado Springs but was shocked to learn the training fee was $135. I'd advertised a youth sewing class so if the class brought in enough to pay the fee, I decided I would take the TM training. The money came in and I enrolled. I didn't tell anyone. Lutherans, especially Andy, would view such a practice as cult activity. I thought meditation sounded closer to the kind of praying I did years ago. Prayer was more meaningful to me as a child, when I composed my own petitions rather than reciting prayers from church liturgy.

Transcendental Meditation became a part of my regular Colorado routine. Too many store and household responsibilities demanded my attention in Kansas.

Although I felt guilty walking away from responsibilities, every time I steered my car onto I-70 west, my spirits lifted. After each Rolfing session, my confidence in the technique increased, though I couldn't explain why.

In Rolfing, I was oftentimes cold—not merely chilled, but freezing. At a session when I couldn't stop shuddering, Don paused. "What are you feeling? What do you need?"

Silence gripped me. He should know; he was the expert. But finally, I said, "I think I'm better now."

"I didn't ask what you're thinking. I want to know what you're feeling." Don's voice was gently prodding, not damning, like I expected from a man.

"Maybe my leg hurts less now."

Don's huge hands dangled at his side. "Are you feeling anxious, angry, or confused?"

Relieved to have direction, I said, "Confused."

When the session was over, Don said, "This is your fifth Rolfing appointment and I'm not finished with the sequence of the third session. The fear in your body impedes progress. It appears you will need more than ten sessions to complete the basic series."

"That's all right with me. I'm still feeling positive. After all the therapies I've tried in the past two years, this is the only one that let me ditch my cane."

Don followed me to the waiting room. "Your emotions, particularly your intense fear reactions, concern me. I don't know how you feel about psychotherapy, but my daughter and I have benefitted from seeing a licensed clinical social worker (LCSW)."

"Andy and I have talked about counseling. I'm open to that possibility. After all, I worked at the community college as an instructor/counselor before I bought my store."

"The LCSW I've worked with is director of Lutheran Social Services. I have her business card."

Andy was pleased I had been referred to a Lutheran practitioner for therapy. I was open to the idea. Still, I felt like the water pail in a bucket brigade. I was so impossible to treat that I was being passed on to another professional—again. But I scheduled counseling.

About the same time, I began seeing an internist with the hope that I could find help for pervasive body pain. On my second visit to Dr. Spradley, he reviewed written reports and lab tests, then said, "There is no clear diagnosis from all these tests."

"I was afraid that's what you would say. I've heard that many times."

"Because I've ruled out other diagnoses, I believe you have fibromyalgia. Unfortunately, I can't offer you a cure. But we can make your life easier. For starters, I'd recommend that you take a sleep med. Your pain should be more tolerable with adequate rest and an anti-inflammatory medication."

Encouraged to have a name for my condition, I agreed to follow his recommendations. I left the doctor's office feeling upbeat and phoned Andy. "After years of searching, we finally have a diagnosis. Dr. Spradley says I have fibromyalgia."

My husband didn't share my enthusiasm when he learned there was no cure.

Back home on February 2, 1992, I dreaded hearing anyone say happy birthday to me. How could the two-year anniversary of my dad's funeral be happy? The lonely ache in my heart seemed to magnify the muscle spasms on my left side.

I started recalling the negative things that had occurred near my birthday. In 1989, Andy went to the farm and sold most of our farmland to his brother without consulting me. And then he constantly reminded me that it was my fault he *had to* quit farming. In 1990, my father was lowered to his grave on my birthday. In 1991, I was in severe pain after the failed epidural injection. For my 52nd birthday in 1992, I learned that I had fibromyalgia, a condition for which there was no cure. Does this look like a birthday curse to anybody but me?

> **Does this look like a birthday curse to anybody but me?**

I returned to Colorado for another Rolfing session and my initial counseling session with Leona Williams, LCSW. The Rolfing session was intense. My trembling turned into compulsive shudders. My feet involuntarily pounded a drum-roll on the treatment table as I felt myself transported to the ceiling light fixture. Perched on the fixture, I heard a distant echo that I recognized as Don's voice. A phantom held me captive in a void where my senses felt anesthetized.

Don stopped working and spoke my name. An invisible force pulled me from the void above and back onto the treatment table.

"Would you like to tell me what just happened?"

No amount of self-talk could keep my legs from their spring-loaded return to the fetal position. "I can't. I have no idea what that was." But I wished I were back on the ceiling fixture.

Continuing his work, Don kept up a constant stream of questions. Before I left the room, he suggested I talk with my new therapist about this session.

At counseling, I recounted being on the ceiling fixture during Rolfing.

> **Dissociation is a God-given gift that helps us survive when something we experience is unbearable.**

"Can you remember that feeling of floating through space any other time?" Leona asked.

"Not really, and yet … it was familiar. That doesn't make sense, does it?"

"Actually, it does make sense. Your involuntary actions in Rolfing suggest to me that something traumatic happened in your past. If you experienced trauma in your childhood, you may have formed a pattern of automatically dissociating when you feel fear."

In a flash, I remembered I did have that pattern. "All my life, I've been teased about getting glassy-eyed. It happened on our first trip overseas. While we were driving through Austria, I missed a mile-long field of roses. Ever since then, whenever I glaze over, Andy teases me about missing the roses."

Leona slapped the arm of her chair. "That's it; that's your pattern. And some day you'll figure out why you learned to do that. Dissociation is a God-given gift that helps us survive when something we experience is unbearable. Continuing to dissociate later in life is dysfunctional. Your job now is to notice when you "check-out" and develop tools to interrupt that process."

I left Leona's office grateful that I could spend the night in the trailer. Driving home the next day, my mind replayed the Rolfing and therapy sessions as I tried to digest the idea of dissociation.

I didn't stay home long; within a week I returned to Colorado. At the next counseling session, Leona again asked about my childhood.

"I remember so little. I know that I couldn't see at a distance until I got glasses in the fifth grade. I thought everyone was smarter than me, because they saw leaves on trees and birds flying. At recess, I never could catch a ball; it always hit me before I saw it. I remember riding Rex, a cranky Shetland pony, to the one-room school. Rex was ornery. He would untie the rope that was supposed to keep him in the little barn behind the school and I'd have to walk home. My brother Roger liked to kick Rex in the flanks, so he would buck me off."

"How did that make you feel? Were you angry? Start there. Journal what you remember about your childhood relationship with Roger. You might want to read Harriett Lerner's *Dance of Anger*."

At Poor Richard's bookstore, I found Lerner's book, and Marianne Williamson's *A Return to Love*. I didn't want to read about anger; the very thought made my body tense. So, I read Williamson's book first, and cried a lot. I longed to feel the kind of love she wrote about ... warm and nurturing attention.

I described my body tremors and emotional tears during Rolfing with my therapist. She explained, "It's well established in the psychological field that all cells of our body contain memory, not only brain cells. When something is too fearful to remain in our conscious memory, it is still in the memory of the traumatized cells. Because your body is revealing fear you don't understand, it could be that cellular memory is trying to bring something into your awareness."

I leaned forward, trying to understand what she had said. "Although I studied theories of counseling for my master's degree in the sixties, I don't remember hearing anything about cellular memory."

"Body Memories is the term we use for what's happening to you when your body is touched. Beyond the phenomenon of body memories is a flashback or the revisiting of an experience that has been repressed. A good reference book to learn about cellular memory and flashbacks is *Courage to Heal*."

"I've heard of that book. But it's about sexual abuse. I've not been abused. I've had a happy, pain-free life until the past few years."

Leona's dark brown eyes drilled into me, as if she saw beyond my words. "Tell me about your childhood."

"Well, I was a spoiled little girl, with two jealous brothers. My family said that I expected to have my cake and eat it, too. My brothers called me daddy's little darling. They even sang a little ditty: *Joycie, sister sweetheart, baby darling dear.*"

Leona urged me to try to journal more about my childhood between therapy sessions.

After about six months of seeing Leona regularly, I finally started sharing images from my dreams. Throughout my life I'd experienced dreams of being chased and feeling fearful, but now—as the weeks passed—the fears in my dreams intensified.

I shared my three most frequently reoccurring dreams. In the first dream, our family is held hostage by uniformed soldiers who surround our farmhouse. In another, I am lying under a lilac bush and Mother is forcing me to drink urine from a Pepsi bottle fitted with a calf nipple—like we used to feed abandoned baby sheep and cows. In the third, we are in my parents' bedroom and my father says, "Gene needs this because he'll soon be in high school."

When Leona asked how I felt when I woke up from those dreams, I told her that I usually woke up anxious and trembling.

"Have any of your recent dreams been sexual in nature?"

"Yes, although I never told anyone. It embarrasses me to admit that."

"It wouldn't hurt for you to look at the *Courage to Heal* book. My clients have found it helpful for all kinds of trauma, not just sexual."

At home my dreams became increasingly vivid, and I remembered more details. Andy would often shake me awake in the middle of the night because I flailed about and struggled to speak. Chase scenes where I tried to escape from an unknown assailant were a common theme. One night I awoke feeling terrified and resisted going back to sleep, fearing the next nightmare would be more violent. I opened *Courage to Heal* and read: *Once you have an insight, it is yours and you'll always know.*

Then I opened the pain book, ready to embrace the exercises. I wrote what I remembered about my childhood home, my brothers, and my school days. I recalled little at first, but more memories surfaced as I wrote. After writing, I bowed my head and asked for courage to face my fears and grace to live with the consequences. Then I wrote in my journal: *I choose to commit to healing. I choose to search for the part of me I've lost.*

While I was home, I moved a lot of heavy fabrics in the store. After I returned to Colorado Springs in July of 1992, I saw Dr. Kelly. She worked on my lower back and then attempted to release tension in my legs. Laying on my back, she placed a hand outside of each of my knees, instructing me to push against them.

Controlling isolated muscles was difficult for me. Dr. Kelly was patient as I struggled. When my knees finally began to inch outward, a guttural moan erupted. A crushing force collapsed my chest. I held my breath and a body memory burst through my resistance. Something beyond my control moved my legs up and down ... slowly at first ... then faster ... kicking frantically until my heels burned.

> **There's a frightened little girl inside you, Joyce. It would be good for you to talk to her.**

"It's safe here. Stay with it, Joyce ... let it all out." Dr. Kelly's words sounded far away. "Keep your chin close to your body; it will help you stay connected."

I found enough control to lower my chin—not enough to stop kicking.

Dr. Kelly spoke. "Let the sounds come out; it's safe here."

I let go of breath I didn't know I was holding. Then I emitted haunting howls that culminated in a piercing shriek.

Dr. Kelly was steadfast. "We're going to stay with this until it all boils out."

We? I wasn't in this by myself? The fear of being alone hit me; a frightening emptiness gripped my gut. I reached out.

Dr. Kelly's fingers closed over my hand. "Keep breathing. You are safe here."

My breath came easier … my body tension dissipated. I sipped the water Dr. Kelly gave me and found my voice. "I've never felt like that before. It must have been hysteria. But hysteria is a term for crazy people."

Dr. Kelly stroked my arm. "You aren't crazy, Joyce. Your sounds were those of a very young child. You revisited something terrifying from childhood, when you were helpless."

"I've had strange nightmares lately. When will this be over?"

"That's hard to tell, but I think we're getting a lot out of the left leg today." She spoke softly, an unruffled witness to my violent outburst.

"Just my leg?"

"Be gentle with yourself, Joyce. Take time to integrate this new information. Get extra rest tonight."

My wobbly legs barely supported me as I moved off the table.

"There's a frightened little girl inside you, Joyce. It would be good for you to talk to her. Tell her there's nothing to fear; that you as an adult, will keep her safe."

Back at the trailer cutting vegetables for supper, I realized my rib cage was so sore that it hurt to inhale. I ate my salad and took a long Epsom salt soak in the tub before I crawled into bed. Snuggling under the quilts, I whispered a prayer of gratitude for this little space in Colorado where I felt safe. I wondered if I would ever have answers to the questions my body evoked. Per Dr. Kelly's suggestion, I tried to talk to the frightened little girl inside me. I closed my eyes and visualized a photo of myself at five years old. A white satin ribbon held my Shirley Temple curls; my pensive blue eyes reflected confusion. I sent reassuring thoughts to my child-self … inaudible thoughts … I couldn't speak aloud to her yet.

My sleep was repeatedly interrupted by nightmares … a rape followed by another rape followed by another. Perhaps that's why my movements, sounds, and feelings changed throughout the night terror. One time my sounds were senseless babbling, another time melodic. At one point, the sounds eased into the tune of "Anchor's Away" and another time "Taps."

I have no idea how long it lasted. Sometimes my body jerked; other times my shoulders pounded the mattress. Later my hips gyrated. One time my mouth made strange popping sounds.

Later I was sucking and couldn't breathe. Afterward, half awake I realized my tongue was cottonmouth dry. Although I thought about getting a drink, I fell back asleep without moving.

It was daylight when I awoke. The sun, shadowed by coral-streaked cloud puffs, shone through the east window of the camper trailer. This world I knew.

Cup of tea in hand, I started writing in my journal. The second sentence was: I watched from my perch atop the bathroom door of the trailer. I reread what I'd written, closed my eyes and examined my thoughts. Yep, that's where I was during the nightmare. I did not know that world of terror, and yet it was familiar.

What I recalled was unbelievable and appalling. *Courage to Heal* says: "If a memory is coming, go to a safe place ... don't go through it alone. You did that once; you don't have to again."

> **Courage to Heal says that feeling crazy is part of the process of finding repressed memories.**

But who would have been a safe witness to the madness I went through last night? Unfamiliar and unwelcome feelings ravaged me. My hands shook as I wrote: At times I felt frightened and tried to escape. Sometimes I felt pleasure. I think I said "more" and "yes" at one point. Is it possible that I wanted sexual stimulation as a child? Surely not ... After the ordeal last night, it seemed clear that I was sexually active at a young age. Shame burned in the tears that streamed onto my journal. Maybe I started to go crazy last night. *Courage to Heal* says that feeling crazy is part of the process of finding repressed memories. How do I know when I've passed the threshold—to being crazy?

Driving to see Leona Williams that afternoon, I pushed away the temptation to keep my nightmare to myself.

When I entered her office, she said, "You look tense. What's up?"

I dropped into a chair. "I am tense. Last night I had a dream ... maybe a night terror."

"When you woke up, how did you feel?"

"Frightened. This is so hard to talk about, but I need your help. In the nightmare that went on and on, I apparently had sexual intercourse, and more than once. At times I was very young, other times more like a teen."

Leona leaned forward. "This sounds like repressed memories coming out."

My skin burned and I felt shame. "There was more sexual activity last night than ever before. At one point I touched myself. I've always considered masturbation unnatural—something done only by crazy people. Was the scenario last night a hallucination because I touched myself?"

Leona shook her head. "Whoa. Let's back up. Masturbation is normal; it satisfies a physical urge. Where did you get the idea it was crazy? Did someone tell you masturbation made you crazy, maybe because that person thought stimulation might make you remember something you were told to forget?"

"I don't remember a warning like that. I have another embarrassing question. My vagina pulsed during the nightmare, when I felt small, like preschool. Could that be? Can a child have an orgasm?"

Leona's expression softened. "A child can be stimulated to climax, but he or she has no words for it. Emotionally, it's very confusing to a child."

Back at the trailer, I struggled with the emotional fallout from my body memories. While my confusing thoughts sought balance, I kept my hands occupied by sewing a coat for Mother. I had brought Ultra-suede to the trailer to sew coats for both of us— eggplant purple for Mother and oyster white for me. Handling sumptuous fabric soothed my troubled spirit. Mother's coat was ready for her 81st birthday. I hadn't even cut out my coat when I left for Kansas a few days later.

The drive to Colby served as a buffer between craziness and normal life. At home, I intended to maintain composure and leave my body memories in Colorado. But Andy pressed me to tell him what happened in therapy as soon as I arrived.

"You haven't used a cane for months. Is there any reason to keep going to Colorado?"

As I poured Coke over ice, I tried to think of a safe answer. Andy might consider my emotional volatility a negative outcome of therapy. I could almost agree. But I felt too unstable to give up seeing Leona, Dr. Kelly, and Don. They all urged me to trust that body memories would eventually set me free from the fear stored in my cells.

"I still have a lot of tension in my shoulders, so I've scheduled more appointments. Now, fill me in on how the fabric shop is doing." I breathed relief at successfully changing the subject and kept our conversation focused on business matters.

Returning to Colorado, I continued to work on exercises in the pain book. The practice of journaling the past year had convinced me of the cathartic value of recording my thoughts. My counselor encouraged me to journal daily, with stream-of-consciousness writing. I took advantage of the Colorado sunshine and sat outside to meditate and write. Winter in the high desert, 6,000-7,000 feet above sea level, was a sharp contrast to winter in Western Kansas. The closer proximity to the sun in Colorado makes it comfortable to be outside without a coat in the mid-fifties.

In addition to writing how I felt about not finding solutions to my body pain, I let my pen process the guilt I still held for attacking my son Ben three years earlier when he uttered the F-bomb. It still made no sense to me that I pounced on him like a wild animal. And his loneliness when I'm in Colorado adds to my guilt. What if all the time I'm spending with out-of-state healers has a far-reaching negative effect on my son? And what if I never get to the point where I can think about my father without crying and feeling like I've lost my best friend? Guilt and grief and physical pain have merged to create a disparaging situation that I am determined to overcome.

Sitting outside that sunny day, I soaked up nature. Watched squirrels scamper along tree limbs and stop to scold invaders, like me. Heard birds softly beckon their partners, while a faint breeze rustled through the woods and delivered the fresh scent of pine. Nature created a soothing contrast to the inner discord I sought to dispel by writing. I closed my eyes and opened my heart to allow the unseen to direct my thoughts. Calm washed over me as I sensed the presence of my Guardian Angel Elizabeth. Behind closed eyelids the gibberish in my mind coalesced into calm, lucid images. Then I felt safe … and basked in a moment of peace.

Thinking will not overcome fear, but action will.
—W. CLEMENT STONE

6

Breakthrough

*When a child is silenced during abuse,
it takes a lot of healing before the frightened
child inside will allow the adult to use her voice.*

I didn't spend all my Colorado days soaking up sunshine; cleaning, cooking, and grocery shopping routines demanded some attention. Browsing shelves at a health food store, I recognized Marilyn Van Derbur on the cover of *Colorado Woman's News*. The headline caught my attention: "Marilyn Van Derbur Atler, Miss America 1959: Incest—Talking Story." Nearby, I spotted a flier for a local event, "Surviving Incest," featuring Marilyn on January 13, 1993, 7:00 p.m. at Calvary United Methodist Church. Without consulting Andy, I sent in my registration before I returned home for Christmas. Night terrors had me wondering if there had indeed been sexual abuse in my past. Could incest be the reason I felt connected to Marilyn?

We completed inventory at Joyce's Fabric the first week of January so I could keep my Colorado commitments. Driving west, I didn't have snowy weather to contend with; instead, my perspective was blurred by the blustering fear-storms in my mind. Although I arrived in the Springs in time for Marilyn's lecture, I got lost driving to the church. When I entered the building and saw that every seat was filled, a flood of tears erupted. A lady with a pasted-on smile stepped from behind the registration table and beckoned me to follow. She ushered me past rows of filled seats to the one vacant aisle seat, in the front row.

Marilyn Van Derbur, now 55, was tall and elegant in a sleek navy dress. She stepped through a side door, paused, and panned the filled auditorium. Stopping inches from me, Marilyn's gaze dropped, and our eyes met. I couldn't dam the tears rolling down my cheeks.

Resting her hand on my shoulder, she said, "I feel your great pain." And with the grace of a model, Marilyn walked to the podium. "My name is Marilyn Van Derbur Atler. I am an incest survivor and I bear no shame."

That simple statement captivated the audience of hundreds. A hush fell over the room as Marilyn related how her incest became public after a survivors' meeting in Denver. Although she did not choose the time when her secret was unleashed, it sparked in her a passion to speak openly of incest so that others might heal.

Marilyn Van Derbur glanced in my direction when she said, "Incest survivors often bond with their perpetrators."

I was in an abyss with Marilyn's words burrowing deep into my psyche. She glanced in my direction when she said incest survivors often bond with their perpetrators. Horrified, I realized I'd always been closer to my father than my mother. Marilyn related how she was consumed with shame until after she'd had years of therapy. The shame of my sexual nightmares pulsated through my body. Marilyn told of months of inexplicable paralysis when her daughter was five, the age when Marilyn's abuse started. And I thought of the years my left leg was numb for an unknown reason. Why had I experienced so many of the same conditions as Marilyn?

A thunderous applause from a standing ovation accompanied Marilyn as she left the podium. She walked out the same path she had entered. Again, she stopped in front of me and her eyes searched mine. Marilyn bent down, so close I could feel her breath. Her long slender fingers circled my clasped hands. "I derived great energy from your presence."

What?

That night I slept fitfully, recycling Marilyn's words and my fears. The next day in counseling I asked, "I'm confused, Leona. What could Marilyn have meant when she said my presence gave her energy? All I did the entire hour was bawl."

"The pain you exhibited with your tears was an affirmation that her work is important. She needs to know that. It isn't easy to stand in front of hundreds of people and admit that your father, a wealthy philanthropist, was guilty of incest."

"Oh … I didn't think of that. Sometimes I think I will never be able to stop crying. I try so hard to be silent. Even when I'm alone I don't make sounds."

"When a child is silenced during abuse, it takes a lot of healing before the frightened child inside will allow the adult to use her voice."

I studied the floor. "I don't know if I was abused. Why can't I remember?"

"Joyce, there is so much fear in your body language. I sense fear in your speech—not only in what you say, but in your tone of voice and facial expressions."

I'd worked for years to mask insecurity, to exude confidence. Leona spoke as if she had seen deep into my psyche; I felt exposed and vulnerable. Tremors erupted that I couldn't quell. Even after Leona wrapped me in a comforter, I felt bone-chilling cold. My body surrendered to internal forces. Convulsive shudders overtook me. I gritted my teeth, stiffened my muscles and sat up straight.

"Oh God, what's happening, Leona?"

"Are you ready for a body memory?" Leona's voice was soothing.

"I don't think so. I need time to absorb stuff from the sexual nightmares."

"That's OK. You are in control of this recovery process. They don't have to be overwhelming, or on any set schedule."

"But what if I never remember? What am I doing wrong?" I tugged the comforter tighter.

Leona spoke with authority, saying, "You don't want to rush the process. You will remember only as fast as your mind and body can absorb the information."

Her advice settled in; my chill subsided. Leona reminded me that whenever I felt afraid, I needed to breathe in deeply and exhale even slower to avoid a panic attack.

After therapy, I walked up a forested knoll in Bear Creek Park. Scrub oak bordering the footpath created a soothing cocoon. On the far side of the hill, a stream crept across the valley. Resting on a boulder, I watched water meandering over rocks and tree roots and thought about how we humans resist change.

What would life be like if we reacted the way water does and let ourselves move with the current? What struggles would water encounter, if it tried to exercise control the way we do? I wondered and wandered and whispered a familiar prayer:
Dear God, give me grace to accept whatever life sends me and the wisdom to learn my lessons.

The spirit world answered by reminding me of a scripture that had strengthened me since I was fourteen years old: *I have learned, in whatever state I am, to be content.*

Problem was, I didn't know how to feel content in the face of terror.

Two days after I heard Marilyn Van Derbur speak, I was heading to Rolfing with Peg. Although happy with Don's work, Leona insisted I would feel my feminine power more with Peg, a Rolfer who worked in the same building.

Generally, I moved in a fog the first hour out of bed, but that morning I felt alert and confident. After a warm bath I meditated for an hour, pleased that mind chatter didn't interrupt my concentration. Breakfasting on Grapenuts, banana, and peppermint tea, I felt good.

Arriving at the Rolfing office early, I strolled around a little park across the street. Morning dew on the dormant grass reminded me of childhood mornings on the farm when I bottle-fed abandoned lambs and piglets before school. That was fun. Then there were the times we stayed up all night to attend to sows birthing baby pigs. That was not fun.

Peg arrived in a bright red and gold skirt. She took up space without apology. She exuded self-assurance. I wondered what that would feel like?

Following her up the winding stairs. we arrived at her treatment room, which was dimly lit from a ceiling fixture and a tiny window. In one corner, a knitted shawl swagged above a shelf holding a Buddha and burning incense.

Peg asked what was on my mind that morning. Sharing that I'd been up several hours and felt peaceful, I reported that I'd been thinking about our childhood farm and how I helped my father farrow hogs. As I remembered it, I needed to help him because he was recovering from a recent heart attack. No one else in the family was available: My brother Gene was married; Roger was in the Navy; and Mom was recovering from a hysterectomy. Dad and I slept on a dirt floor of a lean-to shed, keeping warm under scratchy woolen army blankets. We raked

> **I stiffened every muscle trying to quell the screams exploding in my throat.**

the newborn piglets away from the sows as soon as they popped out—so the sows wouldn't eat them with the afterbirth.

"There was something repulsive about that experience, but I don't think it was related to the birthing process." I added, "By my teens, I'd dressed hundreds of chickens and witnessed the birth of calves and kittens, too. "

"Just hold onto the thought that it was repulsive, and we'll get started." Peg's hands moved inches above my body, scanning from head to toe for tension. She picked up my left arm and began to knead my forearm with her fingers.

I closed my eyes and silently repeated the mantra that had become routine during Rolfing: *Relax, Relax. Let me be open to this healing.*

The pressure of Peg's touch was more intense as she moved to my left leg. She asked me to describe it.

Before I could answer, I recoiled from a perceived blow. "That felt like a hatchet or a hammer on my right side."

"Just breathe through what hurts. I haven't touched your right side." Peg continued to knead.

I breathed deep, and an invisible force held me captive. My body jerked. Something was holding my feet down. "Peg, it felt like when my overshoes got stuck in the mud. Nobody would help me. They laughed when I struggled."

I opened my eyes and looked up. Peg nodded, her hands resting on my left leg.

Telling myself to breathe, words kept flowing, "Something feels sticky, like gum. But it doesn't belong there, like gum doesn't belong under a chair."

Peg was silent; her hands were still.

I closed my eyes. A thick haze of storm clouds crept into the void. Black lines snaked through the clouds and I floated to the ceiling. The suffocating odor of Camel cigarettes filled my nose. I moved my lips to speak and choked on cigarette smoke deliberately blown into my mouth.

"No" eked out from between my clenched teeth—barely a whisper at first. My fingers curled into fists. I stiffened every muscle trying to quell the screams exploding in my throat.

"Breathe—and let the sounds out." Peg's voice was soft, her words urgent.

Moans erupted from deep within me … hopeless, helpless groans and deep gravelly growls. My eyes were riveted shut.

> **"You screamed 'no' for fifteen minutes. What more do you need to be sure?"**

Peg said, "It's safe to make noise."

I unclenched my fists and beat the table until my palms hurt. Thick, salty slime filled my mouth and oozed over my chin. Compelled by an invisible force, my head flung side to side. My feet kicked the table. My screams got louder and deeper.

I heard Little Joyce's voice as a distant echo. "Oh God, no. No, no, no, God no, no—oh no, no, no."

Exhausted, I finally quieted and sucked air in quick gasps. When my breathing became more regular, I had the sensation of floating down through space onto the treatment table. I became aware of Peg's arms on either side of mine. I felt her strength as she gently stroked my arms. Her forehead rested on mine; her tears streamed through my short hair, bathing my scalp.

"I can't believe it," I whispered.

"You must believe your body. Bodies don't make these things up." There was no alarm in Peg's voice—no doubt, either.

I hadn't seen a face or heard a name, but I knew. "How did the table get turned around?" I whispered. "It was facing the north window."

"The treatment table has not moved; it always faced east. And you aren't confused; you have revisited abuse. At that time, your head must have been to the north and by a window."

I begged for balance. My head felt like a feather drifting through the ether.

Peg moved to my side. Clasping my hand, she said, "Joyce, you screamed 'no' for a full fifteen minutes. I watched the clock."

I don't recall anything else about that session. Eventually I slipped off the treatment table. My knees wobbled when I moved toward the chair to dress. Peg urged me to take time to let my mind integrate what had just happened. Silently, I scanned my body. Every muscle was tired. Descending the stairs to the waiting room, Peg walked in front of me so I could steady myself holding onto her shoulders.

"What does this mean?" I asked, the words grating against my wounded vocal cords.

Peg said, "You know. Your body knows."

"I'm not sure." I tried to study Peg, but sunlight streaming through the window blurred her image. My thoughts were as obscure as Peg's silhouette.

Peg said, "You screamed 'no' for fifteen minutes. What more do you need to be sure?"

I shook my head. "Oh God, if that was rape, if it really happened, what now?"

"Feel it." Abruptly, Peg climbed the stairs. Her footsteps faded.

Alone, I shivered and wept. My feelings were raw, my mind numb. My back ached. My heart ached more.

For months, I'd begged to know the source of my sexual nightmares. Now I had an explanation and no idea what to do with it. What would I say to my husband, our friends and neighbors, store staff and in-laws? In merely a one-hour session, would my therapist be able to prepare me to return to Colby? At home, I would be asked repeatedly about my health—especially because we'd be celebrating Andy's birthday with family and friends. Could I ignore what just occurred and talk only about physical aches and pains?

Leona's office was in the same building as Peg's. Before opening my therapist's door, I leaned against the wall, lifted my gaze and whispered, *"Please, God, help me through this."*

> **Would I ever be able to speak the words 'rape' and 'incest' to describe my childhood?**

Leona rose from an overstuffed armchair. "Peg tells me you had a big morning."

Instead of words, tears came out—burning, hot tears. I sunk into the corner of the sofa.

Leona sat down. "So, what do you need, Joyce?"

"I don't know." The grainy whisper didn't sound like me. It hurt when I tried to swallow and the liquid seeping down my throat scratched like sandpaper.

"What are you feeling?"

"Sad. I want to know why. I don't understand why." I dabbed my cheeks. "Why would my father rape me?" I used the "r" word; I felt like a traitor.

"You know that rape is about power, don't you? It's not about sex." She leaned forward.

"I was so little. Why would a grown man …"?

"Rape is always about power, but especially so in pedophilia. When a man feels powerless, he sometimes feels he can get his power back by taking it from a child."

"But why me? Everybody said my dad adored me." I thought: *I don't care whether it's about sex or power. I care about my dad and me.*

"We'd have to think like a pedophile to know that. Since we are not capable of thinking that way, we'll probably never understand."

"But I have to understand. How else can I get through this? I loved my dad. I thought he loved me."

"How would understanding change things? How would that help you go on with your life? Isn't that what you're faced with now?" Leona's voice had changed from soothing to directive.

"You're still in shock. You need time to integrate this. You'll need to postpone that trip a few days."

"But Sunday is Andy's birthday. I must go home today so I'll have Saturday to get ready. I always do something special for his birthday—at least coffee and cake after church. And his family is certain to show up in the evening."

"How will you handle that? You don't look ready to entertain." Leona shook her head.

"Like always, I'll put all this on the back burner and paste on a smile."

"How does that make you feel … to have to stuff your emotions? This rape flashback may be the biggest challenge you've ever faced. Are you telling me that you'll just shelve it?" Leona's voice rose, uncharacteristically high-pitched and staccato.

"I don't have any choice. That's how my life is."

"Then I urge you to rest for a while in our waiting room before you drive home. And give yourself permission to stop and walk along the way."

At the door I hesitated and asked, "What did you call my father, a 'p' word? I think I've seen it in books."

"Pedophile. That's an adult who sexually abuses children."

"I don't believe I ever heard that term in university counseling classes in the sixties."

"That's not surprising. Child abuse laws didn't appear until the sixties."

After an hour's rest, I pointed my car toward Kansas. Stress permeated my body. While driving, my thoughts raced through fear, denial and courage—settling into confusion and shame.

How could I deny incest now? Other women, like Marilyn Van Derbur, had healed from childhood sexual abuse. Surely, I could, too. For months, I yearned to know a name. Now, knowing filled me with alarm. Part of me insisted I should forget what the flashback had revealed.

Another part of me said, one wall of secrecy crumbled, would there be more? The *what ifs* hit me:

> *What if something had snapped inside me?*
>
> *What if my flashback was a crazed illusion?*
>
> *What if what I'm experiencing is insanity?*

What if I slipped from being sane to being insane?

What if no one believes me?

If it's crazy to be out of control, I was there this morning.

But what if the opposite of crazy is my reality?

What if Dad did rape me?

Would I ever be able to speak the words 'rape' and 'incest' to describe my childhood?

How could I integrate that with what I'd always believed? The childhood stories I'd always heard had been consistent. I was an adored and spoiled little girl. My family and even distant relatives said I expected to have my cake and eat it, too. I believed them—until now.

When I arrived in Colby, Andy was going through mail in the kitchen. "You're later than I expected. You didn't have car trouble, did you?"

"Just got a late start; need to bring in more stuff." I wanted to delay his questions.

Andy followed and carried in sacks of groceries. "You had good weather. How about therapy, did you accomplish what you wanted?"

I avoided eye contact. "Mostly. These things take time."

I felt Andy's eyes on me as I put the groceries away. "You know something new. What is it?"

My gut was spinning as though cycling on the Lazy Susan in the cupboard. "I don't think you want to hear."

"You know your abuser, don't you?"

"I haven't seen a face, but I have a knowing."

"It's your dad." His voice was barely above a whisper.

I nodded.

"But you could be wrong. You're not sure …"

"I'm sure," I looked up. Our eyes locked.

"I saw it in your eyes … that it was your father." Andy's blue eyes clouded. "That's the last person I wanted it to be."

Andy paused, his gaze piercing through me. That was Andy; he always thought before he spoke. The silence squashed my chest; my breath came in shallow spurts. I shrunk into someone small and vulnerable.

"So, Sam isn't my son. He's your dad's."

I gasped.

Like a mama bear defending her cub, I garnered strength. "Don't say that, Andy. Don't even think it. At some level, Sam will feel what you've said."

I dropped into a chair, hands shielding my eyes. I didn't want to hear anything more.

"And you lied to me. You told me you were a virgin when we got married."

Andy's words were clipped—raining down hailstones—piercing, icy cold chunks that froze my insides.

Tears seeped through my fingers and trickled down my face. I wondered: *Does knowledge of incest override everything else in our marriage? Dear God, is there anything I can say or do to make this better?*

The sun had set hours ago. Beyond the window, the blackness of nightfall mirrored the dark cloud that rose out of the chilling hailstones my husband had unleashed. Shrouded in my own darkness, I sat staring into the night, trying to gain my equilibrium.

> **You gain strength, courage and confidence by every experience in which you really stop to look fear in the face.**
> —ELEANOR ROOSEVELT

7

Home Sweet Home

There's no way you could have faked that.

A stone tossed into calm waters produces visible ripples that move in an ever-widening circle. Likewise, when a family member speaks out about a forbidden subject, the ripples invade family interactions. Andy's response when I revealed incest haunted me—repeating in my mind like a tape stuck on auto-replay. The second day home, I stuffed my feelings, just as I told my therapist I would. After baking a couple angel food cakes for his birthday, I entertained church friends at noon and then his family until after midnight. My gut wrenched and my mind was elsewhere as I went through the motions of being a gracious hostess. I listened without hearing, smiled without feeling. Numb was what I had become.

The following night I retired early, longing for restful, rejuvenating sleep. That didn't happen. Shortly after midnight, I was awakened by sudden, powerful leg jerks. As I tried to connect the startled reflex to a dream, my shoulders began to pitch. Beside me, Andy continued to snore. I took deep breaths and lay rigid, telling myself I could prevent the intruder from taking over my body. Momentarily, I thought I was successful. Then the shudders returned. I couldn't stop my legs from kicking or stifle the tremors thundering up from my chest and bursting out in shrieks.

Andy sat up and pulled away. "What the hell is going on?"

I couldn't answer. Salty slime clogged my throat. I gagged and spewed out gunk like pus from a boil. I struggled against an invisible assailant until I was limp. Afterward I felt weak and dirty, shamed and soiled. The interlude didn't last as long as three days ago when Peg Rolfed me, but it left me exhausted.

Finally, I stopped wailing.

Andy said, "There's no way you could have faked that." He stood at the foot of the bed, transfixed—as if he were suspended in time and space.

He would never know how much it meant to me to hear those words. I couldn't talk to him yet, but I clung to what he said.

"It's a good thing you told me about the outburst in Rolfing. I almost called 911. The only time I've ever seen anything like that was years ago, when a student had an epileptic seizure in my class."

I was too tired and embarrassed to talk. Andy quickly fell back to sleep; but I laid awake the rest of the night. I wondered if Andy would be more understanding in the morning, or if he would decide I was crazy. At breakfast, he reviewed his plans for the day, then suggested I work from home. I was grateful that he sensed my angst.

I wanted Andy to watch Marilyn Van Derbur's film, *A Story of Hope—Miss America 1959*. The video was part of Marilyn's advocacy for incest survivors after she revealed her abusive childhood.

He watched in silence and then said, "That's a lot to digest," and headed for the kitchen to make popcorn.

That was my husband. Change rooms; change the subject. Though we'd spent the evening at home, watching the video was as close as we came to the subject that monopolized my thoughts. That night, my sleep was interrupted by flashbacks that left me agitated and wide-awake.

After a week at home, I returned to Colorado Springs for therapy. When I told Leona of Andy's reaction, she drew in a deep breath, straightened her back, and puffed up like a runner ready to sprint. She called it verbal abuse and asked why I couldn't feel anger. She didn't understand why I felt compelled to explain that it was not even possible that Sam was my dad's son. I knew our blood types. Besides that, Sam was conceived during final exams when both Andy and I were teaching. My father was more than 200 miles away.

Leona returned many times to how important it was for me to feel righteous anger in the face of injustice. Leona urged me to stand up for myself and asked if I ever said no. Her question stunned me. I couldn't even imagine when that would be appropriate. She instructed me that she would walk toward me, and I should say "no" when she got too close. When I first tried, she said I made "no" sound like a question. When I finally could say "no" to her satisfaction, she had me say "stop" as she approached. I felt like a little kid learning new vocabulary words—no … stop. Where did it come from that "go" was always implied around me?

I wasn't ready to return home after only three days in Colorado, but I felt I had no choice. I was scheduled to teach new owner classes and cut TV commercials.

Andy asked me to watch television with him one evening. He happened to click on a program where Sally Jessie Raphael was interviewing women sexually abused by an Episcopalian minister. Andy thought it was deplorable that a person who called himself a man of God would sexually abuse women.

"But why are we hearing about abuse in churches, but we don't hear about fathers who have abused their daughters? Is the family more sacred than the church?" I asked.

"Maybe not more sacred, but the family is more tightly knit," Andy said. "Even if a child spoke up, she wouldn't be believed. Remember that Marilyn Van Derbur was furious when her neighbor said it was good her attorney sister admitted abuse, because then folks would be more apt to believe Marilyn."

His remark surprised me. So, he did hear what was being said on the video that we watched before he went to make popcorn a few weeks earlier.

I said, "Sometimes I want to shout to the world that survivors must speak up and incest must stop. Other times I feel like I'd be wasting my breath. Does anybody care?"

"You'd have to think long and hard before you speak publicly here. A lot of people might think differently of you and our store if they knew about your incest."

> And I keep remembering that after I processed in group, others wanted to share their abuse story with me.

"A few of our customers know, and they seem supportive. And I keep remembering that after I processed in group, others wanted to share their abuse story with me."

"But that was a cloistered environment," Andy replied.

For months I vacillated between wanting to keep my incest flashbacks known only to a few and wanting the whole world to know. How could anyone know which would be the better choice?

> I hurled the tray of ice at Ben, cubes scattering across the kitchen and down the stairs.

Early in my struggles with incest memories, it was particularly difficult for me to relate to my younger son, Ben. One day after meditating, while I was pulling out a tray of ice cubes, Ben burst through the front door:

"Thanks for nothing." He tossed car keys in my direction.

I caught the keys, which jogged my memory. Ben had driven my car downtown to be serviced and I'd agreed to pick him up. "Ben, I'm sorry. I forgot."

"Yeah, Mom, you've forgotten lots of things." He pivoted and headed for the basement stairs.

I threw the keys in Ben's direction, they landed on the floor with a thud.

He turned to face me. "What the hell?"

I hurled the tray of ice at Ben, scattering cubes across the kitchen and down the stairs.

"Settle down, Mom. Don't get so mad. I just waited until they finished. It's no big deal." Ben walked toward me; his arms outstretched.

My vision blurred. My hands shook. I began to sway. I raced down the hall and dropped onto the bed, pulling a quilt over me.

Ben stood above me and asked, "Mom, what's gotten into you?"

"Go … away … Ben.

Leave now! You don't want to see this.

"Don't get so upset." Ben's hand burned into my back.

I rolled over to push him away. Tremors raced through my arms and legs.

"Leave now! You don't want to see this." Liquid welled up into my mouth and oozed down my chin.

"Oh, God, no, oh no." I was suspended on the doorjamb; my body was held captive by invading forces. I gagged and spit out muck. I smelled cigarette smoke. My arms were restrained but my feet kicked. After the compelling force withdrew, I floated back through space into the body on the bed and rolled the quilt tighter around me.

"Talk to me, Mom." Ben tugged at the quilt. "Are you all right?"

"Do you know what just happened?" My head was still covered; my eyes were closed. I couldn't bear to look at my son. "It's so ugly; I'm so sorry."

"Mom, you were raped." Ben sat motionless. "Dad told me about your flashbacks. Are you going to be okay?"

"Sure. You go, Ben. I'll rest." I really wasn't sure how all right I was, but I didn't want him to worry. I was relieved that Andy had talked with Ben, so I didn't have to speak my shame to my son.

Years ago, Ben said he thought he came into this world to take care of me. At the time, I argued with him, and said I was supposed to care for him, but I realized I wasn't taking care of my son now. I was out of control and he calmly supported me. At seventeen, he should have been out with friends. At some point I fell asleep, my friend, sweet slumber arrived, and prevented me from drowning in regret.

Ben now knew. I needed to connect with Sam and begin the reveal of my past. After talking with my therapist about Sam, I decided to visit him in Las Vegas where he worked … even over Andy's objections. Instead of going when I wanted to, Andy insisted, if I had to go, I had to leave immediately to see Sam.

Andy said he needed me back in time to accompany him on a trip to Topeka where he served on a legislative committee. When I argued that I didn't know anyone on the committee, Andy made it clear that he needed me there. That was the first time I realized being an arm ornament was a command performance. I didn't understand the obligation earlier because I'd never objected to his request.

When I arrived in Las Vegas, I shared a brief, edited version of my experience of flashbacks. Sam said that he suspected something serious because I'd come on short notice. Then Sam said. "I always thought there was something weird about Grandma Hulda. Remember how Dad and I always disappeared to the farm when she came to visit?"

My flashbacks had often included cheering voices in the background.

That was an unexpected reaction. Another surprise was Sam's suggestion that we see a couple of movies: *The Color Purple* and *The Accused*. Both films contained riveting rape scenes. In the latter, I especially identified with Jody Foster when bystanders in the bar goaded her rapist. My flashbacks had often included cheering voices in the background. In *The Color Purple*, Sophie reached my heart when she said: *The more things change, the more they stay the same.*

On a lighter note, we saw a current movie: *Forrest Gump*. Sam kept pressing me for what I got out of that movie. While I was focused on Jennie and her abusive father, Sam was focused on Forrest. Finally, I said that Forrest, despite his handicaps, succeeded at everything he did because he was totally focused on the activity at hand.

"That's it," Sam said. "That's the piece you got that I missed. And that is you, Mom."

Flying from Las Vegas to Denver on my way home, I learned a winter blizzard had moved into Colorado and Kansas. I had to stay overnight near the airport because I-70 was closed. Andy was steaming when I finally arrived in Colby. Within an hour we were driving east toward Topeka for Andy's committee meeting. The blinding snow and the freezing sleet created a slippery roadway that mirrored the uncertainty I felt inside. After only one hundred miles of the two-hundred-mile trip, we had to stop overnight because the interstate was closed. We arrived in Topeka a day late, and Andy wasn't happy. The return trip was still difficult because of the slow-moving storm. With all the weather drama, I didn't dare talk about my troubles.

We arrived home to learn that Ben and his buddy had gotten excused from high school in order to shovel snow off the metal roof of the fabric store. His good judgment and fast action saved us from severe damage to our building and merchandise. I held my tongue when Andy complained that Ben should have phoned us in Topeka. Why couldn't he just commend Ben for a job well done instead of scolding? And why couldn't we laugh together at Ben's sense of humor? He'd placed a large "Ski Colby" sign atop the snow piled ten feet high in the corner of the store parking lot.

When the weather cleared, I returned to Colorado Springs to resume therapy. Because it was too cold to keep the trailer open in Woodland Park, I had rented an apartment. Although Andy came to Colorado to keep me company, he was particularly distant and unwilling to communicate. When my effort to draw him out failed, I focused on cleaning up after dinner.

"Back home, I've set up the dining table for sorting mail," Andy said.

It would be useless to remind him that he already had a file cabinet, a cardboard filing contraption with 72 bins, and a desk. The problem was that all those were stacked with papers he hadn't sorted.

> **"The devil is capable of sending demons to control people."**

While I washed dishes, Andy studied his Bible and took notes. I was grateful for silence. I recognized Proverbs 31 when he read the traits of a virtuous woman. Then he flipped some pages. When I heard *demon-possessed*, my chest constricted. A shallow inhale sent shocks piercing across my heart and throughout my rib cage.

Andy read a long passage aloud before he looked up at me. "The devil is capable of sending demons to control people. The Bible clearly says that."

I managed to speak. "Are you saying that my problem is with demons, not incest?"

"It's possible. Your screams, the way your arms and legs flail, the vile words that come out of your mouth, that's not like you." He paused. "I've heard there's a minister in Menlo who casts out demons. Maybe an exorcist could help you more than all this therapy. Menlo's closer to home than Colorado Springs, and the preacher would be a helluva lot cheaper than all of your therapists." Andy spoke quieter with each word, signaling me to pay attention.

I stifled the urge to throw a plate at him. "How can you say that? The first time you saw me in a flashback, you said I couldn't have faked it."

"I still believe you didn't fake it, but it could be that demons are causing your problems, not incest. Or maybe it's both; maybe incest opens the door for demons. Maybe the devil has gotten into you."

The dishes were done; I wrung out the dishcloth and felt my heart twisting. I watched water drip from the sink and felt hope of Andy's understanding slide down the drain. "That's not fair. Don't talk to me about demons."

To my relief, Andy let the subject drop. In the morning, he gathered papers for his return to Colby and then proceeded to scold me for not having the medical records ready for taxes and not having filed medical claims to the insurance companies. I was also to provide him with a detailed accounting of my expenditures, not just medical but all the expenses that supported my therapy in Colorado.

After Andy left, I walked to Bear Creek Park and wandered around for an hour. Upon returning to my place, I had an uncontrollable craving for chocolate. I inhaled a handful of double chocolate mints and washed them down with Coca-Cola. The sugar high left me drowsy. I fell asleep thinking about how to report to my counselor.

At therapy the next day, I talked about Andy's visit. "I need to integrate what happened while Andy was with me from Tuesday evening until Thursday morning. A couple times he was reassuring and said our decision for me to be in Colorado to heal was a good one, but most of the time he was angry."

Leona raised her eyebrows. "Did he say what he was angry about?"

"He said I was irresponsible. He even read the Bible and suggested that I was demon-possessed, that perhaps I needed an exorcism. When his accusations surprised me, I tried to look blank and not register fear."

"And did he explain what he meant?"

"Sort of ... he said I was unstable."

Her eyes narrowed. "Why do you resist feeling anger? We need to work on anger. Don't you know ... you have a right to be angry, Joyce ... you were attacked?"

"Anger is such unfamiliar behavior for me. Mother always said I must not get mad. Mad people are crazy." My nervous fingers tapped on the chair arm.

Leona placed a pillow on an end table. "Try this. Stand with your feet parallel, hit the pillow with both hands at once and scream."

I looked at the pillow, then at Leona. My mouth opened and closed without a sound. I slammed my knuckles into the pillow.

"Stand up straight and scream." Leona slapped the pillow. "Damn, damn, damn."

I sucked in air, curled my fingers into a fist and with the strongest left I could muster, hit the pillow and said, "Mean, cruel, insulting."

"That's a start, but you need more force. Try writing a letter to Andy telling him how he made you feel. Even if you don't mail it, writing it down could help you get in touch with anger. Perhaps Andy felt his own incompetence, and to avoid claiming it, he projected his limitations on you. Throw it back at him. Tell him: Don't you project your incompetence on to me. Take it back."

"I can't imagine Andy as incompetent. That's my territory." Years ago, in college, I'd heard about projection in psychology classes, but I'd never internalized the concept. I considered projection intellectual jargon, not anything that occurred in my world. Was it possible that Leona was right? Was Andy projecting his denied feelings onto me the past few days?

I garnered courage. "What hurt most was when Andy said he'd considered legal separation because of my financial instability." My anxious fingers wouldn't be still. They tapped rhythm on the arm of the chair to calm myself.

Leona's words poured out, "You tell him 'if you go for legal separation, file for divorce instead. I'll show you how incompetent I am. Just try to prevent me from getting my share by proving me incompetent in the courts. It's my name that's on "my" store— Joyce's Fabric. You can't do it."

Whew! It took a minute for me to absorb my therapist's outburst. "You have no idea how terrified I am of Andy's threats. He's brainwashed me about divorce; saying it's the quickest way for a woman to go from middle-class to low-class. Andy used to threaten to leave me every time we disagreed. Repeatedly he's told me: *You won't get a goddamn dime; I'm smart enough to see to that.* Then he'd stomp out and slam the door."

My thoughts raced. Why did my husband's threats scare me so? I knew Mother was terrified she couldn't support herself. Perhaps my current fears were beliefs she had instilled in me. With a couple college degrees, I certainly should be able to support myself. And surely, I would be entitled to some of the property we own. And, I ran a store and taught many how to sew and use the latest high-tech machines.

My fingers rested. "After I've dealt with incest, I'll work on my marriage."

"No. You must work on your marriage as you heal from incest. Healing incest is working on the past; healing your marriage is working on the present. You can't ignore either one."

At the end of the session, Leona suggested I write what I thought about divorce. Back at the apartment, putting words on paper helped me see how opposed I was to the thought of separation from my husband. *Dance of Anger* by Harriet Lerner lay open on a table. Why did I resist dancing with anger? I reread what I'd highlighted, studied it like a text, and wrote an outline.

I decided to follow Leona's advice and write a note to Andy.

> *Andy, I don't believe I was demon-possessed when I released fear. Fear had been in my cellular structure for fifty years and it came out with vengeance. My cognitive self oversaw the process, not demons. It was a conscious choice to face my flashbacks rather than stuff them into oblivion. It is not appropriate, Andy, for you to read from the Bible and accuse me of being demon-possessed.*

To myself, I wrote:

> *It's hard for me to write that I resent my husband of more than thirty years. But resentment is a feeling and I've read that feelings just are—they are not bad or good. Only our behavior in response to feelings can be judged. I should not have to think about whether my feelings are right or wrong. Why has it always been so hard for me to admit what I feel? These angry words feel foreign to me: shitass, asshole, sonofabitch, bastard, dumbass, dumb shit, shithead, dumb fart, pompous ass, ruler, boss, frickin' smart aleck, vengeful oaf, cruel, condescending know-it-all.*

I skimmed the *Courage to Heal* workbook and read the chapter on anger. I filled out some of the exercises about creating a safe place. My blocks to anger were still strong. Though I wished I could feel seething anger, what I felt was detachment. That night while I tried to read, I kept wondering if I'd ever feel anger.

Though I slept more than twelve hours, I woke up tired. A fierce wind blew outside, parroting the howls inside me. I spent two days in a vacuum, at times exploring anger and at times fearing what I might do with it. Saturday evening the phone startled me. Hearing the excitement in Ben's voice warmed my heart.

"I got a one rating on my vocal solo at state competition today," Ben said. "The judge's comments were all favorable. One judge wrote that mine was the best voice of the day."

"Thanks for calling to tell me, Ben. I'm so happy for you." It was good to hear him express pride in his accomplishment. Leona had urged me to avoid speaking for Ben because that denied him having his own feelings. I was proud of him, but I knew it was more important that he was proud of himself.

Even holiday celebrations changed after my incest memories. When I returned to Colby to celebrate Christmas, Ben was withdrawn. I recalled an earlier Christmas when he encouraged me to join him singing the *Messiah* with the community choir. Not this year.

"You seem so sad, Ben. Please talk to me."

"What difference does it make to you? You'll leave for Colorado soon." Arms crossed; his stony gaze pierced through me.

"But I do care. How can I help?"

"You could stay here and go back to work. You were happy when you worked long hours at the fabric store. You've had enough therapy." His eyes and his voice softened.

"I still need help, Ben."

"And Dad and I need you here. I'm lonely, Mom. I'm so alone all the time."

In that instant, I saw the tenderhearted little boy I once knew. I yearned for the day when I could scoop him up in my arms and rock away his hurts. "I'm sorry you are so alone. I wish I could be two places at once."

"So, stay home and go back to work." Ben's words were clipped.

"You don't understand, Ben. Things have changed in the past eighteen months. I'm no longer walking with a cane, but I have other pain to deal with now. I still need counseling and Rolfing to get well." My heartbeat quickened.

"You've had too much therapy, Mom. You don't need RRRRolfing."

I fought back tears. "I love you so much, Ben. It makes me sad to disappoint you. But I am going to return to Colorado in a few days."

"What the hell. I've given up trying to get along with you. It isn't possible." He bolted from the chair and ran down the stairs.

I had failed again—failed my husband, my son, my business. Still, nothing could stop me from returning to Colorado. My inner voice, the one I'd come to identify as my Guardian Angel Elizabeth, insisted that therapy was essential.

On another trip home, I watched television with Ben and tried to talk about his upcoming cross-country meet.

"Who in the hell do you think you are, telling me what to do? One minute you don't have the guts to give me an opinion on a magazine article for fear of disagreeing with me, and the next minute you're telling me what to do. Don't you know I'm not going to listen?"

I couldn't find my voice.

"Why don't you just get out of here and leave me alone?"

I didn't budge. Ben hit the TV remote and headed to his room. I stretched out on the sofa, too crushed to cry or move.

Ben reappeared. "Please, don't sleep on the sofa, Mom." His voice was gentle.

"I'm okay. I just need a few minutes alone. Do you want the light on or off?"

"Off." Ben crossed the room and scooped me up into his arms.

"I love you, Ben, and sometimes love hurts."

"I know it, Mom. And I know you love me." Ben left for his room.

My whole body felt heavy. I wanted to cry, but tears wouldn't come. I wanted to throw up. It's no wonder I felt sick. I'd stuffed my face with junk food.

I couldn't see where this led. Would I ever again be able to function at home? Did I have to become numb and stop feeling to make marriage and motherhood work? Fear squeezed the life out of me. I didn't know *why* I was falling apart. I just knew I was.

> **I didn't know *why* I was falling apart. I just knew I was.**

As part of my recovery, my therapist encouraged me to plant seedlings in peat pots, so I'd be ready to garden in early spring. The seeds sprouted and leafed quickly, but for some reason they withered and died before I got them into the ground. That seemed a metaphor for motherhood. I'd nurtured my two sons as young seedlings, and as they approached puberty we grew apart and adversarial. Sometimes, I thought that the tender seedlings I birthed were never nurtured well enough to develop life-supporting roots.

Months later when Sam returned to Colby for a week's vacation, I finally had the courage to share my healing paintings with my sons. The process paintings I'd done in Colorado had been tucked away in a closet for months. Sam wondered what I was going to do with them. I admitted I had no idea; just that I was glad I painted them. Ben stormed out of the room. I didn't know what to think about his exit.

> **When can I talk openly about what's going on with you?**

When Ben returned, he said, "This whole thing makes me so angry; it's such a misuse of power."

I didn't know how to respond to my son. A part of me was relieved to have my sons know more about my flashbacks through the images I painted. Another part of me still burned with shame. I hoped that my sons would never take on guilt because they had a mother with such an ugly past.

In May of 1994, I wanted to celebrate Ben's high school graduation; He had won numerous awards with his art and academic achievements. Andy had no interest in planning the celebration. Before the party, I created a wall of Ben's awards and paintings in the dining room above a table filled with homemade goodies. Ben was a genial host and guests seemed to enjoy visiting with him. After folks left, as Andy headed to the garage for a smoke, he paused and said, "That party was just about the dumbest goddamned thing you ever did."

Later, my therapist suggested that Andy might have been angry because it was threatening to him that I appeared to still be capable of functioning.

Fast forward to when Ben came to Colorado to spend a few days with me during his spring break. We had a leisurely nature hike one morning with a friend who identified every birdcall we heard.

Then we went to the movie *Piano*. I tried to remain grounded, but the contrast between a leisurely stroll and the dramatic movie left me feeling vulnerable.

Back at the apartment, Ben asked, "When can I talk openly about what's going on with you? I don't like keeping family secrets and I'm tired of not being able to tell my friends why you're not in Colby."

I gasped. "I've never put any restrictions on who you told. I never intended for it to be a family secret. You may tell anyone you wish."

"That's a relief. Maybe it was Dad … somebody was adamant that this was only family talk. Besides, I didn't think it was fair for people to hear from me why you were in Colorado when you weren't there to give your side of the story."

"Believe me, Ben, it's okay for you to say whatever feels appropriate. The secret of incest caused me grief; I don't want family secrets to trouble you. Some people still think it's taboo to talk about incest and I don't have any control over others. In my opinion, we must talk openly, in order to prevent further abuse."

I have learned that I have a lot to learn.
—MAYA ANGELOU

8

Community Encounters

*I knew at the country club, the night when
you first told us of incest flashbacks,
that you were very close to losing your mind.*

Living in a rural town of fewer than 5,000 for more than thirty years is serious community immersion. We knew and were known by folks in chamber, church, service clubs, American Association of University Women (AAUW), and even school personnel. Every neighborhood encounter, even with individuals I knew well and trusted, was a test of truth or pretense—a contest between my heart and my fear. My choice was either isolate or paste on a false composure to assuage my husband's concern that others shouldn't know about my memories.

Circle back with me to the first week after my flashback to rape while farrowing hogs. Andy insisted that we have dinner with friends at the country club. If you wanted to have drinks with dinner, the two choices in our little Western Kansas town were Ramada Inn or the country club. Although we didn't play golf, we did ante up for guest membership in the club.

When I resisted going out, Andy pleaded. "It would be good for you to get out. Being a hermit is not what you need. And I miss having you with me."

"I'm not sure I'm ready to face people. What if I flip out?"

"Come with me. If you say you need to leave, I'll bring you right home … I promise." Andy rolled me off the sofa and pulled me to my feet.

I relented. So, I dabbed makeup over my puffy eyes and changed clothes. We rode silently on the three-mile drive to the club, listening to the whine of the wind seeping through our truck's windows. There were few guests in the bar where we joined our friends. My gin and tonic arrived as Neva, one of the ladies from our church clan, began to relate a conversation she had earlier in the day with a four-year-old. The child told Neva about a good-touch, bad-touch lesson at her preschool. She'd learned that it was okay to tell her mother or teacher about bad touch.

"Why are they starting so young with sex education?" Katie shook her head and scrunched her nose.

"That should be left to parents. I'd better not hear that my grandkids will be exposed to sex education as toddlers," Velma added.

The chorus of dissent around the table was unanimous.

"It has to start early. It has to be said." My voice teetered, as did my insides.

> **You've got to speak it out loud.**

The conversation continued as if I hadn't spoken.

"I have to leave. You have no idea how close this is to my heart." Tears rolled out as I bolted from my chair.

Neva held onto my hand and tried to pull me back. "Come back, Joyce … come back real soon."

Pulling loose, I moved toward the door, stumbled down the hall and outside. A sharp, numbing cold wind whipped around the building. Numb was a relief.

Andy burst through the door carrying our coats. "Don't stand out here. It's below freezing—not even twenty degrees."

Andy slammed the driver door as I got into the truck and said, "We'll find something to eat at home. I'm not going back."

We drove home in silence. I wondered what our friends were saying. Would I ever be able to face them again? As we neared our house, I began to wish I hadn't left.

"What now, Andy? What's our next step? Everybody at that table is wondering what got into me. What do we do now?" I realized that the longer I waited, the harder it would be to face our friends.

Arriving home, I disappeared into the guest room and sat in the rocker to pray. My petitions were garbled. Finally, I told God and my Guardian Angel Elizabeth that I was too confused to know what to ask for. He'd have to talk, and I'd listen. Instantly I heard: *There are no accidents. It wasn't wrong that the subject of child sexual abuse came up tonight. These are some of your dearest friends. Reveal your secret. Let them support you.*

I begged and Andy reluctantly agreed to return to the club. I hadn't thought about what I would say. One couple was leaving as we entered the club.

I said, "I'm trying to heal from childhood sexual abuse. I didn't intend to tell you tonight, but after Neva's story I couldn't keep it inside."

Velma kissed me on the forehead and whispered, "Come see me; we'll talk."

Katie stepped closer. "You've got to speak it out loud. They say that's really important."

Neva squeezed my hand and held on. "My daughter-in-law was molested by a relative when she was little. My son has gone to therapy with her for years. He's learning to deal with her fears and her night-terrors."

I never imagined a Colby friend would reveal that a member of her family was healing from incest. It comforted me to realize Neva knew the effects of sexual abuse lasted for years. Now I knew one person in Colby I could talk to. That night I felt the possibility that fellowship with these friends could calm some of my doubts about coping with my emotions in Colby. Bidding my friends farewell, I felt no shame coming from them. But shame still burned inside me.

Rita and Kent dropped in to wish me happy birthday. The memory of my father's funeral on my fiftieth birthday three years ago still cast a shadow over February 2nd. A visit from anyone else would have annoyed me, but I didn't have to pretend with this couple with whom we'd developed a close friendship over thirty years. Rita brought her New York cheesecake and we visited as if my world had not been in shambles.

Kent, who dabbled in antiques, spoke of family treasures. Family treasures was a trigger for me. My composure crumbled and through tears I shared that I'd had more body memories about childhood abuse from my dad and others. I asked, "Do some men think they have a right to their daughters' bodies?"

Andy and Kent quickly denied ever knowing a man who thought that way.

Rita chimed in that she sure hoped I could get on with my life real soon. That was hard to hear, again. Didn't she know I would get on with my life … if I could?

One day when I went to pick up a new dress from my seamstress, she inquired how I was.

I didn't hesitate. "Actually, I'm having a tough time coping. Recently, I've had incest flashbacks and …"

"Oh no, not you, too … I have another friend who was abused. She's so depressed she can't face people." Nanci hugged me.

"Really? You have no idea how glad I am to hear that." Knowing that sounded awful, my hand flew over my lips. "That's not what

I meant. I'm not glad your friend was abused, but it helps me to know that I'm not the only person living with this shame."

Nanci shook her head. "It's not your shame."

"That's what my therapists say. Still, that's hard for me to wrap my head around."

Later, after I had a particularly difficult day teaching a class for sewing machine owners, Andy said, "I hope you get rested up when you go to Colorado. You looked so tired when you left the store."

"Teaching today was the worst in a long time. Erma was bitching about learning the buttons on her computerized machine, and Ms. Plume's comments were crude. I tried to keep them from distracting the others. Thank God for Sharon. She performed like a Golden Retriever. After class she suggested we go for a Coke and I shared some of my memories."

"I know, she told me." Andy sounded almost reverent. "Sharon also said I need to be patient. One cannot rush recovery from sexual abuse."

Thank God for another Colby friend who turned out to be supportive.

After we closed the store one evening, I had dinner with a couple of employees who'd been with us for twenty years. Afterward they came to our house where Andy joined us to watch Marilyn Van Derbur's video: *A Story of Hope*.

After the film, the bookkeeper spoke first. "I don't know why there was so much talk about shame in the video. It wasn't Marilyn's shame."

I squirmed. "My head understands that, but not my gut. There's no way to describe how dirty and shamed I feel when I hear myself say I was incested as a child." I couldn't block the stream of tears flowing down my cheeks.

The first time Andy saw the video, he had nothing to say. This time he spoke. "I see many parallels between Marilyn's experience and Joyce's. Marilyn was hospitalized with paralysis and Joyce's leg was numb. Both have struggled with sleeplessness and itchy skin, and both idolized their father before they remembered the abuse."

> How could I convey to anyone that my "old self" didn't exist?

The head clerk said, "Charlie used to be a big part of Joyce's life."

Andy continued, "Marilyn said abuse bonds the victim to the perpetrator and isolates her from the rest of the family. Ever since I first met Joyce's relatives, they talked about how close she was to her dad."

The bookkeeper added, "You just aren't yourself these days, Joyce. And you aren't at the store as much now, so a lot of things aren't getting done that we depended on you to do."

As the employees were leaving, the clerk paused. "I hope you'll soon be able to put this behind you and be your old self."

My rib cage constricted. I couldn't inhale. I couldn't speak. Andy bid the ladies good night and closed the door. I wondered how I could convey to anyone that my "old self" didn't exist; she had been infiltrated with my child self—with the knowledge of childhood experiences that changed my every word, every thought, and every action.

After our employees left, I decided it was time to share with Andy my new understanding of why I had bonded so closely with my dad. "Leona urged me to read up on the Stockholm Syndrome. The name comes from a botched robbery in Sweden, where victims bonded with their captors after they were rescued. Maybe it wasn't crazy for me to feel such a deep connection to my father. In our patriarchal family, nothing happened without his approval. So, although he may not have been my only abuser, he was the authority figure that allowed all the abuse to happen."

> **To tell you to get over it would be like telling our friend who is crippled with arthritis to get over it. You can't force it away.**

"More psychological bullshit," Andy said.

"Really, Andy. I didn't make this up. Face it, I am a walking, talking example of the Stockholm Syndrome."

So much for identifying my dysfunction.

Andy thought he could help me integrate abuse memories with audiotapes from a Christian minister in Dallas. At my husband's insistence, I listened to the tapes. The crux of their message was that turning sexual abuse over to God resulted in short-term dismay. If anyone had long-term consequences from their sexual violation, it was because of the devil's influence. I prayed and meditated, played the piano and sang, contemplated and exercised—still nothing calmed my angst. I felt judged—like I'd failed miserably.

When some church friends urged me to join them at the donut shop, I hoped for some private time with Neva. My dyslexic friend was the most perceptive and the most supportive.

After others left, Neva said, "Katie can't understand why you're having such a rough time because she sees you in good physical health."

"So, what do you think?" I asked.

"Yours is much harder to recover from. I told Katie that to tell you to get over it would be like telling our friend who is crippled with arthritis to get over it. You can't force it away." Neva sighed.

"Thanks, Neva, for being my advocate. It's sometimes hard to face the others. They look at me like I'm from Pluto."

"I knew at the country club, the night when you first told us of incest flashbacks, that you were very close to losing your mind. I don't think the others knew how close you were. But I knew. It would have been easy for you to give up and let your mind go."

Alone that night, I whispered a prayer of gratitude for my friend Neva. She called herself my dumb friend, but I never agreed. Neva was ten years my senior and grew up dyslexic when teachers didn't know how to overcome that condition. Neva was a loyal, considerate friend and a keen observer. Her creativity was enviable; she could paint and draw like a well-trained artist. To me, she was bright and talented. She created a space where I felt loved and validated.

Returning to Colorado Springs, where I was part of a circle of friends that supported each other, helped me avoid total despair. We originally met in group therapy and from that formed smaller circles that gathered informally in my tiny sanctuary. When it was my turn to check in, I admitted that it was easier to confide in them than many folks in Colby that I'd known much longer.

> **I wanted to smash and burn the beast.**

Jill said, "You need to keep yourself safe. It would be further abuse if they didn't believe you or if they ridiculed your memories."

Tina added, "I marvel at how you've come out of your abuse as a loving, caring, and compassionate person. Do you realize how remarkable that is?"

Affirmations from other survivors helped me cope with the fear that my process was taking too long and my dread that healing would alienate me from everyone I loved.

Robin, a friend from group therapy, came by my apartment one day to have me shorten a pair of jeans for her. I was crying when she arrived. I needed to write a store newsletter … and the computer wouldn't save, wouldn't print, wouldn't exit, and wouldn't quit. I wanted to smash and burn the beast.

Robin said, "Why would the computer work if you are denying your reality?"

My tears fell silently at first, but before long I was on the floor sobbing. Robin sat quietly beside me. When I could speak, I said, "Maybe I need to do some connected breathing. If you feel safe as a witness, I feel safe processing."

She agreed. It didn't take long for me to get through the episode and then I felt better. Afterward Robin said, "It's such an honor to watch your process, the way you let yourself go. You don't fight it. You're awesome."

I was strengthened by Robin's presence and her support of my process.

Several survivors from group therapy gathered at my place February 2, 1995, to wish me well on my birthday. Each one presented me with a flower as she told what it meant to have me in her life. I was overcome with gratitude as I heard how much they admired my process and appreciated my "wise woman" words. I didn't see myself as wise. In fact, I thought of myself as making lots of mistakes and having a multitude of shortcomings.

A few months later, I joined Tina and her husband for dinner at their home.

Tina asked, "What was going on between you and Andy when we went to dinner with you? Was there a problem?"

"Not that I remember. Why?" Her tone made me uncomfortable.

"I just have to say this. You're a different person when you're around Andy. You don't seem to have any confidence. You're submissive." Tina shifted in her chair and peered at Bob.

"That's because he doesn't treat you as an equal. He treats you more like a child. The asshole."

Tina muffled a giggle. "I don't know if I'd say that. But I'd sure pop Bob if he treated me that way."

Stunned, I looked from Bob to Tina. "Well, I do try to put on a polite and acquiescent front, and I assume most people don't notice because you're the first ones to say anything to me in years."

Tina shook her head. "But you've been married for a long time. Has he always treated you that way?"

Embarrassment crawled through my insides and burned into my face. "I … guess I really don't know … maybe. I've always felt like I'm not smart enough or efficient enough. And early in our marriage, the husband of a good friend in Colby said something strange after Andy shook his fist at me. This friend asked if I knew that I didn't have to live that way. He didn't explain what he meant. I dismissed his warning at the time. But for some reason, I've remembered it for thirty years."

Afterward I was haunted by the candid observations of my Colorado friends. Were there others who had noticed what Bob and Tina had observed? I tried in vain to remember when I started to fear my husband and submit to his harsh criticism. Scanning my memory bank was new for me, and I didn't seem to have the necessary access codes. It felt risky to even contemplate how I could transition into standing up for myself and being a peer with my husband.

**If you want to go fast, go alone;
if you want to go far, go together.**
—OLD AFRICAN PROVERB

9

Sister Survivors

It would be good to feel what it's like to be with others who've had similar experiences. They will "get you."

In every interpersonal interaction, something changes hands. Sometimes that change shows up as a mirror so that we see parts of our self that we've ignored. As I risked speaking out in groups, I was surprised at what was mirrored back to me from the listeners. I found myself recording reflections in my journal so I could refer to the notes when my spirits needed a boost.

For months, I'd looked forward to speaking to the Lutheran clergy in Colorado Springs. Without warning, Pastor Cane informed me that the board wanted me to send an audiotape; they'd decided it would be too awkward to have me speak about incest in person. In my mind I thought: *not no, but Hell No.*

Most of my life I'd been a night owl and kept up a constant stir of activity to avoid reflection. One morning, when howling wind and rain drummed on the roof, I woke up alert at five and composed a note explaining why I felt an audiotape was not appropriate. The clergy didn't respond. That kind of rejection underscores why survivors keep quiet. If ministers couldn't bear to listen to a survivor talk about incest, who could?

In order to share reactions of other groups, we circle back in time to when I first learned of my incest. Peg, the lady Rolfer who witnessed my first flashback, recommended that I attend group therapy with other survivors in the Springs. When I protested that I needed more time to integrate the new information before I faced other survivors, she disagreed.

> **I just knew that during the flashback, I was only aware of feeling terrified and violated.**

"It would be good to feel what it's like to be with others who've had similar experiences. They will "get you." It's different than seeking support from folks who have no idea what you've gone through."

The theme of the first session was father issues. When I talked about how close I felt to my father growing up, my body went back in time. Again, I screamed—long and low and guttural—in a way that frightened some other survivors in the room. Even so, they seemed to envy the way I allowed the episode to move through me. Some survivors begged me to tell them how I did that. I couldn't. There aren't words to name the inner force that transported me out of present time and fully into a past I hadn't remembered until that moment. I couldn't explain how a flashback differed from calling up a memory of a past event. I just knew that during the flashback, I was only aware of feeling terrified and violated. It confused me that I felt no physical pain; I only felt the overwhelming fear.

Sophia Fair, the therapist leading the group, said that we should be aware of what was happening in our bodies, whether we were processing or witnessing another's experience. The response of others confirmed Peg's suggestion that other survivors would "get it." Even the two who left the room during my venting confessed that they wished they felt safe enough to let themselves process like that. The anger other survivors expressed at my father surprised me. I'd never been in touch with that emotion. Throughout my childhood my mother insisted that I must never be mad ... because mad people are crazy.

March of 1993, a couple months after my first flashback, I knew I needed more help to continue my healing journey. I registered for a weekend retreat. Sophia was the group therapy leader. Knowing that Andy would object to the Battered Women theme, I told him it was a retreat for incest survivors.

Driving from Woodland Park to the retreat campground, my anxiety softened when I spotted deer grazing in a grassy meadow and beavers building a dam in a meandering stream. Chairs were scarce in the meeting room of the retreat cabin, but a mound of floor pillows and lap robes suggested a relaxed atmosphere. I soon learned that all the other ladies were from the Springs area. They marveled that I'd come all the way from Kansas.

At dinner I learned that Jill, in the bunk above me, had left home at fourteen to escape sexual abuse by a stepfather and brother, only to be later violated by her natural father. For most of a decade, her father had denied the incest. Recently, as the family dealt with a double funeral, her birth father apologized for abusing her. Jill's experience was the first instance where I learned of a perpetrator apologizing to an incest victim. There was an ethereal quality in Jill's countenance when she spoke of the profound healing she felt when her abuser acknowledged violating her.

After dinner, Sophia explained the ground rules. She exuded calm confidence and genuine compassion as she prepared to guide twenty wary trauma survivors through two days of intensely personal sharing. Combine a toothy smile that lit up her face with wispy natural curls, add in a broomstick skirt and beaded vest, and the stage was set for openness, acceptance and nonjudgment.

I tried in vain to contact my dad's spirit before I went to sleep. After hearing Jill's story, I wondered if he'd ever felt remorse. Though a part of me wished my father was still alive so I could confront him, another part of me doubted I would ever have that kind of courage.

Early in the morning, I helped Andy compose a store newsletter via phone. Giving up control and leaving the results to him was a relief. By the time I finished the phone call, the other ladies had already found their places on floor pillows. Sophia suggested we each give a brief review of our trauma and healing process. After listening to three others, it was my turn to "check in." I wanted to talk about my recent flashbacks to abuse and the likelihood that I was given a drug.

"I've recently found out ... maybe drugs ... out of control ..." I had difficulty speaking.

Sophia urged, "Stay with your feelings, Joyce. What drug are we talking about?"

I whispered, "Spanish Fly."

**Stay with your feelings.
Let your body talk to you.**

Loretta was the only one in the group who knew that Spanish Fly was considered an aphrodisiac in the 1940s. Suddenly I ran from the room and Loretta followed, leading me off to a small room.

"It's okay," Loretta spoke gently. "You are safe here. Go ahead and lie down on the floor pillows. Let out the feelings and the sounds that are trapped inside."

I writhed and gagged and spit slime. When foam no longer slithered down my chin, I thought the process was over.

Loretta was so close I could feel her breathing, but she didn't touch me. "Stay with your feelings. Let your body talk to you."

"Why did you do that to me, you sonofabitch?" I gasped at my outburst, rolled onto my stomach and hid my face.

After a brief respite, I could breathe freely. I picked up a pillow and pummeled the floor with it. Screams coursed up from my gut, sandpapering my throat. Finally, exhausted, I fell into the floor pillows, closed my eyes and let my breathing normalize. My body now felt calm and peaceful. When I opened my eyes, Loretta, sitting cross-legged nearby, peered at me with a gaze as gentle and compassionate as the voice that had guided me through the ordeal.

Before I could speak, Loretta said, "You can't imagine how much clearer your eyes are ... how much your countenance has softened."

"I hope I didn't freak you out." My voice was raspy, my throat sore.

Loretta smiled and shook her head. "I've been doing process work like this for years. It's my honor to witness your authentic healing work. You have a lot of courage to let yourself feel this pain. That's how it moves out of your body, so you don't have to be sick."

I melted in the heartfelt support of a sister survivor. "You are amazing, Loretta. Thank you for staying with me."

During free time after the evening session we sang, learned an Israeli folk dance and heard this modified version of the Serenity prayer: *God, grant me the serenity to accept the people I cannot change, the courage to change the ones I can, and the wisdom to know they are all me.*

There were many parallels in the lives of all of us who had our power usurped as children. Of the twenty women in this workshop: fourteen were aware of incest; fifteen admitted substance abuse; all experienced sexual dysfunction; and three were bulimic. All confessed to struggling with feelings of inadequacy, depression, self-denial, erratic temper outbursts, and unreasonable compulsions. It seemed we all learned our lessons well: deny self; serve others; strive for unobtainable perfection, and suffer the subsequent outcome—guilt when we fail at perfection. The experience of these ladies mirrored what I'd learned from research: Sexual abuse occurs in all segments of our society. Economic status, social standing, education, parental occupation, or race does not exempt a child from incest.

Before Sophia gave a presentation on addictions Sunday morning, I thought that was one dysfunction I'd escaped. Sophia said addictions can be either chemical or activity; it's anything we use to numb feeling. With her guidance, I could acknowledge my addictive behaviors: compulsive overworking, chocolate, and Coca-Cola. Sophia listed universal characteristics of addictions: dualistic or black-and-white thinking; obsessive preoccupation; judgmental thinking; external reinforcement; lack of integrity or dishonesty; denial; and control-based behavior that is fear-induced and non-negotiable. She added, "Hitting bottom is the beginning of recovery. The crazy stage is the brain's or the ego's most desperate attempt to stay in control. There's usually a frenzy of activity before one admits to having no control over an addiction."

Listening to Sophia made me feel like she'd been following me around the past few years. Her words described my behavior at the store.

As the time drew near for me to leave my first Battered Women's Intensive, I felt a strong connection with the women I'd known for only forty-eight hours. Regardless of the extent of sexual abuse or the age when it occurred, the trauma was a magnet that held us close. After my process with Loretta, so many asked me to sit with them while they processed that I had to turn most of them down. It seemed strange that letting ugly feelings surface drew these women to me instead of pushing them away. I left the seminar feeling grateful for Sophia Fair's guidance. She'd helped me feel comfortable instead of crazy when feelings burst out of me. Now I embraced the spontaneous release of pain and fear as part of the healing journey that would set me free.

Driving from the retreat, I breathed in the tranquility of the Rocky Mountain setting. A shiver of regret tinged with gratitude washed over me as I left, heading down Highway 24 through Ute Pass.

My therapist and Rolfer both urged me to attend a weeklong retreat at the Kripalu Yoga Ashram. Although Andy protested that doing yoga and meditation was akin to being in a cult, I registered for a Kripalu seminar in June 1993. Even though I told my husband that I needed the retreat in order to heal, my inner critic said I was being selfish. As I prepared for my trip, I tried to push away the thought that I was irresponsible.

When I couldn't sleep, I got up and ate a package of Dutch chocolate wafers. Then, with sewing scissors, I cut my short hair shorter. Looking at the sink where hair clung like freshly cut grass on a sidewalk, I realized this wasn't the first time I'd chopped off my hair when I was distraught. With deeper understanding and compassion, my thoughts turned to those I knew who had taken razors or scissors to their skin. Then I felt grateful that I was only compelled to cut my hair.

The flight from Colorado Springs to Chicago O'Hare was smooth; the short hop to Hartford, Connecticut was choppy. The bus from the airport to the Ashram wove its way past well-manicured farmsteads, vastly different from western Kansas, where trees were sparse, and lawns were rare. The farmhouses here sat amidst lush lawns bordered with trimmed hedges. Tree groves separated the dwellings, standing like tall green frames around the stately buildings. The ashram, near the village of Lenox, was built years ago as a Jesuit retreat. Even before I walked through the arched entry door, a wave of calm washed over me, as if awe and serenity swirled out of the bricks, permeating every cell of my being.

The schedule included a workshop each morning and afternoon. Yoga and meditation before breakfast were optional. Listening to the initial presentation, I jotted down two quotes that held special meaning for me. In *The Prophet*, Kahlil Gibran wrote: *Your pain is the breaking of the shell which encloses your understanding.* In *Healing into Life and Death*, Stephen Levine wrote: *Each time we touch suffering with love ... we are healed.*

Twenty-four participants were divided into family groups of eight. Diverse backgrounds and a wide age span seemed insignificant. A series of trust exercises soon put me at ease with my family group. Later, after we had written down warnings we heard as a child, we were to write a letter to our inner child with the dominant hand. The answer from our inner child was to be written with the non-dominant hand.

I felt small and inept as I wrote with my left hand:

Dear Little Joyce, Dear Tade: You are so precious to me; I'm sorry I've ignored you for decades. Thank you for coming to me during meditation this morning. I will do my best to honor what you need. You don't have to stop crying for me to love you. You may do whatever it is you need to do and trust I will protect you.

Love, Big Joyce

Too drained to write a reply with my non-dominant hand, I went outside and walked behind the building where the forested Berkshire Mountains, like mystic blue monuments, wrapped its arms around the medieval-style brick building. A lush green carpet framed the quiet lake in the ravine below and the sweet smell of clover wafted up from under my bare feet. Mother Earth felt tangible.

I returned to my group in time for the last workshop of the day. The first assignment was to work with a partner and hold the mountain pose for twelve minutes. In that pose, you reach your hands and arms toward the sky—straight up from the shoulders. My arms began to get tired, but with encouragement from my partner I held the full pose.

The leader's instructions were to move from the mountain pose to the rag doll and from there into the child position. When I lowered my arms and leaned forward from the waist into the rag doll posture, my body kept moving downward until my hands hit the floor and my knees collapsed. Spontaneous muscle contractions consumed my body; moans eked out when I tried to swallow the screams swirling inside me.

A leader leaned over me. "Stay in your body, Joyce. Breathe and let yourself feel."

Through clenched teeth, I said, "I mustn't; I'll make too much noise."

"You don't need to be quiet. Let the sounds come out of you."

With her permission, I surrendered to the flashback and went through a rape, as I had done so many times. When my body settled down, a clear white light appeared behind my closed eyes and then grew larger until it enveloped me. Wrapped in the cocoon of that white light, I felt a message sweep through my entire being: *You are safe.*

Fortunately, mealtime afterward was a silent experience. The vegetarian fare was foreign to me. I wasn't hungry and I didn't want to make small talk. I slept soundly all night.

I woke up before the alarm on the second day of workshops. After a shower, I felt ready for yoga and meditation. Rather than eat breakfast, I headed for the whirlpool. I took my bathing suit, but was relieved to find it unnecessary because gender specific hot tubs were in opposite corners of the building. The temperature was HOT; the jets were many and strong. Back at my bunk I munched on an apple, dressed and headed to the 8:30 a.m. session.

> **When I resumed the pushing motions, I realized I was beating off my offenders.**

Walking into the room, I felt confident. During the morning group session, we did a series of "letting go" movements. During one of the exercises, I looked around at others and abruptly stopped the pushing and shoving I was doing. Everyone else seemed to be doing a happy dance. As I stared at others, a leader stepped up to me. "Do what your body wants to do."

When I resumed the pushing motions, I realized I was beating off my offenders. The leader urged me to make sounds. The only sound I could make was "no" over and over until my throat was raw. As I crumbled onto the floor, the word "no" continued to come from deep down in my gut until a final loud blood-curdling "NO." When the leader's gentle voice encouraged me to stay with my body, I pounded a pillow until my wrists ached and my fists hurt. Afterward, I rocked and panted until I could breathe normally.

Eventually I sat up and joined the rest who were in the midst of meditation. With closed eyes, I saw a gentle rose color and was aware of the presence of Little Joyce. Silently, I assured her of my love and protection and apologized that I had ignored her for years. I assured her of my compassion for what she had endured and told her that I wanted her to be a part of me. Promising that I would protect her, I said we could work this out together and become an integrated one.

The intimacy I experienced talking to my inner child was greater than earlier when I wrote her a letter. I curled into the fetal position; I didn't want to share with a partner. But I had a partner, so I finally talked with Pamela, a gorgeous twenty-year-old from Brazil. At first, she held me in her arms because I was consumed in tears. When I could speak, we went through three sharing exercises:

How could I get closer to knowing who I am?

1. Who am I?

2. Who is the person I pretend to be?

3. What is difficult for me to reveal?

Instead of talking about incest, I told Pamela that it was difficult for me to reveal how my own dysfunction had created problems in the lives of my two sons. I told her about attacking Ben when he dropped the F-bomb and the guilt I felt. I shared that my immediate thought after attacking Ben was: *Who am I?* Then reality sunk in; I hadn't yet answered that important question. How could I get closer to knowing who I am? But I didn't want to talk about me; I preferred to talk about my sons.

"My heart aches for my younger son who is so lonely and unhappy. And my older son doesn't seem to connect with females. I fear that's because he has seen me so unstable."

After lunch I went for a guided walk to Nathaniel Hawthorne's cottage between Kripalu and Tanglewood resort. In the evening, I walked into the forest above the ashram.

Though I participated in the 6:00 a.m. exercises and meditation on the third day, I had trouble quieting my worries about what others must think of me. When the entire group came together, one of the leaders approached me.

"Would you be willing to share about your processing? Several individuals asked if you are okay; most people have never seen anyone do deep process work. They need to hear from you that letting flashbacks come through is an important part of healing traumatic memories."

After I spoke to the entire group, I had no time alone. Many marveled at how my voice changed as I told of connecting with my inner child—that it became high-pitched and child-like. The response of these strangers surprised me. I thought they'd distance themselves from me, but instead many asked to speak with me—privately.

Laura confided she was gay. Then she admitted that she suspected childhood sexual abuse. As she shared, I sensed it was greater than mere suspicion.

I nodded and said, "You might want to read *Courage to Heal* to help you accept the person you have become. It also could help you understand the abuse you suspect."

Grace sought me out to tell of her violent exposure to rape. She recalled being next to a girl who was raped during an open-air campout. She diminished the impact of being next to a girl who was assaulted, at the same time she wondered if she might have also been raped that night. She spoke in guarded tones, and pain glazed her eyes. As I listened, her expression revealed that she was aware of new details as she heard herself talk. My hunch was that her need to heal from the campout experience was directly related to a recent nervous breakdown.

Grace, whose rigid posture seemed to soften as she shared, also told how she'd become attracted to a religious movement, but when she wrote a paper on it for advanced studies, she was devastated to realize how fake the leaders were. She was further disillusioned working as a nurse when she saw monitors screwed into baby's heads for no reason, and psychotics who were over-sedated to make them compliant. Her reaction to all the shams she witnessed in her chosen career was to spend three months pedaling across the United States all by herself. She said she sometimes rode a hundred miles a day and cried all the way. In nature she found renewal. After her bike trek, she returned to the university to study anthropology.

I looked into Grace's deep green eyes. "Honor yourself and your need to heal from the campout experience. You have much to offer the world if you heal your heart."

She reached out her arms, cradling me in a lingering embrace. "I certainly will. Thank you so much for being here and for being you."

It amazed me to see how my outburst had given others permission to reveal abuse to me. Someone in the group dubbed me "the little grandma" and that moniker stuck with me throughout the seminar. By weeks end, twenty of the twenty-four participants had confessed their sexual abuse experience to me. Few had ever told anyone, not even a therapist.

Many stories had a familiar ring. And the emotional release each experienced from speaking out was evident in their countenance. As they spoke of their assault, their tone changed from fear to confidence. Each person who confided in me confirmed that my sharing had validated to her/him that recovery from trauma was possible.

> **My sharing had validated to her/him that recovery from trauma was possible.**

Repeatedly, I said what my healers had told me: "Trust what your body reveals, not what your mind adds. If body sensations confirm your suspicions, trust them."

When I finally slipped into my bunk after midnight, I asked myself whose needs I had met the past seven hours. In a strange way, my own needs were met listening to the trauma stories of others. The reality that they shared their stories with me after I acknowledged incest, affirmed the efficacy of the healing work I'd done in the past six months.

The still small voice within me, that voice I identify as intuition coming from my Guardian Angel Elizabeth, chose my response to the revelations I witnessed. I also heard the voices of my healers —Leona, Don, Peg, and Sophia—in the words I spoke to others. Their spirit-filled guidance had enriched my life and stirred within me an unquenchable thirst for the meaning of my journey.

The most touching story I heard was from Chester on the last day of the retreat. I looked at the man facing me, trying so hard to look nonchalant. Everything about him spoke paradox, even his snow-white hair, tousled in an unmanageable, boyish way.

"I don't know where to start, Little Grandma. I worshiped my older brother, but I never could win his favor. He was smart, popular, and a good athlete. I was none of those things. I think my brother started abusing me when I was seven. But he was only a year older than me. Could that be? Can boys that young get an erection?"

I swallowed. "According to my therapist, yes, they can—but sexual stimulation of a young child creates a lot of confusion."

Chester garnered courage. "There's more. In high school my brother said: 'I'll give you a blow-job if you'll give me one.' I told him 'only if you go first,' so I don't think it happened."

If nothing happened, I wondered, why had Chester remembered the conversation? I said, "The mere fact that you mentioned this incident is a clue that something is awry."

Chester frowned. "Maybe it was just mutual masturbation. My memory isn't clear. I asked Mom if anything happened when I was seven. All she remembered was that she kept me home from school because I was scared to leave the house."

I explained, "There is a fine line between exploration and exploitation. Curious exploration between brothers only a year apart in age might be normal. But exploitation is an invasion of boundaries."

He looked down and his head dropped. "My problem is … my brother was killed in an auto accident in his late teens."

I gasped. "What does your therapist say about this?"

"She doesn't know about it."

Surely, I heard wrong. I couldn't speak.

Chester shifted in his chair. "I never wanted to tarnish my brother's name."

I leaned forward. "But your therapist can better help you if she knows your family history. Why are you staking your mental health against the memory of your dead brother?"

Chester said he would think about how to tell his therapist.

Then we laughed together about the kids' book, *Grover and the Monster*, a book that was read to us in a workshop. Each page warned of "when you turn the page" and the last page read: Behind the monster is me, Grover.

Chester slapped his knee. "Wouldn't it be great if all of us could realize the monster is us—the part of us that lives in fear."

Janella was waiting for Chester to leave so she could have a turn. She played in the Met orchestra, and despite her great talent, could not speak up for herself in relationships. After we talked about a series of childhood sexual assaults that wounded her, I couldn't resist giving one more piece of advice.

"I wish you would pull your hair back to reveal your beautiful hazel eyes and flawless skin."

The delicate pink of her face framed by light red hair, as soft in texture as in color, was stunning. She drew her head back, her eyes widened in disbelief that anyone would find her features attractive. She reached for a hair clasp and pulled back the hair that hid her forehead and brow. She allowed her vulnerable and beautiful self to emerge.

Repeatedly Janella acclaimed my wisdom, an attribute I'd always assigned to others. Her praise enveloped me like a warm embrace. As we parted, she said, "I'll be looking for you to direct a women's clinic for incest survivors."

Memories of shared conversations the past six days circulated through my mind. I wondered how to interpret the magnetism that drew others to me. Was my time at the ashram a sign that my healing was a gift that I needed to share? If so, how would I best honor that gift? Should I share my healing experience as an avocation or as an occupation? Would I best honor my gift by writing or by speaking … or through a survivor organization?

I marveled at the dynamics that united our group. At the last workshop, one member gave each of us a powerful gift by confronting us with our positive attributes. He insisted that each of us look honestly at our strengths. Everyone in my family group had helped me grow. With our defenses pared down, we spoke of the depths of our pains and the heights of our triumphs.

The last night I walked around the lake with a couple from my family group, a Canadian artist and his wife. I apologized for intruding on what could have been a romantic stroll for them.

He countered, "We have many chances for romantic moments together, but only this moment to be with you, such a wonderfully courageous and warm person."

I was too touched to speak. Between them, with arms entwined, we strolled under a sky lit by an unfettered moon. The tranquil mountain setting imbued me with the same strength and peace as years ago when I went to Dome Lake in Wyoming with the Shepard family. You'll learn more about that experience later.

The Canadian spotted a firefly. Like carefree children, we searched for more of the almost forgotten lightning bug. I shared how I used to catch them to wear as a hair ornament. It felt good to reminisce about happy times—about events that brought joy and laughter. Sleep that night was the most restful and satisfying of my weeklong stay. I guess that says something for fresh air, positive reinforcement, and genuinely connecting with others who honor the light within.

Vivid images in a dream awakened me and I got up at five to record it. First, I saw a soft rose light, then a brilliant violet light with streaks of white light interspersed. The white weaved slowly through the violet background looking like feathery tufts of ripened wheat swaying in the breeze. The violet developed into a circular form. Staring at the circle, I saw a clock with Roman numerals on the face—but no hands to show the time. The image was a timepiece, but why couldn't I tell the time? Was the vision telling me the time of day, or time in eternity? Perhaps the vision was to reveal that some things are timeless.

I reflected on the caution I felt at the outset because Andy had warned me to be wary of the cult influence of East Indian and Yogic traditions. My caution had been transformed into confidence that I'd made a wise decision. I now felt respect and appreciation for yoga and for the leaders at Kripalu.

I marveled at how my processing touched others. It was strange that I traveled to this ashram hundreds of miles from home and stranger still that others shared their trauma experience. Awe bubbled up inside me at the coincidences and synchronicities I witnessed. Support was there when I was devastated. Validation came in a rush when I reached a plateau: a place where I could stand up and speak. I felt both humbled and excited at the prospect of a different dance with trauma survivors in the future.

Affirmations from others had propelled me on a quantum leap … one that said my healing was not only for myself but to serve the greater good of many. I had journaled compulsively for three years. The writing first helped me heal physical pain, then it facilitated the integration of information from flashbacks with my present reality. My experience among strangers this week convinced me that my words, spoken as well as written, had the potential to help others face the demons of their personal trauma and to move into and through the healing process.

> **We don't heal in isolation, but in community.**
> —S. KELLEY HARRELL

10

Inner Child

*Although many healers encouraged me
to dialogue with Little Joyce,
I approached the practice with doubt.*

The idea of an inner child's needs affecting adult behavior was a concept not even in my awareness before flashbacks. When I studied counseling in the sixties for my master's degree, textbooks did not address incest or inner child issues. In order to see how I gradually came to accept Little Joyce's help in retrieving memories, we circle back in time to the spring of 1993 when I first contacted her. Counselors and complementary healers urged me to be gentle with my inner child because she could be my ally in healing.

When I protested that I was uncomfortable talking to my inner child, my therapist Leona countered: *"Your very best efforts brought you to where you are now. It's worth the risk to try something new in order to get to a better place in life. I really think it would be helpful if you found a doll to represent your inner child."*

After weeks of procrastinating, I stopped at Toys R Us and strolled the aisles looking for a doll I could accept. There were baby dolls, Barbie dolls, dolls that cried, and dolls with wardrobes. Nothing was appealing. As I turned to leave, I spotted a pile of rag dolls on an endcap. Rigid arms and legs, no hair, no mouth, no nose or ears … this could be Little Joyce. At home I sewed a pale pink shapeless dress that resembled the feed-sack dresses I wore as a toddler. Now my inner child had form.

Although many healers encouraged me to dialogue with Little Joyce, I approached the practice with doubt. When another survivor confided that her inner child began to share meaningful information after she adopted the practice of rocking her at least fifteen minutes a day, I abandoned caution and began to rock my inner child doll.

My faceless doll brought me messages from "Little Joyce" that confirmed the flashbacks I experienced, revealing my childhood abuse.

CHAPTER TEN: Inner Child

John Bradshaw's books, *Homecoming* and *Healing the Shame that Binds You*, were gifts from a friend. I devoured Bradshaw's two books in a week and came away with a better understanding of the healing process. He wrote that we must contact the hurt and lonely inner child who was abandoned long ago because this child houses our blocked emotional energy. Furthermore, he asserted that grieving what was lost in childhood liberates and integrates your inner child. Bradshaw referred to this inner child process as the hero's journey to wholeness.

Two quotes from Bradshaw resonated with me: 1. *You can bury your feelings, but when you do, you bury them alive.* 2. *You can stuff your feelings, but eventually your body pays the price.* Those two statements made sense of my years of declining health that occurred before I began retrieving repressed incest memories.

The depth of my shame was evident early in my healing process when Don, my Rolfer, placed his infant daughter in my arms. She snuggled in for a moment and I relished in the warmth of the experience—until I remembered who I was.

"How dare you let me touch this innocent being when I am so dirty." No amount of assurance from him convinced me that I was not dirty, and the shame of incest was not my shame.

Bradshaw's explanation of shame resonated with my experience. He said: You feel guilt, but you *are* shame.

Soon after I'd disclosed incest memories to my birth family, Bradshaw offered a workshop in Denver. Four of us from my support group attended. My composure collapsed when Bradshaw listed the components of childhood sexual abuse that complicate recovery. Everything he listed was in my experience:

started young;

lasted a span of years;

included male and female offenders;

involved family members and strangers;

involved threats of violence;

included gang rape; and

included deviant behaviors.

I ran out of the auditorium. A therapist followed and led me to a small room where she supported me as I processed. Within an hour, I was able to return and hear the remainder of Bradshaw's presentation.

Even the therapist who facilitated conscious connected breathing (CCB) urged me to connect with my inner child. When I spoke of leaving the Springs to return to Colby, she asked who would nurture my frightened little girl.

I closed my eyes. "Others can be there for my adult self, but I am the only one who understands Little Joyce—the only one who can nurture and protect her."

I questioned if it was the frightened little girl inside that compelled me to be sad and not mad. I'd studied so many books, even Charles Whitfield's *Healing the Child Within* and Wayne Muller's *Legacy of the Heart: The Spiritual Advantages of a Painful Childhood*. Still, I felt unstable and lost in a sea of memories that I wanted to discredit.

As I struggled to figure out how to repair the broken threads in my relationship with Andy, I remembered John Bradshaw's words from the workshop: *Today's pain is usually about yesterday's unresolved pains.*

Maybe if I convinced Little Joyce that she was safe, she'd let me be an adult with my husband. Holding the doll in my right hand, I wrote with my left.

> *I'm sorry there is little time for us to be together in Colby. Please don't go back into hiding and silence. You have been courageous to reveal your secrets to me and I promise I will never abandon you the way I did for nearly fifty years. I now understand why you were moved at age fourteen when you heard the words: I have learned, in whatever state I am, to be content.*

I realized that scripture had been like a mantra for me. My experience at church camp, when I first internalized that scripture—was not noisy or charismatic. Rather it was a calm assurance that settled in and soothed my entire being. Later, when I married a staunch Lutheran, it did not alter my connection with the Divine. I told Andy he could choose our church because I could find God anywhere.

Andy finally told me that when his father admonished him for marrying a non-Lutheran, he told his dad I was a better Christian than he'd ever thought of being. We'd been married decades when Andy shared that conversation with me. Only then did I realize how much his family disapproved of me because I wasn't Missouri Synod Lutheran. My childhood taught me well: *We only remem-*

ber the good. In other words, *ban from your awareness what is unpleasant.*

On one occasion when Andy phoned me in Colorado, I felt a tugging on my left side, as if I'd developed a side-ache from running. Sitting afterward, I asked what message the pulling in my side wanted to bring me. I closed my eyes and listened the way I did in meditation. In my mind I saw the image of a tinted photo taken when I was five years old. Soft blue eyes squinted sideways and down, too timid to smile. The hint of a dimple softened my chubby cheeks and Shirley Temple curls were pulled off my high forehead with a wide satin ribbon. Flowers shaped with white satin piping trimmed the purple velvet dress.

Tears seeped through my closed eyelids when I realized the photograph answered my question. The pulling on my left side was the frightened Little Joyce, reaching up to say: *Don't forget me.*

I pulled out a drawing pad and began to doodle, lots of swirly-twirly meaningless globs. Later I wrote poetry, angry poetry. That felt good. For days I feverishly studied anger books and meditated on phrases that triggered a strong reaction. The heaviness in my chest tugged me further into melancholy. I tried to recall my first experiences with anger, to see if something happened then to frighten me from ever expressing negative feelings. Serious cracks were breaking down the wall of belief I'd carried since childhood, the belief that good girls don't ever get mad.

Childhood memories were blurred. Relatives used to joke about how much I liked to visit them and stay, whether overnight or for weeks. I thought that was because I was the spoiled and happy baby of the family. Was it really because my little self yearned to escape incest? That was hard for me to grasp. I had never felt so confused about the accuracy of my memory and my beliefs. Was it possible that my inability to get angry with perpetrators during my childhood had prevented me from being appropriately angry as an adult? Would that make sense to anybody else? Why didn't it make sense to me?

Although I was trying to find my own anger, all I could think about was Andy's. Then I remembered, decades earlier when Sam was a baby, I was upset with Andy. I threatened to leave if he didn't stop hitting me. Then instead of hitting me, he began to grit his teeth, shake his fist, and threaten. Sometimes he would kick me. Other times he would twist my left arm and jerk it behind my back until I gave in to his demands. Lingering pain below my left shoulder blade still reminds me of that trauma.

Andy frequently rebuked me because of that one time I'd threatened to leave him. Finally, I countered that I'd only threatened to leave once, while he had threatened dozens of times. He claimed that was different, because he didn't mean it and I did. He was right. I meant it at the time. Years later when he resumed aggressive behavior, I was weak. I stayed.

Visiting with a Colorado friend over café lattes, I talked about how frustrated I was with Andy. His complaints felt unfair. She laughed and cried with me. She said she hated Andy for treating me that way. Afterward, I wondered why I couldn't say I was angry. How would I ever unlearn the lessons I internalized about being mad? Fifty years later I'm still Little Joyce, my mother's programmed robot, living proof that she convinced me: I must never be mad.

I worked at finding anger by reading many books: *Dance of Anger, The Gentle Art of Verbal Defense, Love Is Letting Go of Fear,* and *Living with the Passive-Aggressive Man.* Still, no answers came.

I decided to engage with the faceless rag doll wearing her pink feed-sack dress. We rocked until I had the courage to speak. Maybe I would feel crazier after I spoke to my inner child doll and maybe I'd feel better, either way I had to try.

> *We need to start pulling together, little one. I've told you before that you don't need to be frightened anymore because I will protect you. Now I need you to let me help you change your ideas about being mad at people you love. You learned that it was crazy to get angry, and that is not true. Anger is a feeling, an honest feeling that everyone should have when they've been treated unfairly. You and I deserve to get mad when we are attacked.*

I stopped rocking and looked directly at her featureless face.

> *You have been in charge for a long time, but now you need to let me make the decisions. I need for you to let me be angry when Andy or anyone else says things to us that are unjust. It was unfair of Andy to say we were demon-possessed, and we deserve to be angry. Anger is a source of energy, and we need a lot of energy to heal. We need energy to overcome maladaptive responses. It was appropriate for you to dissociate as a little girl, but as an adult we have choices and it's no longer helpful to leave the present and get lost in dissociation. Together we can become fully functioning and reach our full potential.*
>
> *I'm begging you: Please let me grow.*

It wasn't long after I began routinely talking with my inner child that I faced the reality of my mother's role in fueling the fears that lingered within me. The flashback to my mother abusing me was the most powerful communion I ever had with Little Joyce. After the flashback, I was too confused to think rationally. Until then I thought only my brothers got the razor strap. But I clearly felt the thick leather strap snap across my back and my left arm before her assault. When I failed to satisfy her sexual appetite, I ran up the stairs and shouted at my mother that I hated her guts. Speaking too much information aloud to the therapist supporting me, rendered me weak and trembling.

> **I hate your guts.**

"I've given lip service to the thought that Mother may have been a perpetrator for several weeks. But what my body revealed today is worse than I ever imagined."

"The real hold your mom had on you was guilt," my therapist stated. "You were assigned the guilt for not making things right for her—for being inadequate. Guilt and fear are the two biggies in neurosis."

I remember early in my recovery apologizing for saying my abuse was brutal—because all sexual abuse of children is brutal. I was embarrassed to make it sound like mine was worse than anyone else's. After this, I can say, I hope most sexual abuse survivors didn't endure anything as horrific as my abuse.

I looked through my process paintings back at the apartment until I found the one where I'd painted images of Gene, Roger, Mom, Dad, and me. Mother's face was vivid red. While I was creating the painting, guilt swelled up in me when I remembered shouting to my mother: *I hate your guts.* Before this flashback, I couldn't imagine any good reason that I would have spoken so severely to my poor unhappy mother.

The first year after I faced incest was confusing and chaotic. My Colorado Springs friends insisted that I'd moved at breakneck speed and encouraged me to record the events so I could see for myself all that had transpired. I assured them that I had the details in my journals.

Was there a big truth or a little truth in all this? What is *real* truth? There's personal truth and universal truth, and both are subject to dispute. There's my truth and your truth; both are subject to disagreement. Sometimes even my personal truth is subject to my doubt. I can't jump on a magic carpet and ride it to truth. Truth must seep into my soul and stick before I can own it and claim it as mine.

> **The most courageous act is still to think for yourself. Aloud.**
> —COCO CHANEL

11

Flashes of Insight

Never have I felt so weak and vulnerable.

Flashbacks came frequently and without warning the first six months of 1993. After that they occurred sporadically, accompanied by less angst. This overview of flashbacks might be a rough read. Although many healers urged me to view flashbacks as trustworthy insights to events I'd banned from memory, I found them disorienting. Some survivors see a film of their assault and are done with flashbacks. That wasn't my experience. For me, the memories of more than a decade of sexual abuse came in brief glimpses of smells, feelings, or words. No doubt, some of my progress was from the different modalities I engaged, and some was from time alone, to reflect. Truth is, I sometimes felt like I was climbing up the healing ladder and other times I thought I'd fallen off.

Early in my recovery, Leona told me to make storyboards from magazine clippings. Creating them was an emotional experience. Some of the images made no sense until later when a flashback provided new information. It was weird for me to realize that inner knowing caused me to include meaningful words and images for no apparent logical reason at the time. And, it was reassuring to make the connection between collage images and flashback memories.

As months passed and I had flashbacks at home as well as with therapists, I confided my fears to Leona, "There were many times during and after episodes that I wondered if I was losing my mind. Never before have I felt so weak and vulnerable."

Leona shook her head. "It is strong, not weak, to be able to let flashbacks come through at home without the support you have here."

"When will all this be in my consciousness? Sometimes I want to doubt the body memories." I slumped further down in the sofa and dug my nails into the upholstered arms.

"The cellular memory that you recovered in flashbacks came from your subconscious mind. It may never be in your conscious mind because you were dissociated during the abuse. You were not in your body; you were not there."

"Maybe dissociation is too abstract for me to comprehend. That's stupid, I should be able to understand what I experienced."

"You invalidate yourself every time you say you're stupid, Joyce. You have shown great strength to come this far. Now you need to be patient with yourself. Also, think about what doubt does to your inner child. Why would she trust you with more information when you doubt what she has disclosed?"

"Whew, I hadn't thought of that. It's like living in a land where I don't know the language."

Andy repeatedly witnessed my unreasonable reactions to triggers. One time when I thought I could be a wife, I was suddenly aware of my teeth bearing down on his bearded chin. That didn't do anything good for intimacy.

Afterward, Andy reminded me of a similar situation, years ago. To my horror, I did recall that earlier episode. I'd gotten really aroused reading an erotic novel. Thirty years ago, I was as shocked as I was now to have bitten my husband. I burned the erotic novel the next day in our backyard incinerator. Now I understood why I hadn't read a fiction book for decades.

After my confession, Andy said, "If I'd have known that's what got you excited, I'd have bought you a shitload of novels. I thought I was in bed with a stranger."

Another time Andy winked, thinking that an affectionate gesture. I shouted that I wanted to scratch his eyes out. The wink sent me into a flashback as a preschooler, when a wink meant my brother was going to assault me.

When I read in *Courage to Heal* to reflect on nicknames, I remembered my grade school nickname, Tade. I recalled that when I protested my nickname, Gene explained that it was short for potato. Why would I be called a potato? I kept the word potato in my thoughts and began to free-associate. Oh, my God, was I called Tade because I was a hot potato? That was sick.

In high school my nickname changed to Jug. The change from Tade to Jug was a mystery to me. I used to complain that I'd like to be Veronica from the Archie comics instead of Jughead. Then I recalled that my older brother Gene referred to my developing breasts as milk jugs. Was that the source of the nickname Jug? Conversation with a high school classmate confirmed that everyone else knew the moniker Jug was not about the comic strip. Roger's nickname was always Toady. Was that because he was a horny toad? Where did I first hear that term and when did I learn that it carried sexual connotations?

One time when Andy was visiting me in Colorado, he asked about my father's family—thinking it strange that my dad didn't keep in touch with his dozen siblings. I explained that his sister Fannie accused Dad of giving Spanish Fly to Amy, her pregnant granddaughter. Andy, the analyst, remembered that I'd talked of spending summers with Amy and suggested to me, "If your dad gave her a drug, he probably used it on you, too."

> **You lay still, Tade. You aren't going anywhere.**

I immediately became ill. Andy watched in disbelief as I upchucked my dinner and struggled for hours with diarrhea.

One night at home, I got out of bed without waking Andy and went to the bathroom floor to let a flashback come through. Lying there I witnessed myself float to the top of the shower curtain, aware of my body on the floor.

First, I heard my brother Gene's voice, then two other voices, neighbors Dan and Larry. Gene and neighbor Dan were eight years my senior, Larry was 10 years older. Dan's grin and lopsided smile sent chills up my spine. The rhythm and cadence of a goading voice sounded like a cheerleader. "Fuck her, fuck her, fuck her, man. Get with the program. Pump, man, pump faster."

Then I heard Dan's voice. "You lay still, Tade. You aren't going anywhere. We're all gonna fuck you ..." His voice trailed off, saying, "We're gonna fuck you ... 'til you die."

Instantly, I felt myself swoop down from the curtain rod. My writhing body now lay still. I stumbled to the guest room and found my journal. I had to record the episode before I pushed it out of my mind. Now I understood why I'd attacked my son Ben when he said: *What the fuck*. My inner child felt the fear of death when she heard the F-bomb. No longer does Little Joyce need to control my reactions. That night the word fuck lost its venom.

Moving a memory from the subconscious to the conscious mind can release bondage.

In another flashback, my feet were held down or tied, with my left foot twisted outward putting torque on my left hip. The pain in my hip felt just like the ache that gave me years of agony and eventually caused me to walk with a cane. That physical pain led me into recovering the memories that are making sense out of many things in my life that initially appeared to be nonsensical.

I wanted to shout from the rooftops: This is a clear example of how moving a memory from the subconscious to the conscious mind can release bondage. Simultaneously, I was filled with gratitude for understanding and with fear of what was still unknown. These competing emotions fought a fierce battle as I recorded flashbacks. I couldn't tell my husband. Maybe I could tell my therapist. The following day I stayed home to do household chores and prepare for my trip to Colorado. Like a robot, I vacuumed, dusted, and folded laundry.

Andy came home for lunch and tried to startle me out of my listless state. "You're glassy-eyed today. Looks like you need some fresh air, or maybe a kick in the ass."

"I have a different name for glassy-eyed now. My therapist says that usually indicates a dissociated state. All these years when you've teased me about missing the roses, I probably was dissociated." It felt good to give Andy a clinical explanation.

Andy furrowed his brow. "More psychological bullshit. You were in your own world, like you are most of the time."

Abuse is part of me, but it's not going to hold me in chains anymore.

I wanted Andy to understand, but he was having none of it.

In my first Rolfing session after Kripalu in June of 1993, Peg worked at opening my heart to feel compassion for myself. Her touch felt heavy and intense as I was transported above the doorjamb and moved through a rape.

When I could speak, I said, "I'm confused, I don't know what to say about this flashback."

Peg responded, "From the sounds you made, I'd guess you were too young to have words for what was happening. We call that a flashback to a preverbal experience."

"I'm stunned by the impact of the release, the powerfulness of getting that tension out of my body," I said, getting up from the treatment table. "Abuse is part of me, but it's not going to hold me in chains anymore."

One time in process painting class, I painted several dogs beside shadowy images of little girls, from infant to teen. A lady in the class exclaimed: "I can't believe you actually admitted that dogs were involved in your abuse. I've never told anyone."

"But I think we have to let the world know that people who abuse little children will do things to make the child feel subhuman—perhaps because they think the child who feels less than human won't speak up," I replied.

In group, other survivors shared their experience of being treated in inhumane ways … like being peed on or being forced to eat dirt or worse. We wondered why, although many people watch fantasy movies about inhuman acts, no one wants to hear about the reality of inhumane acts against children. We marveled that recent research revealed that most humans react with more compassion when they view a photo of an abused animal than when they view a photo of an abused child. What is that in our human psyche? And how can we as survivors live openly and authentically in such a culture?

After experiencing repeated flashbacks to violations of every orifice in my body, I asked my therapist if I was wallowing in incest. She assured me that each instance I reported was different. If I were wallowing, I'd be repeating the same flashback over and over. Her explanation was somewhat reassuring.

The fall of 1993, my therapist became directive and told me that I needed to go home and live. She further asserted that I should tell God I didn't need any more memories—that I had enough to be convinced of childhood abuse. In both cases, I disagreed with her. It was a tough position for me to be at odds with my primary therapist. She'd guided me through so many difficult times that I didn't want to contradict her, but my gut told me she was wrong. Even though I felt crazy at times, I felt intuition knocking and chose to listen to my inner compass rather than my therapist. There was some drama in switching therapists. Each thought the other was unprofessional. I let that be. Not taking responsibility for others negative feelings was new freedom for me.

Within a few weeks after switching to a new therapist, my intuition to continue the healing path proved credible. At a painting process session, I painted a family portrait that was weird.

About that time, I read *People of the Lie* by Scott Peck where he explains that we need to be wary of others who project their evil misdeeds onto the innocent. A short time after I created the painting, I flashed back to my mother abusing me. That explained a nightmare I'd had repeatedly, beginning in childhood and continuing into adulthood—where Mother forced me to drink urine from a nipple on a Pepsi bottle. My therapist confirmed that to a small girl, the sex act between females might seem like drinking urine.

The flashback to my appendectomy when I was fifteen was particularly intense. The day before it occurred, I felt what seemed like quickening in my gut … and I knew I wasn't pregnant at my age. Definitely not now. During a therapy session, when I went back in time to the surgery, I shouted that I heard the doctor exclaim, "We are in trouble, the appendix has ruptured." Then he added, "And we need to take care of the baby in this little girl."

A few months later, that same doctor had his wife phone my mother and convince her that they needed a housekeeper. I ended up living with the doctor's family the rest of my high school years, and as a result spent few nights on the farm with my family.

Sometimes when a survivor says she/he doesn't want to know what happened, I agree with them: That is one choice. Then I explain how I could forgive myself for speaking harshly to my mother when I couldn't satisfy her sexually. Furthermore, I could forgive myself for attacking my son when he dropped the F-bomb because I realized the word triggered the fear of death for my inner child.

Rape flashbacks that involved soldiers in uniform helped me understand the dream I'd had since childhood where soldiers surrounded the farmhouse and held our family captive. It's great comfort that, after flashbacks explained the basis for my fear, I no longer had to have those recurring dreams.

Reading statistics about how a high percentage of individuals who report rape to the police do not recall it years later shocked me. Then I had an experience that showed me how easy it was to forget or twist parts of a story. In the presence of a fellow survivor, I had a flashback to my mother telling me during her assault of me that she would kill me if I ever told my precious father. A few days later, this friend and I were in a group where I said that "someone" threatened to kill me. My friend corrected me—that the "someone" was my mother. It was shocking for me to realize how quickly "mother" had disappeared from the version of the story I told the group.

I was stunned. It was sobering for me to hear how quickly my memory had modified what happened in the flashback. Would I ever know what was real? I thought back to the advice to remember only what your body revealed and not what your mind added. Only then did I realize how critical it was for me to promptly journal flashbacks in order to accurately report my healing process.

> **Yesterday I was clever, and I wanted to change the world. Today I am wise, and I want to change myself.**
> —RUMI

12

Healing Partners

*Don't wait for someone
to give you what you need.
You take it.*

I humbly acknowledge that many different therapists supported my healing process and propelled me toward wholeness. Although I often felt like the water bucket in a fire-fighting brigade, that didn't stop me from engaging a variety of modalities. Some techniques improved my physical health; others nourished my mental health. The therapies that helped me most were Rolfing, process painting, and talk therapy. As described earlier, I experienced flashbacks in those three modalities as well as in massage, myofascial release (MFR) physical therapy, yoga, and conscious connected breathing (CCB).

Although I couldn't possibly honor all the incredible healing techniques and practitioners I encountered on my journey, a few stand out. Psychotherapy or talk therapy with Licensed Clinical

Social Workers (LCSW) was significant in my recovery. My first LCSW guided me across the threshold of memory retrieval. She bolstered my spirit when I felt crazy, and she helped my husband and sons understand the complexity of what I was experiencing. Some counseling sessions crept into my difficult relationships with family members. They are not repeated here.

Rolfing is often overlooked to heal trauma because it is reportedly painful. I experienced it as intense, both emotionally and physically, but not painful. Maybe that's because the practitioners I saw were sensitive, intuitive, and client-centered. The questions they posed as they worked to release tension and fear from my body widened the lens through which I viewed the world. Other times, their queries narrowed my focus to include taking care of myself, not just others. Gradually I began to realize how other-centered my thoughts were. One example of my rescuing, caretaking behavior was the fact that I never understood the adage: *A friend in need is a friend indeed.* I tried to understand why a needy friend was a better friend. Eventually a therapist explained that the phrase referred to when someone befriended me.

The flashback where I recognized my father as an offender while on Peg's Rolfing table was just the beginning. Many more flashbacks occurred in Rolfing, some with Peg, others with Don. Their non-judgmental, calm demeanor helped me overcome the fear that engulfed me when I felt a memory episode was imminent. Their unflinching support helped me soften my self-reproach and released the tendency to judge myself harshly. Eventually, I let go of fear and allowed the flashbacks to sweep through me and out of my body.

You should be afraid.

Once after I stopped shuddering on the Rolfing table, I told Don how frightened I felt during a flashback while I was home in Kansas.

Don said, "It's brave of you to have flashbacks when you are in Colby without the support you have here. Hopefully you will get to a place where you can breathe through that moment of onset and postpone the flashback until you are here, surrounded by safe people."

Before his query, personal safety did not enter my thinking. I recalled another time when Peg asked me if I was afraid when Andy shook his fist at me. I quickly answered *never*.

Peg responded: "You should be afraid. He's 6'3" and you are 5'2". He's a farmer—fit and muscular."

After that exchange, I worked on the concept of personal safety. At first, it was foreign, and I felt selfish. Gradually I felt more self-worth and could think about my personal safety without feeling self-absorbed. Later, I listened to a Deepak Chopra lecture where he said that to ignore self-care is self-neglect.

Circling back to before I remembered Mother's abuse, I once asked Don if he had any insights why I felt more pain with Peg's Rolfing than with his work. His response was not what I could have ever anticipated.

He said, "Probably something about Peg triggered your abuse. Who knows what?" He hesitated. "Your mother never comes up in this room unless I bring her up. It's like she's not even in the picture. I understand that she's not the acknowledged perpetrator, but she was there. As an outsider, I had a strong reaction when you showed me your childhood photos." He checked my reaction before he continued. "I zeroed in on your mother right away. There was something different about her, almost a subversive energy."

I was in a daze, or maybe a haze. I couldn't think of any response. I think I went momentarily into the dissociated zone where I was glassy-eyed and lost.

I pulled myself back by talking about the stiffness in my legs and arms. Don wasn't surprised with my report. He said that he'd been working on the abdominal stuff, releasing toxins. And those toxins had nowhere to go. He said that the stuff from the bladder and kidney area needed to move out. So, in that session he worked on the five points of the star: the arms, legs, and head.

It was near the end of the hour when he was working either side of my neck that I first saw colors. Then the dark hole in my throat began to constrict. Before the throat closed, I was aware that the motions he did with my neck were mirrored under my rib cage. As I stayed in touch with that feeling, it became rhythmical in my torso. Don was still Rolfing my neck.

I had an urge to dismiss the connection, but instead I forced myself to acknowledge it out loud. That was pivotal in my ability to release, because then the body processing became more compelling. I floated up to the door jamb and watched as I flung my head from side to side. Don let me be in charge. At first my head would only move a little and ever so slowly. I moaned deep in my gut as I felt oxygen cut off in my throat. An invading force pressed deeper and deeper into my throat, stretching the roof of my mouth and denying life-sustaining breath.

Far in the distance I heard Don's assurance, "It's safe here; it's okay. Breathe in through your nose and out through your mouth. Remember where you are. It's safe here."

This time I didn't scream no. It didn't even occur to me to try. I could scarcely breathe, let alone scream. My body was pressed to the table. My hands were free and clutched the sheet beneath me as I choked and desperately gasped for air. I finally exhaled and then I held my breath, afraid to inhale. Don gently reminded me to breathe.

By the time I left the Rolfing office, I'd stabilized and felt the relief that follows release. Still my body and mind were screaming fatigue and all I wanted to do was sleep.

Another time, when I gagged after an ugly oral rape, Don held a wastebasket under my chin and said, "Go ahead, do what you need to do. You aren't the first person to upchuck in this room."

After the Rolfing session, I saw my therapist.

Early in the session, I said, "Maybe I still want to have my cake and eat it, too."

She puffed up and slapped the chair arm. "That invalidates all the good things you've said."

"I guess I should know that by now." I stared at the floor.

"Stop saying what you should do. What I need to hear from you now is: How you plan to maintain your centeredness when you go back home? Who are you right now, this minute? What do you really want for yourself?"

"Write, meditate, practice yoga, and read."

"How will you go about doing those activities when you return to Kansas?"

"I can't work seven days a week or spend all my energies trying to second-guess what those around me want from me and still have time for myself."

> **If your marriage fails, Joyce, where would you be? Who would you be?**

"Are you going to go home and try to second-guess people?"

I looked down, shook my head, and fumbled for words.

"How are you going to do what you need, Joyce?" With crescendo, she said, "How? How?"

"I'd have to get up really early."

"Oh sure, Joyce, do what you need on your own time, so no one notices, and then you can still do everything others want you to do. Don't wait for someone to give you what you need. You take it."

I tried to absorb my therapist's words.

"If your marriage fails, Joyce, where would you be? Who would you be?"

I found my voice. "I'd still be me—warm, creative, capable. I'd lose a relationship. That's all. I wouldn't lose me. But I'm worried that Andy wants me to come back and be the old me. I know in my gut that being the old me would kill me. My body would give me so much pain I would soon be crippled again."

"So, the key issue is, what price are you willing to pay to maintain this marriage?"

As we batted words back and forth, I realized that I had to release control of others. Ultimately, I could control only myself and my reactions. If I trusted my ability to maintain boundaries, there was no need to control others."

"What I dread most about going home is having sex. It's such a sham."

"You don't trust Andy yet, so you aren't ready for sexual intimacy. But be careful that you don't slip into using sexual contact as a means of control. That's a fine line, to maintain your own boundaries and still avoid controlling others.

Many bodyworkers do their technique without revealing much about themselves or their thoughts. All forms of bodywork were effective in releasing the tension that contributed to my body pain. Initially, I was surprised when some of the bodyworkers shared the images they saw as I released pent-up emotions. I came to appreciate the fact that their insights confirmed information that came to me through flashbacks. I viewed their perceptions, not as a psychic phenomenon, but more as an indication that these healers were tuned into their intuition, their own inner guidance system.

> **Your abuse is mind boggling to me.**

Both a Rolfer and a physical therapist commented on breast torture, something I'd briefly glimpsed in flashback. That helped me understand why I'd always loathed my heavy breasts.

A massage therapist said she couldn't believe that the man she saw on top of me was my father because he was a big man, fair-skinned—not like a farmer—and dressed in black. Her sharing confirmed the minister I remembered. Additionally, her vision affirmed that my abuse started at an early age because that preacher left our community about the time I turned five.

A female physical therapist commented on how my sacrum was skewed to one side, that she saw a large penis banging against it when I was a toddler. This accomplished practitioner internally repositioned my tailbone. Her work alleviated low back pain.

After flashbacks of being given the drug Spanish Fly, a naturopath physician suggested I take homeopathic doses of cantharis. Homeopathy uses extremely small amounts of a product to overcome symptoms. The theory behind homeopathy bears some similarity to vaccination. The doctor directed me to a Hippocrates medical book where I read that Spanish Fly, or cantharis, is residual in the kidneys. After a couple rounds of homeopathic cantharis, I have never had recurrence of the inflammation/infections (UTIs) that plagued me in my thirties and forties.

Another time when I consulted the naturopath, I reviewed recent flashbacks and asserted how much I wanted to be done with healing.

The doctor shook her head. "Your abuse is mind-boggling to me. No wonder it took such intense pain to wake you up. Now that you are awake, you might as well finish this and not have to come back again to learn these lessons."

"But I've cried so much; I'm sick of grief work. My first certain memory of incest was in January. A year of tears should be enough."

"You've remembered all this in one year? You didn't just open the door and take a peek ... you flung the door wide open and dove right in!"

"It seems to me I should be done by now."

"You've remembered as fast as your body and your nervous system could handle the new information. Any faster and you would not have survived; you would have short-circuited. You couldn't have stayed in the body. Either you would have left this earth or let go of sanity. Neither are good choices for healing."

During frustration and doubt, reassurance from my team of healers kept me focused on hope that I could recover to normal functioning. Process painting, creative art like stream of consciousness writing, was a powerful healing modality for me. We never started a painting with an image in mind, but let our feelings direct the brush strokes and our intuition choose the colors.

My first class was disorienting. With no guidance and no painting background, I wanted to bolt. With dogged determination, I stayed with process painting until I figured it out. In classes over a couple of years, I painted images of events that were not in my conscious awareness. Later, after flashbacks, the meaning of the images became clear. Most noteworthy were the abortion that accompanied my ruptured appendix, my mother's assault, and effects of Spanish Fly. Years later, about twenty of those paintings became the anchor for my advocacy presentations.

Writing in many forms—journaling, affirmations, and poetry—was all part of my healing process and continue to be important to me today. It amazes me how clarity emerges as words stream onto paper. I have dozens of journals where I recorded events during my healing crisis. Those journals informed the events and dialogue in this memoir.

I'm grateful that affirmations were recommended in the pain book I studied and in the writings of Louise Hay. The facilitator for Conscious Connected Breathing (CCB) expanded the process of affirmations by suggesting that I write responses to them. The responses helped to identify the root beliefs under my faulty assumptions. I've since read that it's important to recognize that our beliefs as well as our inner critic are not our own voice but from authority figures in our childhood. What we hear before six years of age enters the memory unfiltered and settles in our unconscious as a belief. From then on, these unfiltered beliefs will direct our thoughts and behavior until we release the faulty thinking. Uncovering the faulty beliefs that had directed my thoughts and actions evolved into an ongoing process that will likely continue as long as I breathe.

> **As a child, you froze because you had no ability to escape the danger.**

Poetry was something I did on my own; words just appeared in my thoughts. My poetry is folksy and my proclivity to rhyme didn't earn me any accolades when I enrolled in poetry classes. I've continued to create my kind of poetry, even though it isn't modern. To this day I yearn to write with reckless abandon and prefer to compose with pen in hand rather than fingers on a keyboard.

Oh, the joy of giving up perfection! Releasing the drive to be perfect helped me overcome the propensity to procrastinate. Finally understanding that procrastinators are often perfectionists, I became aware of internal thoughts that told me I would surely do better tomorrow or next week. Silencing that inner voice helped me act instead of ruminating and procrastinating.

I'm grateful for my experience with Conscious Connected Breathing (CCB), Pranayama Yoga, and somatic healing techniques. All emphasize the power of the breath in healing trauma. Prior to dealing with incest, I had no idea that my breathing was shallow. More recently, the process of circular breathing I experienced in CCB is identified as Transformational Breath Work. One of the hallmarks of this modality for me was feeling energy pulse through my body. Also, I found releasing fear through cold-water breathing profoundly effective.

The CCB facilitator who worked with me introduced new ideas when she stated: The world thinks we have thoughts because of our experiences, but more accurately we have experiences because of our thoughts. New discoveries in neuroscience affirm the accuracy of those statements that fell on my ears as speculative ideas in the 1990s.

Healing therapies from other cultures also had merit for me. One time a counselor accompanied me to a session with a Native American shaman. The shaman's sensitivity gripped me. Integrating the session afterward, my therapist shuddered. "The darkness, the heaviness, I felt in that room when you released pressure from your head … I can't put words to it…but it shook my entire body. I felt sick."

I said, "It amazed me that the shaman sensed that pressure before I spoke about it."

"You must remember that Andy may be frustrating, but he is not evil. Your birth family showed you evil. From them you learned psychological fear that overrides instinctual fear." She continued, "When you feel fear now, it is imperative to identify the source and ask yourself if it really merits fear. As a child, you froze because you had no ability to escape the danger. Now you freeze when the fear stimulus is insignificant. Your goal is to recognize appropriate instinctual fear and separate it from learned fear that paralyzes."

Yoga practitioners introduced me to Ayurvedic traditions. A weeklong stay at a Vedic center in New Mexico was a profound healing experience. My body responded well to the treatments and to a diet that contained all six tastes at every meal: sweet, sour, salty, bitter, pungent, and astringent. Vedics believe that spices are healing and keep us in balance. One week of a very limited and controlled eating pattern convinced me that food can be medicine. As I learn of new research on the importance of nutrition for optimum health, I look back to my Ayurvedic experience with gratitude.

Looking at the many different modalities I tried, you may think me a healing junkie. Could be. In my experience, healing junkies are stuck in repetitive cycles. It's true that I am still searching for new information on trauma and healing, still examining the latest insights on health and nutrition, still nurturing my spirit with meditation and contemplation. I don't feel like a healing junkie. Truth is, I'm determined to continue learning, so long as I'm in earth school.

The pains you feel are messengers. Listen to them.
—RUMI

13

Family Talk

*I have no idea ... what ... you ...
are talking about.*

Although I lived 230 miles from the Kohl relatives, I viewed our family ties as tight prior to incest memories. We celebrated holidays together and followed each other's health challenges. I'd had enough insight from flashbacks to believe that my entire birth family was involved in the dysfunction. What I wanted more than anything was for all of us to heal together. I'd heard of many instances of families being torn apart by abuse allegations, but I couldn't see that happening in the Kohl family. I knew that my traveling many miles for holiday dinners had held the Kohls together when there was tension between my brothers, and I believed that I could hold us together through this crisis.

Is this truth mine alone?

When I first wanted to reveal incest to my birth family in February 1993, my therapist discouraged me. By late July 1993, she and

I both felt like disclosure to my family was a risk worth taking. Because I viewed us as closely knit and supportive of each other, I felt certain disclosure to the Kohl family was safe. When I shared with my friend Robin that I planned to confront my mother and brothers, she wisely suggested that I think of confront as "turn and face" and hold in my mind the intention that the conversation need not lead to animosity.

Driving from the Springs to Colby, I recalled Leona's earlier advice to not speak with my family until I was certain I would not react with guilt, in the face of either denial or confirmation. I reflected on the eerie synchronicity in Peg's advice to keep my eyes open during Rolfing and the affirmation of the Yoga therapist: I can open my eyes to truth. Thinking deeply about truth, I asked myself: *Is this truth mine alone? Is it possible that my birth family will be able to see the collective truth?*

Moments with my mother over the past three years circled through my mind. I recalled how stoic Mother was in 1992 when we were decorating Dad's grave. In contrast, I couldn't hold back tears. By then, I'd been immersed in therapy for two years, yet Mother never asked how I was feeling. She knew I sought relief from physical pain when I was walking with a cane in 1990, soon after my father's death. Still, she never inquired how it happened that I no longer needed a cane. I had purposely avoided telling her about Rolfing, psychotherapy, or flashbacks.

Mother's gaze froze beyond me.

Questions about my childhood from my counselor had aroused my curiosity. I longed to seek Mother's help in remembering, but an inner voice cautioned me to wait every time I was tempted to approach her. I trusted my gut feeling that it would be risky to tell her that many therapists had observed fear in my body.

As I contemplated approaching my mother about incest in July of '93, I remembered a face-to-face conversation from the past May. I had asked her if she remembered the rash on my hands and forearms that plagued me during grade school. When she acknowledged the rash, I pressed on: "Do you also remember, I think it was during first grade, I had hard red welts on the inside of my thighs? I couldn't wear clothes for a while and had to miss school."

Mother's gaze froze beyond me; her presence evaporated.

A shudder shook her out of her trance. She cleared her throat and spoke with measured deliberation. "I have no idea ... what ... you ... are talking about."

My shoulders pitched forward, squeezing my heart against my spine. I forced an inhale and pasted on an empty expression. I'd had years of practice freezing my emotions under a blank face. I resisted the temptation to tell her that I'd read in a medical book that Spanish Fly on the skin can cause hard red welts. Following that encounter, I'd spent some time regretting that I'd tested her. So, it surprised me to realize how much stronger I felt now—only two months later.

Then I remembered how distraught I was when photos arrived a couple weeks later. I had asked if she had any childhood pictures of me. She couldn't remember where they were, but promised to mail them soon. I was disappointed to find that most of the photos she sent were of my sons, Ben and Sam. Only two small Kodak photos were of my childhood.

When my Colby friend Neva learned I planned to visit the Kohls again, she was visibly shaken. Like my son Sam, she worried about my safety. I assured her that was not my concern. I wanted Ben to know of my plan to talk to my birth family. When he came home from work, I shared my mission and asked if he had any words of wisdom before I left.

What good will it do to confront them?

"What good will it do to confront them? Do you really think that will make you feel closer to your family?" Ben asked.

"We've always been close. I want to be honest with the Kohls. And I want all of our family to heal together."

"They will perceive this as a threat. You need to think about how to present it, so it doesn't come across that way. Consider how to make it easier on them because this will be hard for them to hear. Life is not the same for any two people because of their own perceptions and interpretations." Ben paused. "Things like you've been remembering are usually inventions of the mind to cover up worse realities that have been repressed. It's hard to imagine if worse things could have happened. So maybe you've gotten deep enough to face repressed stuff. It's difficult to believe that the mind could invent all you've remembered … if nothing had occurred."

Ben's insights gave me comfort. His comments were validation that he accepted my memories. Now I felt ready to proceed, even though I knew it was risky to defy the three cardinal rules of dysfunctional families that Bradshaw shared in his workshop:

1. Don't talk.
2. Don't feel.
3. Don't trust.

CHAPTER THIRTEEN: Family Talk

Driving from Colby to Prairie Center, I turned on the radio more than once, but mostly preferred my own thoughts versus the canned noise. When I tuned in to a PBS presentation of Beethoven's "Ode to Joy," the announcer explained that it was originally titled "Ode to Freedom." The change from freedom to joy occurred because it was politically dangerous to use the word freedom.

> I reveled in the powerfulness of the musical composition, and it dawned on me that I was on a journey to claim my freedom.

I reveled in the powerfulness of the musical composition, and it dawned on me that I was on a journey to claim my freedom. I wanted to be free of the bondage of deception, repression, and secrecy. Though not culturally or politically safe, I'd decided to take the risk to claim my truth and to own my freedom.

Ben's advice swirled in my mind: "Consider how to make this easier for them." An allegory emerged that could soften my words: *In this life, we are much like the three blind men who argued about the essence of an elephant because each was touching a different part of the animal. I could add that each of us is unique and each of us will view my childhood through different filters.*

It was a beautiful Saturday drive. An hour from my destination, I stretched my legs at a park and my thoughts began to gel. I would meet with Mother, Gene, and Roger, each one privately. I'd approach the subject cautiously, setting the stage for understanding by asking only that that person *hear what I had to say.*

I would say ... I was not able to face you until now because I wanted to be certain of what I believed, and because I've known for some time that I cannot continue to be in your presence and pretend nothing had changed. Out loud I affirmed to myself that I must tell Mother and each brother: I realize I may not be welcome after this conversation.

I arrived at Mother's house about 4:00 p.m. and she greeted me at the door, saying, "Well, my darling Joyce, you're here."

That was almost enough for me to turn heel and forget my purpose. Endearing platitudes were not what I wanted to hear. They reminded me of the many times I'd heard Mother speak to others about me as her "precious daughter." I never felt precious. I'd always hated Precious Moments figurines.

Did it not seem uncanny that my mother would call me precious, when she could never say I love you? Breathing deep and slow, I chose to rise above the platitudes and get on with the purpose of my visit. We had small talk and looked at photo albums until about 9:00 p.m., then I called each of my brothers and decided to see Gene in the morning and Roger for lunch.

I knew I had to tell Mother that evening. About 10:00 p.m. over a cup of tea, I called up my bravest self, referring first to my sleep disturbances and my internist's diagnosis of fibromyalgia in January 1992. I acknowledged that meds helped me progress to more restful sleep at night.

Then I plunged deeper. "As I slept better, I became aware of nightmares and suffered night terrors. These sleep interruptions often repeated a similar pattern ... one of sexual activity ... as a child. I was devastated by this information and had to work through it myself before I could share it. I have done that, and now there's no doubt in my mind." I took a deep breath. "I'm convinced I experienced incest as a child."

There, I'd said it.

Mother said, "Joyce, I'm not denying anything. Why didn't you come to me earlier?"

Really? She's handing me guilt? I struggled to keep my expression neutral. Finally, I replied: "I've only known it for a few months, Mother. It was too painful for me to see. I repressed it."

"I feel like such a failure." She sighed and lowered her head.

Now, am I supposed to jump in and assure her she's not a failure? Is it beyond her capacity to think about how this has affected my life? I thought about Ben's advice and redirected my thoughts to how I could make this easier for her. "We can't change the past. I only ask that you hear me."

She said that she had no higher education and she had no way to support herself and three little children. I acknowledged that and added that even if she had known, there were no laws in place in the 1940s to protect children from incest. Those laws first appeared in our country in the 1960s.

There were other tense moments during our discussion that my ego was tempted to blot out. To support my revelation, I asked if she recalled my helping Dad during hog farrowing season after his heart attack. Mom's eyes widened, but she remained silent.

"My dad raped me one night as we waited for the sows to deliver. That was my first clear memory of incest."

Her response was: "Joyce! Joyce!"

My therapist's words of warning strengthened me at that moment. Although I longed to hear her say she was sorry to hear that, I told myself to accept that Mother couldn't go there.

I'm not denying anything. A few minutes later she tried to counterattack, circling back to the fact that I lived with Dr. Fritz and Vi Shepard my last two years of high school. Then she told how she and Dad had read and destroyed the cards that Fritz had sent me while I was in college.

"Well," she said. "You know what was said in those letters and it wasn't good."

I had learned to trust my body. I breathed deep and observed my body. I had no reaction. No diarrhea like at the mention of Spanish Fly, no clutching in my gut like when Andy winked, and no constriction of my breathing. My body was at ease.

I thought of Scott Peck's *People of the Lie* explanation: Those who do evil project their deeds onto the innocent in order to preserve their own innocence. The words that came to me were simple. "But Mother, was there anything sexual in those cards … any romantic or sexual innuendos?"

"No, but they were very mushy," was her terse answer.

My mother's interpretation of "mushy" was what most would think "mushy" was. She felt that if anyone said they cared for someone or wished them success—it was too mushy! I told her firmly that I didn't believe there was anything unseemly with Dr. Shepard because I felt no fear or defensiveness in my body.

I got back on track with some references to Mother's reality. I said, "There's some good in all this pain I've experienced. I've been able to recognize some of my father's negative traits and some of the pain you've endured over the years."

She nodded in agreement.

"I remember how jealous he was of you, unreasonably jealous. Remember how you couldn't go shoe shopping without him because he didn't want men touching your legs? He was upset about makeup and he wouldn't allow you to shave your legs. When I was fourteen, I remember visiting cousin Rene in Texas and you said that Dad was angry because she'd taught me to shave my legs."

Mother chimed in: "And perfume, I couldn't use any perfume or cologne."

I continued, "He accused you of affairs with different men in church, and still you continued to attend and take me. You grounded me in the Christian faith. That faith has helped me survive. It helped me first as a little child and it has helped me work through these memories."

She pursed her lips in a familiar pout as she exclaimed, "I refused to give up my church, even in the face of repeated attacks. You don't know how severe your father's attacks were!"

As she spoke about her unhappiness, she shared that her maternal grandmother told her Charlie was not the man for her. But she was young and in love. She further explained that getting through high school had been a struggle for her. She wasn't smart. Her sister, Margot, was bright and was salutatorian of her class. I gently suggested that must have been hard, being a year older than Margot and watching her excel. Mother shook her head. She couldn't speak of her pain as it related to her dear departed sister. They supported each other in the absence of the loving mother they had lost as little girls.

> **Why was I never told the truth?**

Mother continued, "Charlie wanted to marry me, and I knew my dad could only afford to educate one daughter. It should be Margot because she was the good student, and she wanted to be a nurse."

I seized the occasion to seek truth about her sister's death. I locked eyes with Mother and said, "About Margot … she didn't die in an automobile accident."

Mother didn't flinch under my steady gaze. "No, she didn't."

I asked why I was never told the truth. She passed the buck, saying that the auto accident tale in the official obituary was a decision made by Aunt Ester and Dad Elder.

Oh sure, give up your power! Let others make your decisions. I spared her the fact that I'd read the death notice in the Dallas newspaper that revealed Margot had split her wrists, taken morphine, and turned on the gas oven without lighting the pilot.

"Mother, I'm 53 years old. Why was I never told the truth?"

"You never asked."

I thought, here we go again; it's my fault because I never asked.

"Do you feel cheated?" she implored. "What difference would it possibly have made in your life? What good would it have done for you to know that my sister took her own life?"

I am looking directly at her, my gaze unflinching. "It would have been the truth."

Assuming a defiant pose, she said, "There are things about your father and about the past I vowed I would take to my grave. I will NOT change my mind."

"You have a right to make that choice. But please know, if you ever change your mind, it might speed up my healing."

I asked about Dad's falling out with Aunt Fanny. I told her what I remembered, how she had told me Aunt Fanny accused him of giving Spanish Fly to Amy, contributing to the pregnancy that forced her to get married. She looked at me blankly. I knew she knew. I remembered her telling me that Aunt Fanny's Spanish Fly accusation was the reason I couldn't visit my cousin after serving as her bridesmaid.

Mother rambled on about her plight. She shared how Dad would embrace and kiss other women in front of her. She even related attending a funeral where Dad ignored her and gave all his attention to another woman. Obviously, she intended to take to her grave what she knew about my abuse, but was willing to share what made her life unpleasant.

That led to a discussion of the time when Dad asked her for a divorce, and she refused because she felt that she had too much to lose.

The biggest surprise for me was when Mother said he threatened to kill himself if she didn't sue him for divorce. According to my memory, Dad told me that Mother had threatened suicide. There was no divorce, they just continued living together and hating each other. I shared that she had told me years ago that Dad demanded sex several times a night.

She shuddered. "Oh Joyce, you don't know. You just don't know what it was like. Yes, he insisted on sex every night; sometimes many times per night. And that's why I insisted you must have a college education. I couldn't support myself. I wanted you to always know you could."

Interesting. What she remembers is vastly different than what I remember. I thought it was my own drive, good grades, and the influence of Dr. Fritz and Vi Shepard that got me to Kansas State. Neither of my brothers went to college, or even considered it a possibility. Before living with the Shepard family, college wasn't even a pipe dream for me.

Whose memory is more credible, Mother's or mine? Until recently, I would never have considered my memory more reliable. Have I not been giving Mother the credit she is due for my college education, or is she lying to make herself look good? Recovering incest memories has made me feel more compassion for my mother and opened my heart to see her pain. Simultaneously, it has caused me to consider her words suspect. Tonight, she appeared fully open to sharing her strife, but unwilling to share any clues that might help me understand my past.

When Mother had heard all she could take, she bowed her head.

I asked if she would like to pray.

She bristled. "I am praying."

"Yes, I know. But would you like to pray out loud, for both of us?"

As she began to speak, I knelt at her feet and clasped her hands in mine.

As she concluded her prayer, I offered my own. Up to this point, only an occasional tear had fallen as I presented my story as boldly as my being would allow. But now, as I invoked God's grace and mercy, I was totally humbled and wept openly, but it didn't interrupt my flow of words. I closed with a plea for forgiveness for each of us. We know that's possible because His forgiveness is Divine; ours is only human, and it's much harder for us. And the most difficult forgiveness of all is to forgive ourselves. I asked His mercy as we struggled to follow His forgiving example.

It was after midnight when we retired. I slept soundly. I felt like I'd stayed in my power when she challenged me. I consciously chose to resist the temptation to lie awake and analyze her response to my revelations.

There were many moments that could have led to disastrous separation. I trusted God and my Guardian Angel Elizabeth to supply the thoughts and words I needed. That trust was rewarded. There was no way I could have anticipated some of her responses.

The next morning, I drove twelve miles south of town to meet Gene. We sat in my car to talk. Gene registered surprise when I told him I remembered incest. He claimed that he didn't remember anything like that. Then I asked Gene what he remembered about Amy's pregnancy and marriage. He said that Aunt Fanny accused our father of molesting Amy. That the baby she was carrying when she married Bill was Dad's child, not Bill's. What a saga. This was soap opera material.

Then I told Gene my Spanish Fly story. That I had residual of that drug in my system, and it was likely responsible for my recurring bladder and kidney disturbances for years.

He said, "Gee, Sis, that's hard to believe. How would a poor farmer, out here in the country, get his hands on drugs like that?"

I decided not to share that I remembered Dad had supplemented the farm income during the war by working at Fort Riley Army Base, which was only twenty-five miles from the farm. Additionally, I'd read that farmers sometimes used Spanish Fly to get cows to breed.

As Gene and I parted, he started to get out of my car and then settled back in. He reached across the console to give me a hug and assured me of how sorry he was that I had to go through this. I felt his genuine concern, even as I considered that he must be in denial of his involvement. I thought I would hate him when I took this step. Instead, I pitied him for what he hadn't acknowledged to himself ... for the distance he would have to move in order to heal. I was glad that I didn't tell him that I'd remembered his part in my abuse. My therapist had warned me to avoid details because that could invite arguments and defensiveness.

CHAPTER THIRTEEN: Family Talk

I drove back with mixed emotions. Mother was not home so I started to drive to Roger's office when I met her a couple blocks away. She told me that Roger needed to postpone his meeting with me. Mother and I had tea and small talk. She didn't ask any questions about Gene's response, so I kept that to myself. It never occurred to me to ask where she had been, or how she happened to learn that Roger needed to postpone our meeting.

I met Roger at the Pizza Hut just an hour later, as she had told me to do. As we left the Pizza Hut, I revealed the purpose of why I had come. Lowering his voice, he asked that we talk in the privacy of his home, and not at Pizza Hut.

Seated in the comfort of Roger's home, I started the same as with Mother and Gene—by relating the story of the three blind men arguing about the elephant. I said that I thought life was like that, subject to different interpretations. Then I talked about my back pain, my sleep disturbances, and my flashbacks of sexual activity as a child.

Roger didn't register surprise. Like Gene, when I said that my first clear flashback to incest was this January, his question was: "You mean Dad?"

Roger repeatedly asked if I was talking about Dad, and then cautioned me to exercise discretion. He could appreciate that it was an important part of my healing, but it appeared that I pretty much had my life in order now. And he hoped I would be aware of how this could affect so many other people.

Roger remembered Dad working at Fort Riley before his first heart attack. Dad was too weak to drill wheat in the fall of 1955.

In order to plant that crop, Roger missed football season his senior year in high school.

When I brought up the Amy story, Roger was visibly agitated and reminded me of how Dad could get frighteningly angry. My brother didn't have to tell me that he was also capable of seething anger. I could see it coming in his clenched jaw and his twitching forehead. I began to feel unsafe and chose to quit sharing. This one-on-one conversation with Roger felt dangerous.

> **You should have kept the family secret ... secret.**

Rising from my chair, I indicated I was ready to go. Roger remained seated, staring above the chair I'd vacated and out through the window. Clearly, he had something more to say.

"I hope you will treat with discretion this new information you have and realize how devastating it could be to others." Roger rose and walked me to the door.

There was no warmth in our parting, like with Gene. I clearly absorbed one message: You have broken out of your assigned role in this family. *You should have kept the family secret ... secret.*

Driving back to Mother's house, reality settled in. In view of the calm with which Roger received the news of incest, I should have realized that she had rushed over to prepare Roger before I talked to him.

Driving the four hours back to Colby, I tried to understand the responses I heard from my birth family. Clearly, I was overly optimistic when I thought we could all heal together. Others viewed the need to heal as belonging solely to me. There were only guarded comments that I was believed, and no one offered to share anything that would further my healing. I recalled feeling isolated on an island after Dad's funeral. Three years later, my island had drifted further from the mainland. From my vantage point, I could barely see the mainland and my bond with those dwelling there had been stretched to the breaking point.

After I returned from revealing incest memories to my mother and brothers, Andy accompanied me to the Springs. He acknowledged that he'd had several breakthroughs recently. He talked about the phenomenon of bonding with the parent who hurt us most. He told how he identified with and tried to please his dad, even though his mother was much kinder to him. I shared that Leona had suggested that we respond to the parent who gives us the most attention—be it positive or negative.

Andy also talked about his role as peacemaker. He remembered that role emerged when he was young, and his parents were bickering. Andy affirmed to me that he thought we were both here to stop the generational cycle of abuse. That didn't come as a surprise to me because we had skirted around that subject before. I was really astounded when he said he thought he chose to be a part of my healing a long time ago. He spoke with certainty and conviction. I asked if he meant on the unconscious level and he nodded agreement. A few months ago, his acknowledging the mere existence of the unconscious realm would have been utterly impossible.

Andy's solemn sharing warmed my heart and gave me hope for better times ahead.

While in the Springs, Leona helped me to integrate my conversations with my mother and brothers. My report brought tears to her eyes, especially as I told her of Gene's compassion. She was touched by the fact that Mother and I could pray together. Leona said that prayer was possible because I approached Mother with love rather than blame.

I felt emancipated.

Leona reminded me of the distance I'd covered. Just a week ago, I'd been in her office discussing my plan to disclose incest. Leona asked what was next for me and I told her I wanted to work on defining my restructured self. Although I realized my incest issues weren't over, I wanted to think beyond memory retrieval.

After therapy, Andy broached the subject of timetables. I confessed that I was unwilling to make any promises about when I would return to full-time work, as well as daily commitments as wife and mother. I took a deep slow breath. "I can live with uncertainty. If you can't, then you'll have to decide what to do about that."

He said, "You've given me your answer."

At one time, that would have struck terror in my heart. But as we drove peacefully down Gold Camp Road and then strolled up the path to Helen Hunt Falls, I could speak honestly to my husband and accept his response without fear or judgment. I felt emancipated.

It seemed like other people in my support system were more awed by the outcome with my mother and brothers than I was. It's almost like I couldn't be happy that I wasn't rejected. Truthfully, a part of me expected denial from all three members of the Kohl family. A part of me would have been more comfortable with their denial, because it would have given me a reason to discount my memories. Even though I trusted that my body revealed truth, a part of me still wished it weren't true.

I grieved over my mother and brothers' ability to completely abandon any responsibility, not only for the abuse but for any need to help me heal. The implications of Mother's comment: *I'm not denying anything*, lingered in my mind and left me curious—wondering how different she might have responded if I had given more details.

Changing paradigms regarding spirituality helped to diffuse some of the turmoil associated with incest memories. Others in my healing circle had shared how they believe we come to this earth to learn our lessons. The more years I live, and the more books I read, the more open I am to the belief that we come here to learn lessons and we come many times. It's curious that even before I experienced incest memories and encountered new paradigms, I repeatedly prayed: Dear God, give me grace to endure what comes my way and the wisdom to learn my lessons.

There is a voice that doesn't use words. Listen.
—RUMI

14

Family Repercussions

I don't know why in the hell Joyce and Rob couldn't keep their mouths shut like the rest of us.

After speaking of incest memories with my family, I didn't expect much communication. Any family gatherings were always near Prairie Center, not where I lived. In the day of only landline phones, long distance calls were rare and expensive, and 200 miles was far.

Carrie, my brother Gene's wife, phoned me a couple weeks after I disclosed incest to my birth family. She asked, "Are you okay?"

Something in her voice startled me. "Yes, Carrie, is something wrong?"

I pictured my sister-in-law—short, always smiling, moving too fast for extra pounds to settle in. My inner voice whispered, *don't give away your power.*

"Joyce, I have some questions … just for me." She gained momentum. "Gene's in the field and he won't be back for a while and I need to ask you some questions." She drew in a slow breath. "I might not tell Gene we talked. Gene gets things mixed up. When something is hard to handle, he just goes to work. You know that's always his answer to anything hard to face. Also, Gene forgets things. Whenever something unpleasant happens, it doesn't take long, sometimes just a few days, and Gene completely forgets it. I mean … it's gone. Sometimes when he's fixing fences with a neighbor and they disagree, I'll ask him about it a few days later, and he's already forgotten." Another pause. "Can you tell me, Joyce, how did the memories come to you? Are you sure?"

Trusting that still small voice, the one I attribute to my Guardian Angel Elizabeth, I listened for guidance.

When I hesitated, Carrie offered, "Joyce, I am not doubting you, really. I just need some help. I need to know some things for me."

Then she asked, "Did you see things? Did you know where you were? Who was with you?"

"Sometimes I knew; sometimes I smelled Dad's Camel cigarettes, other times I smelled hay or fresh cow's milk."

Oh, Joyce, I believe you!

"So, you're sure it happened more than once?"

"Definitely." I stopped myself. Leona said to be careful about sharing details—that invites argument.

Carrie said, "Uh huh. Oh, Joyce, this all makes so much sense."

I launched into an explanation of traumatic memories and repression. She assured me that she heard those terms watching the *Phil Donahue Show*.

Then I told Carrie my diagnosis was PTSD, a diagnosis shared with Vietnam vets. When my voice broke, she quickly asked if she was upsetting me. I assured her that I'd cried a lot and it didn't upset me to do so.

Carrie referred to my high school days. "I believe Dr. Shepard knew about this. I remember he took out your appendix shortly before he gave you a job at his house."

"My therapist had the same thought as you, Carrie. She said there were no laws protecting children from sexual abuse until the sixties. The Shepards did the only thing they could do in the mid-fifties."

"Oh, Joyce, I believe you! I didn't at first. But with a little time to think about it, so many other things make sense now."

My sister-in-law couldn't possibly know how important it was for me to hear her words. I thought about the scripture: *I have learned, in whatever state I am, to be content.* Even in this miserable time of feeling damaged and confused, I'd received unexpected and loving support from Carrie.

What difference would it make?

Rob, Gene and Carrie's son, called me within a week to tell me he had no difficulty believing me because no one suspected he was beaten as a child. Rob revealed that he used to run and hide in the fields to avoid being beaten by his father. The severity of the beatings was recently confirmed when Rob had X-rays because he thought he'd broken a rib. The physician asked if he grew up in a foster home. The doctor went on to explain that Rob didn't have a broken rib now, but the test revealed that all his ribs had been broken as a child. Rob assured me that he'd talked with his dad about his childhood and they'd reconciled their relationship. Rob said he'd learned from his experience to be a different kind of dad to his two sons. That he hugged them often and told them how much he loved them.

Rob told me that after he learned of my abuse, he'd begged Grandma Hulda to share what she remembered about my childhood. My mother responded to Rob's plea by saying: My memory doesn't serve me.

Another time Carrie phoned Andy with a stern warning. "Don't let Hulda come between the two of you. Many times, she has said cruel things about me and my family. Gene always sides with his mother, but I've refused to let it change our marriage."

After Andy hung up the phone from talking with Carrie, he said, "Doesn't your mother know that you would get hurt more if we split up?"

"You think she'd care? Mother is only interested in appearances. She'd be right if we split, because she didn't approve of you when we got married. Then she'd be without fault. She could deny everything and say I made up the incest story to disguise a bad marriage. Mother will protect her righteous image at all costs. My feelings aren't any more important to her now than they were when I was little." My outburst shocked even me.

On another call, Carrie said she always knew Mother's sister Margot had committed suicide, but Gene denied it until he read it in a neighbor's family history book. I told her that Mother got huffy with me and asked what difference it could possibly have made for me to know how Margot died.

Carrie sounded exasperated. "What difference would it make? You would have known the truth!"

"That's exactly what I told Mom. The word 'truth' was lost on her."

Carrie wanted to know more about Amy and the Spanish Fly rumor. She said when Aunt Fanny died, she asked my brother Gene what could possibly be so bad that his parents would miss his aunt's funeral. At the time, Gene said he didn't know.

I doubted Gene's denial, but I didn't say so. Instead, I continued to listen.

Carrie thought I should visit Amy in Texas and find out what she knew. I didn't argue, but my hunch was Amy would likely have repressed any abuse.

Carrie changed the subject. "How did your brother Roger react? Did he believe you?"

I struggled not to sound judgmental. "His concern was that I use this information with discretion; that I realize how devastating it could be to others."

Carrie asked again, "Did he believe you? Did he ever say he believed you?"

"He never said he believed me. He didn't call me a liar, either."

Carrie repeated, "I believe you. What is your mother going to do about this?"

"Nothing. I didn't ask for anything."

"How can she do nothing? I wanted Gene to go to Hulda right away. I told him: If you're sure it isn't true, you need to say so. And if it is true, you need to do everything you can to help Joyce."

"I don't expect help, Carrie. I wanted us all to heal together, but Mother said she vowed to take these things to her grave and she wouldn't change her mind. I agreed to respect her wishes."

"That's not fair to you. Your mother can't change the past. What she could do now is tell you anything that would help you get through this."

I told her I'd been angry with God because I hadn't faced this earlier so I could protect my sons. I regretted that I'd sent my boys to visit my parents.

I felt like I'd been given an hour-long embrace.

Carrie picked up steam. "You don't know how much my kids resented not staying overnight with the Kohl grandparents. I always thought it was because of me, and that my kids weren't good enough. Now I understand."

My composure collapsed. Why was it okay for my sons to be in harm's way? I couldn't say another word. My mind was spinning, and my knees were shaking. What had I done to my sons? What should I do with this revelation from my sister-in-law?

Carrie's confidence had grown as she poured out her heart over the past hour.

"Gene would die if he knew I told you this, but he's just not very affectionate. Sometimes I call my kids and tell them I need a hug. Gene loves me; I know he does. But he just can't give me a hug. And I don't think we've had intercourse for three years."

Again, I was too stunned to reply. That's how long our dad had been gone. Gene's withholding intimacy could be a sign his memories were surfacing.

"Thanks for talking to me. You've answered a lot of my questions and made me feel a lot better. I believe you, Joyce, and I love you. Take care of yourself."

I felt like I'd been given an hour-long embrace. Tears of grief and joy poured out.

Weeks later, Carrie called Andy and reported that she and Gene had visited with Hulda and begged her to talk to Joyce. Carrie was so upset over what she heard that she had written down Hulda's words so she could repeat it accurately.

> *Joyce has been having mental problems and had a nervous breakdown. You can believe whatever you want, but I will not lose my daughter over this.*

Andy was so upset with the way Hulda twisted the facts, that he wrote her a four-page letter in September of 1993, pleading with her to help me. Since I was in Colorado, he faxed me a copy. I was touched my husband wanted to help me but felt certain his efforts were futile. My mother would never sacrifice her reputation to help me heal. Andy included lots of Bible quotes to win her cooperation. She willingly prayed aloud during Sunday School and church services, regularly read the Bible, and often quoted scripture. Reading Andy's last page, I wept.

What has happened in the past cannot be changed, it can only be accepted. It is now part of history. Hulda, the Bible is full of passages telling us to speak in love and truth. You could really help your children and grandchildren a lot by telling them what you remember. It would take a lot of courage on your part to tell them what really did occur in the past. However, with your help they could know so much more about their childhood and heal so much faster. In the fall of 1991, I thought Joyce would be gone by now. In the past year, with memories coming back, she has started the slow process of healing.

I was home when Hulda's response came a week later. Andy knew I wasn't strong enough to read it alone, so we read it together.

Andy, dear
Your certified letter I must answer. Andy, whatever our daughter has told you, I have nothing to add or subtract. I am not a suspicious person, and there is no way I could explain my compassion and love for Joyce, my daughter.

> *Joyce to me is a precious girl—woman where I am concerned. But my memory doesn't serve me. One of the nicest things a man can do for his children is to respect and love his children's mother.*
>
> —*Joyce's Mother*

November 1993, just two months later, I was teaching a machine embroidery class when a basket of blue carnations and white daisies was delivered to Joyce's Fabric.

The card on the basket read: *Remembering. Love, Mother*

What the hell was that supposed to mean? Earlier she'd told me unequivocally that she would not discuss my abuse. During the ensuing weeks she'd responded to my brother Gene and his wife, Carrie, as well as their son Rob—that her memory didn't serve her. She'd even gone to great lengths to convince them I was having mental problems. Additionally, her response to Andy's letter confirmed she would not take responsibility.

What was the remembering about?

I penned a simple thank-you. I couldn't phone yet. The days slipped by and I forgot to rock my inner child or meditate. After a week in Colby, I'd caught up enough at the store to spend a few waking hours at the house. Sunday afternoon I garnered the courage to phone her. I sensed the basket of flowers was intended to evoke guilt in some twisted way. I doubted it meant she was remembering my abuse, but I had to ask.

"Oh, Joyce! It's good to hear your voice." Mother's tone was pleasant.

I steeled myself and didn't scream, "Will you ever ask how I am?" Instead I listened as she carried on about her cats and the weather.

"The bouquet you sent is still lovely. What was the remembering about?"

"Why, Joyce," she cleared her throat, her voice uncharacteristically upbeat, and said, "I remembered that you used to say, when your ship came in, you'd have fresh flowers on your table every day."

I recalled that as a child I thought it strange that our neighbor lady used to proclaim her wishes by saying: "When my ship comes in, I will have a big house and a new car…and on and on."

Always loving fresh flowers, maybe I did say that. Maybe I didn't. Either way, the card simply signed "Remembering" was a trigger I didn't need. She had to know what I wished it meant. My goodbye wasn't upbeat.

> **I must have the strength to stay away from my mother.**

I have a new script for interpreting my relationship with my mother. The script comes from reading Peck's book, *People of the Lie*. My mother's skill, mastery, and persistence at lying are too great a match for me … even after hundreds of hours of therapy. Scott Peck says in his practice of psychiatry, he learned to be quick to diagnose … and firm in confronting … evil.

Never been able to think fast in a conflict, a good comeback would occur to me a day late. I don't believe I could ever be quick enough with Hulda to dispel her lies. She bemoans that I am a better cook and seamstress. She starts with the victim stance, declaring that she doesn't have the education I have, and then she attacks the way I go about my work. Is her goal to make me feel wicked and selfish because I have a college education?

I must have the strength to stay away from my mother. I am not trained enough or widely experienced enough to stand up to people of the lie. Hulda's pattern of deceit is superb. Her ability to back up her lies with her own victimization and pious stature is without dispute. Dear God, is this honoring my mother? In a few minutes I have spit out accusations I never would have dreamed of a few months ago. Webster says: "Honor: a sense of high respect; renown glory; reputation; a sense of what is right or due..."

A sense of what is right or due? That I can agree with. I have high respect for Hulda's ability to tell lies and draw us kids into animosity and distrust for each other. I've come to expect her to whisper that she doesn't think Roger is giving her the full owner's share of hay bales, or that Gene might not be showing her all the elevator tickets from the wheat harvest. I have no idea what she says about me, but I'm certain it's something to create distrust. I have high respect for that behavior and recognize my inability to rise above her clutches. I believe a protective distance is necessary for my own sanity and safety.

I confessed to my therapist that I feared I wasn't honoring my parents with the thoughts I had after reading Peck's book. She responded, "You honor your parents for giving you life. You honor yourself and God by healing and transforming into the best human being that you can be."

Months later, Andy told me that Carrie called him while I was in Colorado and asked if I had remembered my brothers abusing me.

He reported telling her, "You're asking the wrong person. But what if they did? Wouldn't they have just been following a pattern shown them by their father?"

I was touched by my husband's compassionate answer.

Eventually I did relent and admit to Carrie that I remembered Gene, along with neighbor boys, Dan and Larry, taking turns. My gut snarled as I spoke. I knew I was giving too much information, but it just poured out. My therapist had warned me to avoid sharing details.

Later that day, I was mulling over what I told Carrie when my brother Gene phoned me.

"At first, I could straddle the fence on this thing with Dad, but now you are accusing a dead man who can't defend himself. Well, I'm alive and I can defend myself. Those things you told Carrie did NOT happen."

Gene's tone was different than I'd ever heard. I said, "I hear that you think nothing happened."

"No! I'm saying nothing happened. My mind is fine. I remember. I can't imagine how you could let a therapist plant those crazy ideas in your head." Gene's words struck me with the sting of a cattle prod.

"Nobody planted them. The memories came out of my body."

"You need help. You need a new therapist," Gene barked.

"I've had flashbacks with many different professionals, not just one," I said.

"Sis, really, you need help. Different help than you are getting now." Gene paused. "You are my sister and I love you, but I've drawn a line in the sand." And he hung up.

I thought that was the end of it. Wrong. The next day Gene's wife called. Carrie spoke slowly, in a measured tone I didn't recognize. "Joyce, it didn't happen."

I mumbled something about hearing her. I could hear Gene in the background: *Tell her it did NOT happen.*

Carrie repeated as Gene commanded.

I couldn't undo the damage I'd done by telling too many details. My challenge was to continue therapy and try to find my balance. After particularly difficult therapy sessions in the Springs, I arrived home in despair. Andy held me while I cried. He wanted to know what new memories I'd had, and I wasn't sure I should tell.

"I don't want to fill you with hate by what I have to say. I have decided that my therapists are right, forgiving my perpetrators is for my healing, not theirs. It releases me from the love/hate bond with them." The rest just oozed out of me, in no sensible order. Andy listened, transfixed. I had shared only a few incidents from the many flashbacks the past four days when Andy interrupted.

"I've been thinking about the Kohls and I have some thoughts to share. When your brother Roger and his wife joined us on the trip to the Husqvarna sewing machine factories in Sweden, Roger and I were a few steps behind you girls in Stockholm when hookers propositioned us. Your brother's response was: "*Why would I pay a hooker? I can have any woman I want because I know how to do it."* Andy continued, "I never told you about that incident because I figured you were too naive to notice we were propositioned."

"But what did he mean by 'I know how to have any woman I want?'" I asked.

Andy shrugged. "I don't know what he meant, but now I wonder who put that idea in his head. And that's not the only incident that makes me wonder about Roger. Last Thanksgiving when Roger came to our house to take your mother back home, he chided me for letting you make too many decisions."

I shook my head. "Chided doesn't sound like my brother. I'm guessing he said you were pussy-whipped." Clenching my teeth, I flinched as pain shot down from my jaw through my neck and bounced off my collarbone.

"That is exactly what he said."

Roger was always more distant than Gene, and knowledge of my incest memories resulted in greater separation. Months of silence from Gene and Carrie had passed when Gene called me to report that Mother and Roger planned to establish a trust for her property. Gene had attended a meeting at the attorney's office where Mother and the attorney both said that I shouldn't know about the new trust because of my condition. From Gene, I learned that she made certain that she could change beneficiaries. Initially, Roger and the attorney were to be trustees. Somehow that got changed so that Roger and Gene were trustees. Gene assured me that it was his intent that I get my share of Mother's estate if she passed.

Just the fact that Gene phoned me to alert me of her plan warmed my heart. He may have drawn a line in the sand earlier, but he was still my brother.

Andy and I were surprised at Roger's animosity, because we had set up Faye, Roger's wife, with a fabric shop after they experienced a financial disaster on the farm.

Eventually, Mother phoned me repeatedly, trying to convince me to merge the Western Kansas trust by combining it with her trust. Before Dad's passing, he and Mother had set up a trust for a parcel of Western Kansas land that Dad inherited from his father. Dad appointed me trustee, supposedly because I lived closer to the property than my brothers and could more easily supervise it.

In response to her request, I consulted with my attorney. I learned that the irrevocable trust Dad set up couldn't be changed until three years after Hulda's death, since she was the second grantor. Mother tearfully pleaded that this was a family matter; that we should all just agree. She argued that we didn't need an attorney for this family matter. Following the advice of my attorney, I countered that I wasn't willing to do something illegal. November 1995, I told her that my attorney had requested that her attorney send a letter explaining how to legally transfer an irrevocable trust. My request ended Hulda's pleading.

Hulda had a stroke December 24, 1995. My brothers notified me of Mother's condition midday, when Sam and Ben were in Colorado Springs with me. Because Roger reported that Hulda was in a coma, I decided not to travel immediately. I asked to be notified if she regained consciousness.

I immediately phoned Andy. At the time of our divorce three months earlier, (you'll learn more about that later) we'd agreed that we would welcome each other as family when either mother passed. Not hearing anything from my brothers, I phoned the nurses' station on December 27 and learned that she was visiting with my brother Gene. I was prepared to leave on short notice, but before I left, I phoned Andy to tell him Mother was no longer in a coma. I learned from a staff member at Joyce's Fabric that Andy had been summoned earlier and was already with my mother. That smacked of betrayal.

I arrived at the hospital to find Mother's brother at her bedside. Apparently, Andy left before I arrived. Gene and Roger were distant and cold. I was not allowed to stay at Hulda's house but drove thirty-five miles to Manhattan to stay overnight with Ben's girlfriend. On December 31, Mother was trying to say something to me. She kept repeating: *can't*. I tried a lot of different phrases, and when I asked, "You can't get well?" she blinked.

I said, "That's okay, Mother. If you need to stay on earth, we'll find someone to take care of you. If you and God are ready for you to go to the other side, it's okay. I know you did the best you could."

Mother closed her eyes and seemed to breathe easier. Later when Mother's brother and Gene and Roger met me in the lobby, I told them what I had said. Her brother nodded agreement. Gene said, "I'm not a praying man, but this is no way to live. I told God it was okay to take her. But I wouldn't say that to her."

Roger said, "I agree with Gene. I can't believe you were so callous. But then, that's who you are."

I left without reacting and drove the 500 miles back to Colorado. On January 2, I was making lentil soup about 8:00pm when I decided to contact Mother and tell her what Gene and Roger had said about releasing her. I felt her presence for several minutes, and then I seemed to lose her. A little after 11:00 that evening my cousin from Fort Collins phoned to say she was sorry about my mother. She'd received a phone call from her aunt in Kansas that my mother had passed about 8:15 pm

> Her effort to disinherit me failed.

The Western Kansas trust was never transferred. When we gathered at Hulda's house after her funeral, Roger informed me that Mother had drawn up a trust with the intention to disinherit me. She was waiting for the transfer of the Western Kansas land before finalizing it. Roger said he intended to honor her wishes.

Gene said, "You are my sister and you will get your share from me."

Roger went on to say that I was not needed to prepare for Mother's estate sale. I didn't argue. I didn't even attend.

Again, my angels protected me. Because I did not transfer the Western Kansas land, Mother's trust was never finalized. Her effort to disinherit me failed.

Backing up to her funeral service, there were some tense moments. Because I was divorced three months earlier, I attended Mother's funeral without a partner. I was confused when some extended family members and neighbors turned to exit the receiving line after shaking hands with my brothers. As I stood in the receiving line, my Colby friend Neva appeared by my side. She insisted I sit beside her. She couldn't bear to see folks snub me at my mother's funeral.

Later I learned that Mother had carefully planted seeds of doubt that grew into walls of distrust with folks who knew me. One neighbor later told me she was pleased to see me, after all the things she'd heard. To my inquiry, she mumbled something about mental problems. A few months later, a cousin expressed shock that I attended the funeral. She was under the impression that I was confined to a mental hospital in Colorado. An aunt whom I adored confided in me that she was told that I couldn't be trusted because I was a member of a cult.

Fast-forward almost a decade. In 2003, Gene was diagnosed with kidney cancer that spread to his brain. In 2004, as his health declined, I heard from his wife, Carrie, and his children that there wasn't much time to reconcile. I wrote a couple of letters, hoping Gene would be able to pass in peace. Meanwhile, Carrie wrote that my exile would be over when Gene passed.

My last letter to Gene arrived a couple weeks before his death. Carrie, as well as their son Rob, insisted I attend the funeral and sit with the family. Remember that Rob is the nephew who was one of the first to believe me, because Gene had beaten him as a child.

After Gene's service, Carrie and I had a genial visit in her home. She told me that Gene let her read my last letter to him. Carrie thought I should know his response to that letter. He said, *I don't know why in the hell Joyce and Rob couldn't keep their mouths shut like the rest of us.*

CHAPTER FOURTEEN: Family Repercussions

My heart filled with gratitude for Carrie. She gifted me with the most direct confirmation of incest I've ever had from my birth family. I drove west toward Colorado, but the 500-mile trip was too much to do in one stretch. I pulled out my journal after checking into a motel and let words come through my pen.

> *The rolling hills and the bluegrass prairies of central Kansas disappeared in the rearview mirror of my aging Toyota Camry. I was driving away, never expecting to return. This last visit was all I would ever need to connect me to bygone days. As the stately beards of wheat waved their farewell, I resolved to put all this behind me. As the grain had matured in readiness for harvest, I felt the fall of my lifetime upon me. Like the standing grain, the stalk would weaken and decay after it yielded ripe grain. I, too, would yield up the parts of me that had been used up, dried out, and no longer served me. This release would allow new gifts to be revealed. As the breeze blows the chaff from the grain during harvest, so would the winds of time clean the irritants from my psyche.*

Doubt crept in. Would my thoughts ever be free; would my movements ever be unfettered and untethered? Would the lingering voices of the past ever be quieted? More than sixty years had passed since I first opened my eyes to the windswept horizon of central Kansas, and what I had refused to see for the first fifty years haunted my living far more than I wanted to admit. Dissociation was a delicious gift and a bitter curse. At times I struggled with a hunger to return to that state of selective knowing. But like the rock broken asunder in

> **Dissociation was a delicious gift and a bitter curse.**

the face of rushing waters, my memory bank cannot be restored to its former state.

Just as a broken boulder can reveal precious stones, so do hidden gems emerge after the crushing waters of personal transformation. Yes, the flow of life crushes in on our hidden elements releasing dormant talents, distant memories, and forgotten skills. Life's blows open cracks and crevices in our darkness, so the light of truth can illuminate our living. Light reflected from the gems imparts wisdom and perspective and invites forgiveness, the balm of the soul, so that authentic freedom settles in.

Judgment can creep in and stall the march to freedom. Sometimes it wins the battle and we're left to live in anger and resentment. When we persevere, surrender peeks through the judgment clouds and the light is bright enough to enliven the latent quality of forgiveness that releases us from agony.

> **Rise above the storm and you will find the sunshine.**
> —MARIO FERNANDEZ

15

Relative Echoes

*Facing the betrayal of childhood incest
opened my eyes to the good as well
as the traumatic.*

Like sounds echo against canyon walls, spoken words reverberate and repeat farther than the sound of an individual voice. Relatives with whom I had frequent conversations, as well as those at a distance, learned of my new insights in a myriad of ways—ways that were known to me and ways I never imagined possible. In turn, their voices bounced back to me in echoes that I did not anticipate.

I digress now and circle back to the early days when I was flooded with flashbacks. I worried about explaining the source of my dysfunction to relatives on Andy's side of the family. My physical health was no secret, but the conundrum was when and what to reveal about my abuse memories. A few months after my first flashbacks, Andy's brother Eric and wife Elaine came to talk about Grandpa Meier's dementia. Earlier, I had discouraged Andy from telling his brother about my incest. After the candid discussion about their dad's welfare, I had the courage to open up to my in-laws. They sat transfixed as I skimmed the surface of memories retrieved from flashbacks.

"I wondered about the possibility of incest because the way you grieved your dad's death wasn't normal." Eric pulled his Farmer's Union Co-op cap forward, tousling his full head of graying blond hair as his words spilled out. His huge hands gripped a beer mug like mine would hold a shot glass.

Elaine's hands shook as she reached for her diet Pepsi. "I'm so sorry to hear that, Joyce. I understand it's really difficult to get over abuse from a family member."

Andy seemed relieved to be able to talk to his brother about the chaos that my memories had created for him. And for us. As I listened to Andy and Eric, I was glad I followed my intuition. My in-laws didn't appear to gloat over my ugly past. Like my therapist said, Andy was a co-victim; he needed support. He'd put up with my craziness, my absence from the store, and my frequent trips to Colorado.

My mother-in-law phoned me frequently, whether I was in Colby or Colorado Springs. She always asked how I was doing and always said she loved me. She even traveled to Colorado to spend time with me. As a young bride, I feared my mother-in-law, but over the years I'd come to admire her wisdom and appreciated her help in raising our sons. She was ahead of her time in many ways. She gleaned information on nutrition and household management from the County Extension Service and every source she could get her hands on. And her memory for facts was enviable. Her warmth and concern won me over years before I was accosted by incest memories. Her loving concern supported me when love wasn't forthcoming from my own mother. When my heart resisted addressing Hulda as Mother, it swelled with affection when I referred to Vera as Mother.

January 1994, just a year after my first flashback to rape, I started seeing Nora, a psychologist for process therapy. I was nervous because my birthday was coming up on Groundhog's Day, and every birthday since 1989 was linked to something dreadful. Andy was distraught because his father's health was rapidly declining, and I felt helpless to relieve his stress. Sam phoned the morning of my birthday, February 2, to report that he'd had a car accident in Las Vegas. After midnight, Andy phoned to let me know that his father's struggle was over. It was poignant to hear Andy say that he thought his dad waited until after midnight to leave because Grandpa knew I couldn't take another blow on my birthday.

Overwhelmed by the two phone calls, I asked for an emergency session with my new therapist. Nora encouraged me to feel my feelings. I hadn't pounded and screamed for weeks, and the release felt great. Nora kept reassuring me that she was there, and she wasn't going away. She sat silently on the floor beside me as I screamed and shuddered and moaned. I felt supported as I released built-up tension. Her style of process therapy differed from Sophia Fair's in that she touched me during the process. Afterward, she offered to hold me, but I wasn't ready for that. I did let her caress my hand as I settled down. Nora recommended that I take Bach's Rose Water for terror and fear. I shared that I'd been using Bach's Rescue Remedy for months.

Sam arranged to fly into Colorado Springs so he could drive to the funeral in Kansas with me. By six that evening, Sam and I had completed the 350-mile drive to the farm. Anthony Meier's funeral was to be the next morning. Grandpa had spent months lost in dementia and family members were resigned to releasing him. Ben would miss the services. He had traveled to New York with his high school choral group.

When we arrived at the church, I went to the basement and joined my niece. Andy mingled outside with neighbors. My brother-in-law Eric appeared and motioned me to follow him.

With uncharacteristic hesitation, he said, "I thought you should know … your mother and Roger … are upstairs."

Dread clogged my throat. I dropped into a chair. Why would Mother and Roger drive 200 miles to attend a funeral in the middle of winter? My niece must have left to summon Andy. Eric was on his knees beside me. His hand—a huge farmer's hand—rested on my shoulder.

"Are you going to be all right? Should I ask them to leave?"

Andy arrived; his mouth drawn tight. "What do we do now?"

"Nothing. I'll be okay. But I don't want to see them. Don't make me talk to them."

"You don't have to. Our family will walk in last and out first. We'll see to it that there's no chance for them to reach you," Eric said.

Andy looked as upset as I felt.

After the service we gathered at Eric's home on the farm. We grazed on food left by neighbors. Like a robot, I watched my in-laws going through motions that seemed foreign. I slipped into the background whenever possible. Shoestring relatives were leaving and only Eric's family and ours remained when the phone rang.

It was Ben. Andy was summoned to the phone. I sensed growing anxiety as he spoke—Ben had been held up at gunpoint in a Burger King. The thieves had taken his spending money and a fake Rolex watch. He called to let us know that he was all right, not harmed and that a sponsor had loaned him money for food. Clearly, he was rattled by the experience.

Oh God, I thought. My prayer had been incomplete. I asked that my child be brought home safely. I should have asked that he be kept out of harm's way.

There was too much to absorb in one day. My father-in-law's funeral, Sam's car wreck, Mother and Roger showing up without notice, and Ben robbed in New York. My eyes burned; I could barely breathe. My heart wrenched. Fog moved in and the room began to sway.

> **I'm feeling the swirls I'd painted weeks ago.**

Seeing my reaction, Andy immediately asked, "What do you need? What can I do?"

I knew what I wanted. Did I dare ask? From someplace I didn't recognize, a voice said: "I need to stretch out on the floor … with pillows."

Eric's wife Elaine opened the double doors to the master bedroom and raked pillows off the bed. Sam appeared with throw pillows from the living room. Andy sat on the carpet beside me. The wails building inside me started moving out of captivity. Screams from a broken-hearted little girl erupted—hopeless, helpless, and futile. The initially guarded sounds intensified until the shrill cries echoed off the walls.

Oh God, I thought. I'm feeling the swirls I'd painted weeks ago. Only when breathless and exhausted did I stop to imagine what folks on the other side of the closed doors might think. When I stopped flailing and began to gasp, Andy scooped me into his arms. Depleted, I melted into his embrace. He caressed my face and tried to brush away my snot and tears. When my breathing normalized, Andy suggested perhaps we should go.

"Not yet. Maybe I have more to process."

I rolled out of his arms and began to pound pillows with my fists. Andy moved more pillows under my feet. I pounded and kicked until my arms and legs were limp. That wave of release passed more quickly than the shrieks. Then I sat up and shook off the process.

"Now I'm ready to face the others." With Andy's arm supporting me, I stumbled into the living room to face in-laws.

I tried to focus and see others, but the room and the people in it appeared to be wavering—the furniture and walls tottering like trees in a windstorm.

A niece, the youngest in the room, spoke first. "Aunt Joyce, if your mother could have heard you, she would talk. She would help you if she knew."

I shook my head. "You don't know my mother."

Sam reappeared. He'd gone for a walk around the farmstead to avoid witnessing my process. We stayed overnight. The next morning, all the extended family went to the Lutheran church together. Sam's return flight wasn't until midnight so there was time to relax after the noon meal before we left for Colorado.

The next few months I spent a lot of time in Colorado in psychotherapy, Rolfing, and process painting classes. My progress was irregular, and Andy became increasingly impatient with my inability to resume normal life.

The fall of 1994, we needed to travel to Dallas, Texas, to learn about a new model of Viking sewing machine. Since Ben was in his first year at KSU in Manhattan, Kansas, we planned the route so we could visit him on the way. We were scheduled to arrive in Dallas a day early to spend time with Rene, a cousin of my mother, who knew about my incest. She was compassionate and supportive but repeated what she told me on the phone and in letters—that she had no knowledge of my abuse. The one helpful insight she shared was that she never understood why I spent so much time crouched in a corner, crying and sucking my thumb as a toddler. She thought my behavior strange—since I was the spoiled and coddled only daughter. Soon after we left Rene's home and checked into the meeting hotel, Rene's daughter Nellie phoned.

"I'd like to see you tomorrow evening," Nellie said in her slow southern drawl.

It had been years since I'd seen Nellie and her unexpected phone call was intriguing. I suggested she have dinner with us at the hotel after our meetings finished at 6:00 p.m.

"No ... I want to see you alone and catch up on old times. You tell that husband of yours to have dinner with friends. We'll order room service so we can visit in private."

> **This was our little secret and no one else needed to know.**

What unfolded was unexpected. Nellie revealed that, at fourteen, she was sent to our farm for two weeks to learn about life in rural Kansas. She reminded me that I was on summer vacation in Wyoming with Dr. Shepard's family when she visited the farm.

"I'm going to tell you something that I've never told anyone else, Joyce. My mother told me about your flashbacks and there's something I want you to know." Darkness clouded her round face.

"I guess you realize my brothers don't believe me," I spoke quietly.

"I believe you, Joyce. The summer I went to Kansas, your dad was teaching me to drive the little Ford tractor on the schoolhouse quarter when suddenly his hands were inside my jeans. Now I was a city girl; I'd been taught that wasn't right. I cussed him out, jumped off the tractor, and ran the half mile back to the house. When Charlie returned on the tractor, I was sitting under the black walnut tree, crying. He came right over to me and said this was our little secret and no one else needed to know."

My eyes were fixed on Nellie. I never expected to hear an abuse story from this relative. "Oh, my goodness, Nellie, I'm so sorry. I didn't know."

"Of course, you didn't. I never told my mothuh, my fathuh, my brothuh or my lovuhs. But I'm telling you because I know there will be folks saying Charlie would never do that to a little girl. But I know better; and so do you."

"I'm so sorry Nellie. I thought it was only me." I dug my nails into the arms of the chair. Then I recalled that several therapists had suggested that I was not only healing myself. Eventually, I would come to understand I was healing for many in my circle.

I opened my eyes to see pain ripple up from Nellie's pug nose and narrow her dark eyes.

"That wasn't the end of it. The next day Charlie said I had to clean the chicken house and that's what I did, despite my asthma. When I finished that chore, he told me there were too many cats in the barn and I needed to get rid of the kittens he had captured in a gunny sack. Now you know how I loved cats, and Charlie knew that, too. But he let me know I could drown them or hit each one in the head with a hammer. I choose drowning and cried my eyes out as I did it. He stood behind me to make sure I complied. I knew why I was being punished and he knew that I knew."

I gasped and my heart raced. I reached for Nellie's hand and shook my head in disbelief.

> **I would come to understand I was healing for many in my circle.**

"Now, I don't want you to think that had anything to do with my being a lesbian." Nellie paused. "I knew in kindergarten I liked girls better than boys."

We spent another hour catching up on how our adult lives had evolved. Nellie left soon after Andy returned. When I told him the purpose of her visit, he shook his head. "If all that happened, your dad was certainly a good actor. It's still hard for me to believe he could be so cruel."

I particularly noticed Andy used the word "if."

The following evening, I met with Amy May, the cousin on Dad's side of the family that Carrie expected to confirm my abuse. I didn't tell Amy that her grandmother had accused my dad of getting her pregnant at the time she got married. I did tell her I'd had flashbacks to sexual abuse. Her reaction was that she'd have killed somebody if she'd known I was being abused. Her response convinced me: She was either in total denial or Aunt Fanny's accusation was false. Either way, I had no need to disrupt Amy's life by sharing too much information.

In Colorado Springs, my therapist smiled when I explained that a relative on my mother's side of the family, not Dad's, had confirmed that my father was a pedophile.

"When you follow your intuition, the universe often gives you unexpected results." She smiled. "You went to Texas believing a cousin would affirm your sexual abuse, and a cousin did."

My father's cruelty had been validated by more relatives than I ever expected.

During Thanksgiving of '94, I was home from Colorado and Ben was home from the University. A blizzard moved in as we returned from dinner at the farm with Andy's family. My cousin Sonnie, from Fort Collins, Colorado, and her husband were traveling through Kansas on I-70 when the storm moved in. They ended up snowbound with us for the weekend.

Sonnie said she'd recently learned something from her mother, Hazel, that was pertinent to my abuse. Hazel said that none of her six sisters could babysit my brothers and me, because my dad made passes at the oldest sister when she came to watch us three kids. My father's cruelty had been validated by more relatives than I ever expected. Last month I learned that he'd fondled Nellie in the 1950s, and now I learn his lurid appetite was evident in the 1940s. Would I ever know how many more were victims of his perversion?

Fast-forward to May 1995 when I felt a strong urge to connect with some Kohl family members. Memorial weekend I drove to Salina to visit, Aunt Anna, my father's youngest sister. She lived in a rest home where she could get regular dialysis, but her spirits were upbeat, and her mind was alert.

She seemed eager to talk about my parents. "Charlie had a violent temper; Hulda had to have experienced it."

"Really?" I asked.

"Oh yes, he was beaten so much by Papa and by my two oldest sisters. It's not surprising he was angry all his life. Charlie was the scapegoat for all of us kids when we were growing up. But he was also a good worker, the one neighbors wanted to hire. Elmer, our eldest brother, was lazy and everybody knew it. Elmer never had to work out. Charlie hired out a lot."

> **Nobody taught us about right and wrong.**

"Dad didn't talk about his childhood."

"Oh! Without a mother, we grew up like animals. We worked the farm and garden without shoes and all of us could cuss a blue streak." Aunt Anna grimaced.

"It must have been hard for you growing up without a mother. Now that you know about my incest memories, was there anything like that when you were little?"

"Honey, I told you, we were animals. Your dad just did what he learned as a kid, being raised by other kids—selfish ones at that. Nobody taught us about right and wrong."

That was enough for me. I didn't press Aunt Anna to share specifics. Instead I asked, "Did you know anything about the rift between Dad and Aunt Fanny, when Amy got married?"

"I know about it, of course. What I don't know is, which one was lying. Both were mad as hell, so I avoided the subject. But tell me, honey, are you doing all right? Will you get back to your fabric store soon?"

"I'm doing okay. But it may be a while before I'm running the store. Andy's been in charge the past few years, and it's a little rocky when we're both there."

"Oh honey, don't soft-pedal your life for me. I saw how Andy treated you back when Ben was a baby. It broke my heart the way you cowered when he spoke."

"Really, Aunt Anna, nineteen years ago? I thought I'd put up a better front than that."

"You stayed with us in our trailer at the 1976 Kohl reunion in Wakefield. You were still nursing little Ben. Andy ordered you around like a child."

"Oh, my goodness. I should have been talking to you long ago, instead of Hulda."

"I notice you don't call her mother anymore. I can understand that. But just remember that she had a hard life, too." Aunt Anna lowered her gaze and let out a long, slow sigh—as if she'd just witnessed a tragedy.

Aunt Anna's candid revelations replayed in my mind as I drove home that evening. I kept reminding myself it was just information about my past. I didn't need to do anything about it. Then I had a sobering thought: Was it only about my past? Or did I still cower when my husband spoke? Did the universe want me to hear Aunt Anna's observation and take it to heart?

All I could manage at that point was to feel gratitude that my dear aunt was willing to be honest with me. I gave thanks for the intuitive push from my Guardian Angel Elizabeth that gave me the courage to connect with Aunt Anna before my trip to Arizona for MFR therapy. I gripped the steering wheel and asked for grace to endure what came my way and the wisdom to learn the lessons I needed to learn.

I reminisce on other Earth Angels, on how instrumental Dr. Fritz and Viola Shepard were in shaping my adulthood, although I didn't realize the extent of their influence until after I had flashbacks. My therapist alluded to their impact when she told me there weren't laws against child sexual abuse until the 1960s—that the Shepards did what they could do to protect me in the 1950s.

Although I cannot claim being related to either Vi or Fritz, I include them here as if they were family. Traveling this road to recovery, I've become aware of the term "chosen family" to refer to people who function in the supportive and nurturing manner that we culturally expect to be the role of family. I believe that angels appear in novel forms on this earth. Fritz and Vi, as they asked to be called, didn't sport wings. Even so, they lifted me up.

Vi liked to entertain her bridge club and other ladies' groups. She always told me: I enjoy my company, because guests have a good time when the hostess is relaxed and enjoying herself. All my adult life I've heeded her advice and followed the model she provided for entertaining. With Vi, I learned to set up an inviting buffet, bake luscious desserts, and enjoy company.

She made me a trendy poodle skirt to wear to parties. She taught me to dance the jitterbug, the fox trot, the waltz, and to swing and sway to The Inchworm. Frequently, Vi would call my mother on Friday and explain she needed me in town on Saturday evening. She'd offer to bring me to the farm Sunday morning in time for church. Those weekends, my mother would take me back to town Sunday evening. Interesting. Those weeks I did not spend even one night on the farm. Vi found me a summer job, clerking at a ladies' ready-to-wear store. That meant that I spent most of my summer nights in town with the Shepards, rather than on the farm.

Fritz helped me to appreciate a juicy steak. He encouraged me to be at ease mingling with both the affluent and the humble folks. Joking, but ultimately serious, he said that we all put on our pants the same way—one leg at a time. He advised me, if you make one or two good loyal friends in a lifetime, you will be among the most fortunate. I am deeply grateful for many loyal friends. And I acknowledge that I am securely held in a circle of sisterhood.

One night when a date stood me up—for good reason, he was in wheat harvest—Fritz tossed me the keys to his Cadillac and said: *Don't waste time on that stinker, take my purple pigeon for a spin.* Driving to the baseball diamond, I soon chauffeured a carload of girls to the ice cream shop.

When the Shepards traveled to their cabin at Dome Lake above Sheridan, Wyoming, Vi told my mother that she needed me to help cook. I spent a lot of time writing poetry and daydreaming by the lake. Vi had my Dome Lake poem printed in calligraphy and framed; it hung like a trophy in the cabin's great room.

On my 18th birthday, she surprised me with a sock-hop in the garage. She invited my friends, had music for dancing, and made a freezer of homemade ice cream. Bill Avery, Kansas governor at the time, was among the guests who signed my autograph hound, a stuffed animal that was a popular memory token in those days.

A country bumpkin, I would never have considered trying out for the class plays. Vi insisted I try out and I had a small part. The Shepards had season tickets to K-State basketball and football games. Accompanying them to those events spurred my interest in attending college. Both Fritz and Vi encouraged me to aspire to a college education, and they supported me when I felt discouraged my first couple years at K-State. Fritz sent me cards with bills tucked inside and sometimes came down on his day off to take me to dinner. Usually I spent the dollars on books, but one time I splurged and bought a baby blue dyed-to-match wool skirt and sweater that made me feel like Lana Turner.

During my early college years, Vi occasionally took me to a department store to buy me clothes. Most memorable was an emerald green, princess-style dress, with an embroidered bolero jacket. Vi wanted to pay my fees to go through sorority rush. That, I declined. Timid as I was in those days, I knew I was better suited to be a gol-darned-independent.

When I told them of my engagement, Fritz said, "It's gonna be crowded with me and Charlie both walking you down the aisle." Doc didn't get to walk me, he had a medical emergency and arrived at my wedding midway through the ceremony. Vi was there the entire time and poured punch at the reception.

Facing the betrayal of childhood incest opened my eyes to the good as well as the traumatic. Prior to incest memories, I encountered extended family members only occasionally at weddings, funerals, and family reunions.

I am enormously grateful.

During recovery, I experienced deep understanding and genuine support from aunts and cousins in surprising ways. And, it was only after incest memories surfaced that I came to appreciate all that Fritz and Vi Shepard did to move me into adulthood where

I could experience career success. At the time it didn't occur to me that they were keeping me away from my birth family, for my own safety. Now when I think about how my chosen family stepped up to love and support me when my parents and brothers couldn't and didn't, I am enormously grateful.

Out of suffering have emerged the strongest souls.
—KAHLIL GIBRAN

16

Sparks

*You don't even know where
you are safe and supported.*

I spent so much time in Colorado Springs throughout 1994 that it felt important to put down some roots. I rented a post office box and opened a bank account. In January 1995, I stopped at the bank to make a deposit and fell on the entry steps. The security guard helped me to a chair and offered to call 911. I felt a little dizzy and assured him I just needed some ice. The lady who appeared with ice urged me to let them call for help. Still, I declined. She asked if she could phone someone to come get me. I protested that I'd soon be okay.

She frowned. "Do you realize you can't drive? Look at your arm. That bone is broken."

Surprised, I looked down to see the bone in my left wrist pushing against the skin. I don't know what happened after that. The next thing I knew, an EMT in the emergency vehicle was explaining that she was giving me another morphine shot. She urged me to stay awake.

It was after midnight when a friend came and took me to her house from the emergency room. Still high on morphine, I couldn't walk and had to be carried into her house. Now, I had another midwinter crisis to add to my list of stressful events near my birthday.

1989	Andy sells farmland and blames me	
	I attack my son for dropping the F-bomb	
1990	Dad's funeral on my 50th birthday	
1991	Failed epidural injection and doctor's Rx is a cane	
1992	Fibromyalgia diagnoses for which there's no cure	
1993	First rape flashback	
1994	Father-in-law passes, Hulda and Roger appear uninvited; Sam: car accident in Las Vegas; Ben: robbed in New York	
1995	Broken wrist	

I'm beginning to wonder: *I must not be learning the lessons I'm supposed to learn. What must I do differently to stop the annual calamity of one sort or another around my birthday?*

Not only did I have difficulty using my nondominant hand for eating and writing, more complications ensued. I couldn't use a sling because of shooting pain, so I held the cast at shoulder level.

When I complained to the orthopedic doctor, he said, "Lady, at your age, you need to learn to live with some pain."

That's what I did. And I used a lot of ice on my arm and back to numb the pain.

A few days after my fall, Eric and Elaine brought Andy to the Springs so he could drive me home. The pain was more severe than I had expected, but then I hadn't had a broken bone since college days when I broke some bones in my foot. Andy seemed to be seething with anger in Colorado, and soon after we arrived home, the anger burst out.

"Before you went and broke your wrist, I was ready to kick your lazy ass out. Now what am I supposed to do? Keep on being a nice guy?" He stormed out to smoke.

I didn't even try to protest. I couldn't undo the broken arm. The shooting pain in my arm and shoulder seemed to shrink under the weight of my husband's outburst. Six weeks later when the cast was removed, I was shocked at the sight of my shrunken arm. And the pain in my shoulder was still unreasonable after the cast came off.

> **You don't know where home is.**

In dismay, I stayed in the Springs longer than intended and saw Sophia for therapy. I dreaded going back to Kansas. I was certain I would be even more miserable there. After I vented and processed, Sophia suggested I walk in Bear Creek Park after the session. She reasoned that if I stopped searching for why and paid attention to the present, the answer would come to me. No answer came during my meditative stroll. That afternoon when I saw Don for Rolfing, I was still trying to decide whether to drive home to Colby or stay in the Springs.

Don paused in his work. "Home is more than a place where you hang your hat, Joyce. It's where you feel safe and supported—protected and nurtured. Have you ever had that?"

"I've never thought of home that way. I've always felt like I didn't quite belong—wasn't good enough, smart enough, big enough or successful enough."

"Look what you've created now. You don't know where home is. You don't even know where you are safe and supported."

The Rolfing session was good for my emotions, as well as my aching hand and shoulder. My left hand was swollen and painful, even though I iced it several times a day. Physical therapists in both Colby and Colorado Springs described my shoulder as "frozen" because of holding up the heavy cast instead of resting it in a sling. A hand specialist confirmed that bone fragments floating in the area of the break were responsible for the pain I experienced when I tried to use a sling. He assured me the bone fragments would eventually dissolve.

I made a choice. I phoned Andy and told him the pain was too great for me to make the four-hour drive. At first, Andy seemed to accept my explanation, but the next morning he called saying he was unable to sleep. I felt angry barbs coming through the phone.

I listened to a string of insults before I spoke. "I hope you can get your strength back by yourself, without making me responsible …"

"I don't think you being responsible is something apt to happen these days," Andy said.

My resolve to be strong was drowned by his quick answer. I didn't argue, just said we couldn't solve this on the phone. Andy hung up.

Tina, a friend from a battered women's group took me to dinner that evening. "I'm worried about you, Joyce. I have a sense that you need to feel your support here and develop more inner strength before you face Andy."

Through a rush of tears, I managed to speak. "But I've been working on this so many years, why does it take me so long?"

"You've spent a lot of years being codependent. One doesn't undo that quickly or easily. Remember that healing doesn't move straight upward. It spirals; there are setbacks."

Even with journaling and meditating, it was impossible to integrate all the advice I'd received in Colorado Springs. I decided to stay a couple days longer and was still scattered when I went to physical therapy (PT) the next day. Adele, who did the massage after PT, said she thought the swelling and inflammation in my wrist and hand were about interrupting the flow of energy.

"Andy is still abusing you, isn't he?" Adele's gaze drilled through me.

My whole body tensed. "He's not hitting me like early in our marriage."

"How do you feel when you are with your husband?" Adele asked.

"I … I have trouble separating thoughts from feelings." With my hand over my eyes, I hoped my weakness wouldn't seep out.

Wanting to change the subject, I told her of Tina's phone call and dinner invitation.

"Look at you. You are animated and enthusiastic as you just spoke of Tina. There is a significant contrast to how you looked when I asked how you felt when you were in Kansas … with Andy."

"But I didn't intend …"

"Of course, you didn't intend to act differently, you just did. When you go to Kansas, do so consciously. Notice how you feel as you drive away from Colorado and how you feel when you arrive in Colby. Then when you return, again notice your feelings each place."

After a day of rest, I headed back to Kansas. For the entire four-hour trip, I kept telling myself that going home was the right thing to do. Staying in Colorado longer would look like I'd given up on my marriage. I hadn't.

Andy was sitting at the kitchen table when I walked in the front door. His face looked as drawn as a little girl with a too-tight ponytail, his lips curled inward. His eyes were fixed in the distance.

"So, you finally decided to come home. How long are you going to stay this time? Or would that be too much to ask?"

My head felt light enough to disconnect. I dropped onto the piano bench. "I'm sorry you're angry."

"Sure, you're sorry that I have feelings. You're the only one entitled to that."

"You are as entitled to feelings as anyone. It's the blame I object to, not your anger."

"And who the hell should I blame? You abandoned us."

Tina was right; I wasn't strong enough to face Andy. "My shoulder hurts. I'm going to the hot tub to relax. It was difficult to drive today with the strong side wind."

Ben arrived home from college for spring break later that Friday night. I spent every minute I could with him because in a couple days he would join K-State friends to snowboard in the Rocky Mountains. We went for a long walk on Saturday and Ben talked about his classes and work at the scholarship house. In church, I sat between Andy and Ben, so I could hear Ben's mellow baritone voice singing hymns.

Ben left for the mountains Monday morning and I had physical therapy at the Colby hospital. A different physical therapy assistant (PTA) worked with me that morning, using a technique she called myofascial release (MFR). Although the pain in my shoulder was intense, I was impressed with Lila and the progress we made. She insisted that I should see Dr. Fischer about the intensity of my shoulder pain before I came for more physical therapy.

Back home, Andy announced that instead of going to the store, he planned to organize tax records before the housekeeper came on Tuesday. Andy worked on taxes until midnight.

Mother phoned the next day to tell me about Aunt Anna's deteriorating health. "It's just so hard when we get older and don't have our kids near. I guess you aren't planning to come home for Easter?" Mother's voice teetered.

Mother's guilt trip didn't rattle me like it used to. "We're staying here. Ben's on spring break and Andy will be helping with the Easter services."

In the afternoon I went to see Dr. Fischer about my hand and shoulder pain. He studied a bone scan and reported that the break in my wrist had healed, and I had good range of motion considering where the break occurred. "But you should have had physical therapy while you were in the cast to prevent the frozen shoulder. It could take six weeks of physical therapy to overcome that, maybe more."

Lila's approach was so much more effective than any other PT I'd worked with that I scheduled a series of 7:00 a.m. appointments so I could see her consistently. The second session she urged me to consult a physical therapist in Holdridge, Nebraska, who had more training in MFR.

Lila maintained that she didn't move my shoulder, that she just provided safety. With Lila guiding my movements, I was able to lift my hand above my head for the first time since the break four months ago. I was so shaken afterward that I staggered walking from the room. I found a ladies' room, leaned against the locked door, and wept. After driving the two miles home, I dropped onto the sofa—still shaking, still shivering, and still wearing my coat.

Sometime later Andy walked in. "What's wrong? Are you okay?"

"I'm cold."

Andy tucked a blanket around me, and I fell into a deep sleep. When I woke up two hours later, Andy was standing over me.

"We're supposed to be on the road to Oberlin to take care of farm business, or did you forget?"

I heard resentment. Ben had returned from snowboarding in Colorado, and apparently Andy and Ben had been arguing while I slept. Everyone was tense as Andy drove the seventy miles to Oberlin. Andy took care of farm business at the bank and a couple other businesses. Ben drove us home. From the back seat I witnessed Andy criticizing everything Ben did: following too close; driving too fast one mile; driving too slowly the next; signaling too late; and braking too hard at a stop sign. Ben white-knuckled the steering wheel and said little, but he started wheezing.

> **Dad, don't you see what your rigidity does to this family?**

In the house Ben spoke. "Dad, don't you see what your rigidity does to this family? Why do you have to find fault with everything we do?"

> **Maybe it's bailout time for me.**

"Because somebody has to be in charge," Andy said. "Somebody has to see to it things get done right."

"I've had enough. I'm going back to K-State." Ben disappeared to pack his car.

I hated that he would be driving three hundred miles in the dark, but I didn't argue.

Andy and I spent most of Sunday listening to Barbara DeAngelis' taped program: *Making Love Work*, recommended to us by a marriage counselor in Colorado. DeAngelis stressed honesty.

We wrote out some exercises and candidly shared what we wrote. Tension mounted when I read what I'd written to Andy. While I prepared some popcorn and drinks, Andy spewed out a string of my shortcomings—spending too much money, away from home too much, not caring about anyone but myself, no time to be a wife.

I shivered, sucked into a spin, with my roots ripped out of grounding as surely as trees are uprooted in a tornado. I dropped into a chair.

"Maybe it's bailout time for me."

Andy's eyes widened; his forehead furrows deepened. "I promised Ben I'd try to talk with you, but it's hopeless. You only think about yourself. You never listen to reason. I don't think you want to get well." He crunched popcorn and gulped Scotch. He sighed, long and deep. "I've been lied to for years—about everything that matters." He sighed. "And a prostitute would be a helluva lot cheaper than a wife and kids."

"It's impossible for me to negotiate when I'm waist-deep in guilt. I need to be alone. Maybe time in the hot tub will help." I couldn't think of any way to de-escalate the conversation. Grateful the spa was private inside the cedar shed, I stripped and slipped down into the bubbly hot water, letting it ripple over my bare skin and thaw the chill that tensed my muscles.

Back in the house, I wrote a note to the supervising physical therapist at the Colby Hospital. I ended the note with:

> *Many who don't understand body memories or stored trauma prefer to pretend trauma doesn't linger in the body. Maybe I'm the first or only PTSD patient your clinic will*

treat, but I doubt it. Most of my treatment has been in Colorado Springs, and it is reassuring for me to know there is a place here that fosters healing of the whole person.

Later, Andy agreed to take me for MFR in Holdrege, Nebraska. The physical therapist there worked on me with an assistant. As they held space for me to move my frozen shoulder, I slipped out of present reality and perched on the light fixture. My thoughts flashed back to toddlerhood when my older brother Gene and his friends dropped me into a posthole. Now I screamed and was back in that posthole. Terror gripped me as I clawed at the earth and tried in vain to reach daylight.

After the MFR session, the physical therapist helped Andy and I integrate my processing and shared his reaction with us.

"Andy Meier, your wife is one of the bravest, wisest people I've ever known. I'm not just talking about my physical therapy practice. I will look for her to run a program for other survivors one day."

We were both speechless.

Before I retired that night, I wrote in my journal:

> *Everything is as it should be. The universe will provide me with all that I need. I have what is necessary at this moment and will have what is essential at the next moment. If I remain in my integrity, those around me can do the same. I won't attempt to rescue them; so that they will have the chance to face their own issues. What once seemed a tough, if not impossible challenge now seems reasonable, plausible and inviting. It's what I want for my life and what I want for*

my loved ones. Let go of judgments. Let go of expectations. Let go of control of others. Let go of my fears, all of them. My tasks are simple. Trust the universe. Trust Andy to deal with his issues. Trust Ben to face his demons. Trust myself to evolve. Let go and let God in.

> **I am not this hair. I am not this skin.**
> **I am the soul that lies within.**
> —RUMI

17

Overload

Animosity spun through the room like a Kansas dirt-devil that spins in a vortex.

Early in the summer of 1995, I had a particularly heavy teaching schedule at the store. At the end of the day, I grabbed my purse from the office, hoping to escape to the house where I could unwind.

Andy looked up from the machine he was repairing. "You need to be ready to cut TV commercials tomorrow morning at nine. And after that I've scheduled you to work with a notions salesman."

I hadn't worked with a sales rep for years, but I didn't argue. Instead of going home, I began to draft the television commercial. I'd barely started that when Andy's mother showed up with her sister. We dined at a restaurant and then continued our visit at our house. As the eight o'clock hour neared, Andy announced he needed to leave for a church voters' meeting.

Only recently had women been accepted as voting members at our church. I regretted that I would not be able to make my voice heard, but I knew I had work to do.

Andy said, "I'll only stay for the first hour, then I'll go to the store and help."

Alone in the house, I took a short power nap and then walked a few blocks to Westside Park before heading to the store. Resting in a swing, I relished the sounds of silence and yet again asked for God's guidance. Andy didn't show up to help. By 10:00 p.m., I'd finished writing copy and setting up displays for a television commercial.

The next day I got through everything I'd been assigned and after dinner, packed for my Colorado trip and looked at my inspirational calendar:

> *Let today be the day you learn the grace of letting go and the power of moving on.*
>
> —Steve Maraboli

Andy phoned me in Colorado a few days later. "I realize some mistakes I've made. I shouldn't have dumped the television commercials and notions rep on you with no notice." He spoke gently, with uncharacteristic tenderness.

I swallowed the retort I was thinking. Instead, I said, "I got through it, Andy. But I appreciate you acknowledging that it was a heavy load."

We both were procrastinators when it came to paperwork and the mail was always a source of tension. A reliable bookkeeper kept store records in order. At home, it was my responsibility to sort the mail into piles, because Andy wanted to open most of it. I objected to any involvement in stocks and commodities trading, a sideline he relished.

One time when Ben and Andy visited me in Colorado, Andy reminded me I wasn't doing my share. He said, "I don't know if you have to work at the store, but you sure as hell need to pay more attention to responsibilities at home … like the mail."

"What mail are we talking about, Andy?" I set out soup bowls.

"All the mail. You left without taking care of important papers, and I don't know what you did with them." Andy pulled the Salems from his shirt pocket and tapped a cigarette on the back of his left hand.

"What I remember is that I moved a stack of mail off the kitchen table to serve dinner. Afterward I sorted out the bills that needed paying and wrote the checks. When you forgot to take the envelopes to the store to be stamped and mailed, I did that, too."

"There's important mail other than bills, and I don't know where to find it." Andy stomped out to the balcony to smoke.

I felt myself snorting shallow breaths and consciously slowed my inhale and exhale. The subject of my irresponsibility had been dropped, but not settled. With Andy angry about mail and Ben disgusted with therapy, they'd probably both be fighting indigestion on the ride home.

We packed the car to return to Kansas, and I offered to drive so Andy could relax. The trip was uneventful until past Limon, where huge potholes on I-70 rocked the car so severely that I steered the car into the left lane of the divided highway.

Andy bolted upright in the back seat. "You'll get a goddamned ticket if a highway patrol sees you in the left lane."

I squeezed the steering wheel. "There are signs telling truck drivers to use the left lane because of irregular pavement. That's what I'm doing."

"Have it your way, know-it-all. You aren't driving a truck."

I felt Andy's breath as he looked over my shoulder, probably checking the speedometer.

I swallowed the retort I wanted to give and guided the car onto the shoulder. "Someone else can drive."

Without a word, Ben took the wheel. After two hours of tense silence, we arrived home.

I wasn't the only family member with body pain. Andy carried a lot of tension in his body and there were times when I worked the store so he could travel to Colorado for Rolfing. One time when he had been in the Springs for a few days respite, he was upset that I wasn't at the house when he returned. In response to his angry phone summons, I excused myself from the store and rushed to the house. Andy was smoking in the garage when I arrived.

"You're feeling discouraged, really in pain?"

"I don't know why I do this. You never have time to be a wife and mother." His tone was angry, his words clipped.

What exactly did "this" mean? Why does he start to share and then clam up? I sat at the table and tried to mirror him and repeat what he said to draw him out. When he wouldn't answer, I went downstairs to do laundry. Later I prepared dinner and tried to eat. Animosity spun through the room like a Kansas dirt-devil that spins in a vortex, depositing dust clouds that choke out life-sustaining air.

> **I've been lied to about everything that counts.**

Andy flung himself onto the living room carpet. "You don't have to take responsibility for anything."

"Just what responsibilities do you mean?" I waited for a response. "Are you feeling overwhelmed?"

"Dammit, Joyce, you put me here. I've been lied to about everything that counts." Andy got up and went for another smoke.

I headed for the basement to take clothes out of the dryer. Laundry doesn't blame. Wide awake at three the next morning, I decided to leave for Colorado. I wrote a brief note and left it on the kitchen table: *Did I ever tell you that you were a poor husband and father?*

Andy didn't acknowledge the note I left. Back in Colorado, I walked in Bear Creek Park and tried to sort out how to communicate better with Andy.

At my therapist's request, I told Andy I needed to spend a few extra days in Colorado. As a result, he announced he was coming. Later, he walked into the apartment complaining and slammed a box of papers down on the kitchen table. "I had to ask the accountant to file an extension for our income taxes."

I poured iced tea in glasses. "Filing an extension is not the end of the world. It's the first time we've ever done that."

"You always oversimplify things."

I sipped my tea and thought about the little book: *Who Moved My Cheese*? "Broad sweeping issues are overwhelming for me to deal with. I need to segment problems into smaller parts in order to deal with them."

Andy's voice quieted. "You're so unstable. I probably will have to file for legal separation."

This wasn't the first time I'd heard that threat. "Could you be specific? What exactly are you referring to now?"

"In general. This has been going on for years." He leaned back, tipping his chair off the front legs.

I pondered the significance of Andy's unstable chair, thinking he looked like a kid on a teeter-totter. "I need direction on what you want to be different."

Andy's tone turned nonchalant. "I shouldn't have mentioned it, but … it's a big concern of mine." He began to lift papers from the box, separating them into stacks on the table.

I felt foolish to be agitated, but I wasn't going to let him drop the subject.

"If it's a big concern, then it needs to be examined, not glossed over. We need to stay with it until we have some meaningful understanding. Are we talking store finances or personal?

He kept stacking papers, avoiding eye contact. "Overall."

Was he smug because he'd riled me? It took great effort to not raise my voice. I answered some of Andy's questions about fabric suppliers and delivery choices.

He took notes. "I'm not the walking encyclopedia you are about all these companies."

What could have been a compliment from my husband felt more like a punch in the gut. Nothing I said seemed to generate any agreement, so I waited in silence.

Andy went to the bathroom to get Alka-Seltzer. After he gulped it down, I stood silent in the kitchen with the meal ready to set on the table.

> **I'll make that decision; you aren't capable.**

"What are you waiting on? Aren't we going to eat?" Andy's voice rose.

I gestured at the papers littering the table. "It's not appetizing to have the plates squashed between piles of papers."

Andy grabbed papers and started tossing them toward the box he just took them from.

"You don't have to do that. I could help you separate the piles, so you don't have to start over after dinner."

Andy continued throwing papers, missing the box. "What else is on your mind?"

"I've always felt responsible for your gut aches and your need for antacids. I'm trying to let go of that and give responsibility back to you. You had ulcers when we got married and you continued to have problems, even though I tried to serve nutritious meals. I don't know what else I can do to help you with your stomach. Since my efforts haven't been successful, the responsibility is yours." I placed the pot roast on the table and sat down.

"I never blamed you for my digestive problems. It's a Meier thing." Andy ate heartily.

Clearing the table, I said, "It's only a few weeks until Easter. Let's decide what to do for the holiday."

Andy pulled out a Salem. "I'll make that decision; you aren't capable."

I struggled to maintain a calm outward appearance as my mind raced. What bullshit. I was expected to keep working on store business as I engaged in healing, but I couldn't say how I wanted to spend a holiday? Meaningful conversation with my husband seemed futile, so I began to make a list of tasks I needed to do.

To my relief, Andy let the subject drop. In the morning he gathered his papers for the return trip. "As usual, you haven't given me complete medical records or the receipts for all your Colorado expenses. I can't file taxes until you do your part."

"I've always given you credit for managing money, Andy. Perhaps I should get some of the credit. I sort and compile papers for you. Also, you had my cooperation in living frugally so we could save and invest. If I had spent money like some of our friends, we would never have invested my paychecks over the years."

Andy banged the box of papers down by the door. "If you would have spent money like you are now, or like your friends always have, we wouldn't still be married."

I followed Andy out the door. "But I'm feeling much better. I will soon be able to contribute to our income, like I did before flashbacks."

He paused on the balcony and shook his head. "Never before have we spent more money than we earned. Your therapy in Colorado is draining our reserves."

I began to follow his logic. It was typical for him to blow up about something trivial before we got to the real issue. "Perhaps that's the reason God has blessed our investments. Maybe the man upstairs knew we would need funds for therapy without jeopardizing our retirement."

Andy continued toward the parking lot, ignoring what I'd said. "There aren't enough hours in a day for me to be both man and woman of the house." He paused to light a Salem. "I vowed a couple years ago that I'd never put off the whole accounting process until the end of the year. I guess my frustration now is that I didn't keep up with paperwork during the year."

> **Your therapy in Colorado is draining our reserves.**

We'd reached his truck. "Maybe you should give up some responsibilities. Even if you were at peak effectiveness, you couldn't keep up with everything. With the store, the farm, the school board, the church and home, you've got a lot of responsibility."

Andy shook his head and sped away.

Heading back to the apartment, I felt conflicted about our time together. At least Andy talked to me. In the past, he would start to share and then draw back. If I disagreed with him, avoided his eyes, or looked too anxious—he'd either clam up or walk out. Now that he's started to talk, maybe we could work through our differences.

A few days later, Andy phoned to tell me he'd hired a high-school girl to work at the store and then he began his usual interrogation. "What appointments do you have coming up? Is therapy really doing you any good?"

"I really don't want to give you a blow-by-blow account."

"If I don't ask, how am I supposed to know what's going on?"

"You should have a pretty good idea by the tone of my voice." My words came out more caustic than I intended.

"You sound awfully noncommittal."

I wanted to hang up, but I didn't. "That's how I feel."

It surprised me when Andy backed off; I expected an angry outburst.

The next day winter returned. The wind howled; the overcast sky whispered dreary. Dismal weather echoed my heartache. Why couldn't I stand up for myself? Why did my therapist have to urge me to speak up in my own defense? I wrestled with whether to tell Andy he was projecting his denied feelings onto me. It helped when I considered the possibility that not only was Andy requiring perfectionism in me, but perhaps I fell short of my own expectations. Was I beginning to comprehend how sly the concept of projection played out in relationships? Perhaps we'd all failed to own our feelings and instead projected the denied feeling as coming from someone else.

Within a week, I returned to Colby, motivated to try to work effectively at the store. Alone in the hot tub one evening, I scratched my skin to see if I still could feel myself. I journaled the questions circling in my mind: Where was me? Was the real me the person who lived through the pain of remembering incest or was real me the robot who did her jobs well—as saleslady, manager, organizer, one who cleans up others' messes, the one who deals with the public and sends them away content with their buying decisions?

Can all these different me's possibly be inside the same skin? Can an integrated me emerge from the vastly contrasting me's? As I merge into oneness, can I stay centered and not reject an important part of me? A clutch in my gut startled me as I sat journaling without my faceless doll. I realized my inner child was still vulnerable, afraid I'd leave her out of the integrated me. I found the doll and held her as I continued writing.

In the midst of vacillating between confidence and fear, change had been consistent. My confidence in truth and honesty grew as

I mustered the courage to confront my fears of inadequacy and to plunge into work at the fabric shop. The past few days I'd jumped high hurdles.

Many previous times in Colby, I'd felt scattered and unable to accomplish anything. This time I felt more grounded and managed to catch up on jobs long neglected. I cleaned the back storeroom and organized the attic where we kept out-of-season merchandise. I directed the "Bag the Bargain" sale, starting at 5:00 a.m. the first day of pheasant season, and planned for the first fashion show we'd had in two years.

At our biannual fashion shows, we generally used garments sewn by our customers, but this time I'd invited a former Hollywood dress designer to create fashions from fabric lengths, live on-stage. Every seat was filled for the fashion show and the audience loved the stunning designs. We sold a lot of fabric and the designer sold several of his paintings. Andy's response was dismal.

"What in the hell were you thinking, bringing a goddamned recycled dress designer to this little town?" He stomped out of the building.

I turned off the store lights and locked the front door.

> **The truth will set you free, but first it will piss you off.**
> —GLORIA STEINEM

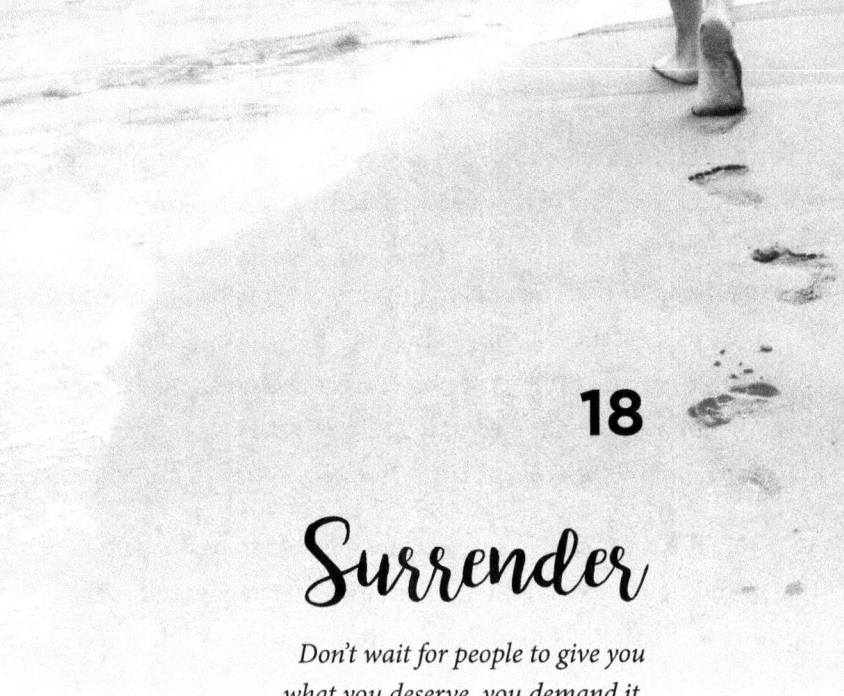

18

Surrender

*Don't wait for people to give you
what you deserve, you demand it.*

Midsummer of 1995, I had lunch with my friend Adele between Colorado appointments. She expressed concern that I was so distraught after spending a week in Colby. Adele's words repeated in my thoughts for hours after we parted. I wanted to own my part in the dysfunction, to take responsibility for my shortcomings.

How much of the friction with my husband was because of our different expectations? He still wanted to have the old Joyce as his partner, and I wished he could accept the changed me. It didn't matter how many times I reminded him that we were supposed to learn as children that we couldn't put Humpty Dumpty back together again. I couldn't erase incest memories or the insights I'd gleaned on the journey into my Self.

A part of me felt primed to adjust my priorities in preparation for a transition. I wrote in my journal: *I don't know where I'm going or what I'll do, but I feel change lurking nearby.* At a process painting workshop in July, I heard concepts I'd never heard before, or maybe I understood words differently than before. Alice, the facilitator, said, "Over the past eight years I've touched previously unknown parts of myself." She explained that process painting is a way for artists and non-artists alike to access an essential creativity within. She encouraged us to surrender the ego, to suspend judgment, and in the process, allow trapped energy to move.

Alice said life and death is a dance in which we all participate. That every night we die to the possibilities of that day, and every morning we live in the possibilities of the new dawn. With process painting, we can access unity, which means bypassing the upper strata of intellect and the second strata of the unconscious to reach the third strata—unity.

The paintings I created in that workshop were bolder, with brighter colors than I'd previously used. The first two had scattered images of shadows, spirits, and disconnected parts of bodies. The last was a brightly colored, segmented heart.

After the painting workshop, I participated in a Native American sweat lodge near Victor. My friend Robin saw the crooked little finger on my left hand.

"Louise Hay says the little finger represents family and pretending. Does that fit for you, Joyce?"

"I believe so. You know that I recently broke my left wrist. What does Louise say about accidents?"

"Accidents are rebellion against authority and inability to speak up for self."

'I guess that fits, too. I bite my tongue for a long time before I have the courage to speak up. Still I've been unable to follow the advice given me years ago by my therapist. She said you don't wait for people to give you what you deserve, you demand it."

"So, who is the authority figure you can't speak up to?" Robin asked.

"My husband. I've told you that before." I studied the floor.

'I know, but it still doesn't make sense to me. Why isn't he your peer?"

"Because he's always been more level-headed than me. And he looks at the big picture and the future more than I do. And because he reminds me of poor decisions I've made. Also, he's working at the store a lot more than I am right now."

My friend didn't seem convinced, but she let the subject rest. The following day, while I drove from Colorado to Kansas, I tried to remember when I started seeing my husband as an authority figure. After all, this was 1995 and women weren't property. Still, my conservative church background contributed to my submissive attitude. From religious authorities in my past, I soaked up the idea that the man should be head of the household. That, combined with my mother's ideas, contributed to my attitudes. She used to purse her lips, make a fist, and proclaim: *Women have to do what men want.*

After a couple of days in Colby, Andy accompanied me back to Colorado Springs where he had a Rolfing appointment. While he was in session, I had lunch with my friend Adele, who startled me by asking, "Are you okay with Andy being here?"

I tried to answer, but my lips moved in silence and tears seeped out.

"You're not okay." Adele's frown deepened and she reached over and squeezed my hand.

"Yes, I am—I really am. I don't expect much out of life anymore."

Adele released her grip. "I haven't seen you this emotional in months. You need to think about what you're doing to yourself."

I thanked my friend for caring. But I couldn't figure out how to undo what I was doing to myself.

> **Why do you do such damn fool things?**

Andy napped after Rolfing and I journaled. Conversation was tense at dinner, and I didn't want to spend the next day arguing. "Do you think we could hike North Cheyenne Cañon Park? It's one of my favorite mountain vistas, with gentle streams and picturesque waterfalls."

Andy agreed and by 8:30 in the morning we were on the trail. After a brief stop at Helen Hunt Falls, we drove to the upper parking lot and set out with our water bottles for Saint Mary's Falls. Andy fretted about a rainstorm and lightning that never materialized. I didn't realize how upset he was until he paused, leaned against a pine tree, and heaved his breakfast.

Back at the apartment, I fed him chicken bouillon and encouraged him to nap until he felt better. After a dose of Alka-Seltzer and a long nap, he was ready for a meal. He ate his chicken sandwich slowly and gulped Seven-Up.

"Why do you do such damn fool things? If you plan to hike for three hours, you need to be prepared, with some food and more than a quart of water."

'I've done that hike many times, with only a quart of water. At any point you could have said you wanted to turn back, and I would have. Instead of rehashing this morning, could we plan our trip to Vegas next week? We should tell Sam the days we want to be at his place and when we plan to be at the sewing machine convention."

"You're the one who needs a schedule; you figure it out."

"I'm tired of making all the decisions and then getting blamed when something goes wrong," I said.

"I have other things to think about. You don't think about anything but yourself."

We finally settled on making a schedule together. Andy agreed we could drive the southern route to Las Vegas, so I could get physical therapy at the clinic in Sedona. Then we would spend a couple days with Sam before we moved to Harrah's Casino for the convention.

That evening we took turns driving and napping on the trip from the Springs back to Colby. We'd only been in the house an hour when Andy pulled out three weeks of mail he had ignored.

"Why don't you make popcorn and we can work on the mail?" he said.

I complied and by midnight we were done. We went to the store together the next morning, but I left at ten to have coffee with a few women from our church clan.

After the others left, I chose a table in the corner to visit with wise woman Neva—my astute dyslexic friend.

"Neva, I've been talking with my therapist about trying to teach a few classes for a Viking dealer in the Springs. She thinks that might be a good transition to returning to work at my fabric shop here."

> You can never come back here.

"Joyce, you don't really think you can come back, do you?" Neva frowned.

"That's what I've been trying to do for months. I believe I'm strong enough now."

Neva shook her head. With a sweeping gesture she pulled in the entire town. "But not here, Joyce, you can never come back here."

"Why do you say that? What do you know that I don't?"

"This is a little town. Everybody here thinks you have a mental problem and they'll always treat you that way. Sometimes I just want to reach out and strangle the ladies at church when they ask you when you're coming home. I can see how deeply that hurts."

"You understand so much, Neva. You're ahead of me."

"I've told those women many times that your problem is like any other disease, the time it takes to heal, is the time it takes. You can't predict and you can't control illness, each develops, and each heals at its own pace."

Neva's words sunk in and recycled in my thoughts in moments of quiet. A couple days later we were traveling 1-25 south in Colorado on our way to Sedona, Arizona. Six weeks ago, I drove this road by myself and thoroughly enjoyed the drive and the scenery. But this trip, Andy was physically sick and emotionally explosive whenever Ben or I drove, although he claimed he needed rest.

Andy's words to Ben sounded bitter and condescending. Ben put up a shield, but I wasn't fooled. I could see Andy's criticism eating through Ben's outer crust. What could I say to my husband that would help him understand that although his anger hurts us, it hurts him more?

Knowing we planned two days in Sedona, I made an appointment with a counselor in addition to physical therapy at the MFR Clinic. The three weeks I'd spent getting myofascial release treatments a few months earlier had relieved my frozen shoulder and boosted my spirits.

The therapist I consulted with was perceptive and intuitive. She welcomed me and even before she sat down, she said: "You are dealing with an adult throwing two-year-old temper tantrums. It's up to you to set boundaries of what you will, and will not, tolerate. Life will be easier for both of you if you take responsibility—because he can't."

As if to drive home the therapist's admonition, Andy was furious when I was thirty minutes late getting back to the motel.

"What the fuck were you doing anyway? I figured you forgot we were here. We drive two thousand miles so you can get physical therapy, and you screw it up. You are more irresponsible than a two-year-old."

I kept to myself the fact that my counselor had spoken of a two-year-old on the other side of the equation. I said, "We only drove two hundred extra miles, Andy. And I'm sure I'll still get physical therapy at the MFR clinic. They're not uptight about schedules."

At the clinic, I learned my hunch was correct. Even if I'd arrived on time, Brian would not have been able to work on me because he had been called into an emergency meeting. Jonathan had agreed to treat me. Fortunately, I waited a few more minutes; time enough to release some of the tension in my body.

After the session, I was pleased when Jonathan invited me to come back tomorrow because he had an hour at 9:00 and Brian a half hour at 11:00. The drive back to the motel was only a few miles, but it felt like I had left a safety zone and entered a combat zone.

Andy couldn't eat much because his stomach was still upset. After dinner he went to sleep, giving Ben and me an opportunity to sit by the motel pool and talk. A frown crossed Ben's young face. "Mom, when are you going to figure out that you have to confront Dad? This isn't going to stop until you speak up."

Ben's sage advice to set boundaries replayed in my mind.

"You aren't the first to tell me that, Ben. Earlier today, someone else told me I must set boundaries because your dad can't. I'll try to speak up, but I get tongue-tied when he's mad."

"And what is this family going to do about finances? Should I stay out of college for a year or two and work, so I can pay my own way? I feel guilty, being financially dependent on you and Dad."

"Don't even think about that. There's money for your bachelor's degree. We started saving for your college education before you were born. That's part of your birthright."

"But you've spent so much money on healing the past few years and Dad needs to get therapy, too. Maybe his therapy is more important than my college."

"Never, Ben! We are not broke! We had a windfall of more than twenty thousand dollars this past month from unexpected sources. Mom sent us $10,000 from Dad's estate and AAL disability insurance paid us $10,600. We had given up on collecting disability insurance, so both of those incomes were like pennies from heaven."

"Are you sure? Why didn't Dad tell me that when I asked about finances?"

"You'd have to ask him why he didn't share that news with you."

Ben's sage advice to set boundaries replayed in my mind and it was hours before I fell asleep. Friday morning at the clinic, both Jonathan and Brian sensed how much more tension and pain I had in my body. Each offered to work on me an extra half-hour. Shortly into the session, Jonathan stopped working and his beady dark eyes drilled through my façade.

"What has happened to you in the past six weeks? When you left here in June, I thought your muscle spasms were gone. You were relaxed."

"Things are pretty dismal right now. Andy is so full of rage; he can't hold it in. He cussed me out because I was late getting back from a counseling appointment. He's been cruel, not just to me but Ben, too. When Ben or I tried to drive coming here, Andy bitched so much we gave up and let him drive. Last night Ben said these conflicts weren't going to stop until I confronted Andy. I wish I could, but I'm scared, and that doesn't make any sense. I'm fifty-five years old. And Andy hasn't hit me for a long time."

"It makes sense to be afraid when a man rages out of control, even if he never hits you." Jonathan paused. "Your energy is not that of a fifty-five-year old, Joyce. It's much, much, much younger. You are alive and vibrant and aware. You really are much, much younger."

After the treatment I fell into a deep sleep, only to be awakened by the receptionist knocking on the door to tell me that my husband and son were waiting for me. Quickly I dressed and stumbled into the waiting room where Andy announced he was going to the hot tub before his massage at eleven.

Ben was waiting for me in the car. We drove to the old walled area of Sedona and strolled the shops until it was time to return to the clinic for my treatment with Brian.

After my final session, I begged to stop at the Chapel on the Rocks, a structure designed by Frank Lloyd Wright's daughter. The setting was majestic, and I wanted to light a candle and ask for guidance. Fortunately, Andy was in the gift shop, so he didn't witness that ritual. He would fail to see the non-Lutheran practice as having integrity.

Driving to Las Vegas the next morning, we stopped at Hoover Dam to see it and take photos. Andy scowled. "All the damn fools running around the parking lot, it's dangerous."

Ben and I got out of the car and walked toward the railing where we could look down on the gigantic dam and the sprawling lake below.

Andy shouted, "Ben, get your ass back here; it's a long way down if you fall."

Ben looked at me. "This is the conflict I'm talking about, Mom. It's not going to stop until you confront him."

Silently, I walked back to the car. What could I say to my son? What should I say to my husband? Resolution seemed improbable; harmony impossible.

Andy slept fitfully at Sam's place. Although Sam sleeps on a futon on the floor, he had purchased an inflatable bed for us. I found it adequate; Andy didn't. Saturday morning Sam took us to Mount Charleston where we hiked to a small but majestic waterfall. Sitting at the base of the falls and listening to the gentle splash soothed my angst. Afterward, we ate at a lodge with a small oom-pah band. Andy is capable of a great polka, but he refused to step onto the dance floor. Instead, Sam and I did the chicken dance.

We made it through another night at Sam's before we were scheduled to go to Harrah's for the sewing machine conference. Sunday morning Andy started to drill Sam about where we could attend church.

I decided it was time to take Ben's advice. "Sam said he didn't know of any Lutheran church nearby. We have to leave midday to get settled into the hotel, so let's skip church today."

"No church any day if you have your way." Andy stormed outside to smoke.

Ben stayed with Sam the five days Andy and I were attending New Home Sewing Machine meetings. Even when we had a break from workshops, I couldn't force myself to follow Ben's advice to confront. Every morning I crawled out of bed, I felt sicker than the previous day.

Driving 1-70 across Utah to Grand Junction on Friday, I drank a lot of soda to avoid throwing up. It was clear that spending so many days with my husband was not good for my health.

Andy got us up at four-thirty in the morning, so we'd make it to Colby in time for church. Even though I'd successfully skirted going to church in Vegas a week earlier, I didn't have the gumption to protest leaving Colorado at o-dark-thirty. After church, we met the coffee clan for lunch at the Deep Rock Café, a good ol' meatloaf, mashed potatoes and corn buffet. In the afternoon we sweltered in the backyard of former teachers who were celebrating their fiftieth wedding anniversary.

I wanted to puke.

I was barely moving by the time we arrived at the home of a church friend at 6:00 p.m. for a barbeque. I volunteered to make posters for an upcoming fundraiser, expecting to slip quietly into a corner. Although I moved to another room, I heard Lula's booming voice.

"Every one of you should write your family history and give it to your kids, like I did. We owe it to our ancestors to inform our children. All you have to do is start with your first memory as a child and tell it all."

She knew I'd been dealing with incest for years. I wanted to puke. Maybe I should just ask her, are you rude or just plain stupid? Instead, I reminded myself I had no control over what she said, only my reaction.

The next day I stayed home with flulike symptoms and tackled decluttering the house. Dutifully, I phoned the florist and wired flowers to Mother, who would turn eighty-four on August 14, 1995. I didn't feel anger toward her, but I couldn't bear to listen to small talk about her lawn and kittens.

I accomplished little between naps and soaking in the hot tub. Moving aggravated my nausea. Late afternoon I put a roast in the oven and sorted some mail. After Andy closed the store, he devoured supper so he could get to the Church Elders' meeting. Andy paused at the door to say I should read an article in *Forbes*— about trust-fund kids.

What did that mean? Yes, we provided some funds for college, but not the entire cost. Sam earned college funds working harder than any hired hand on the farm. Ben flipped burgers and fried chicken during his high school days. College wasn't a free ride for either one.

After Andy left, I ignored his request to read *Forbes* and began to journal events of the past week, searching for when everything went sour in my stomach and life. I was capturing my therapist's words via my pen. Sophia told me I must focus on myself—that focusing on Andy would never solve my problems. It was painful to record the rapid spiral of my physical demise.

> **Think of confrontation as turning to face, rather than combat.**

I phoned Robin in Colorado and blubbered. Robin urged me to be gentle with myself. "Listen to how judgmental you are. You said you are crying for no reason, and I don't believe that. There is always a reason."

"Oh, I guess self-reproach is so natural, I don't even recognize it as judgmental. I feel guilty for not cleaning this messy house. All I want to do is go from sofa to hot tub. I feel so inept dealing with my husband's outbursts." I shared that Ben recently urged me to confront Andy. "Ben's right, but I can't speak up because I don't think fast enough. Even though I've studied *Living with the Passive-Aggressive Man* like a text, I freeze instead of doing what it says. I can't even pinpoint the assumptions under Andy's complaints."

Robin reminded me to think of confrontation as turning to face, rather than combat.

After Robin's phone call I walked to the Westside Park where I sat on the merry-go-round, closed my eyes and thought back to days when I came here with my toddlers. The momentary warm rush of those sweet memories disappeared when I opened my eyes and scanned the empty playground. Outside and inside, emptiness was pervasive. I pressed my hand against my chest to quell the surging pain in my heart. I heard a phantom quietly whisper: *Time for goodbyes—this era is over.*

Walking back to the house I shed a few tears, but a nagging feeling that I needed to be tough made me shut them down. I pulled sheet music out of the piano bench. For more than an hour I played—sometimes softly, sometimes pounding the keys—and prayed for a way to stop hurting. Andy came home while I was at the piano.

"Where the hell were you? When I came home at noon, you had disappeared."

"I didn't know you were coming home. I'd walked to the Westside Park." I closed the piano and went to the kitchen, rattling pans and dishes to drown out conversation.

A couple days later I was at the store preparing for a sewing machine class while Andy and the quilt teacher were buying quilt fabrics from the Hoffman of California sales rep. Walking past the trio, my eyes fell on a stunning print. I commented on the brilliant colors and told the rep that I'd always thought his company did the best dye job in the industry.

Andy stepped out of the quilt corner and said, "Meet me in the office, Joyce."

I followed. He shoved the door shut. "When you are at the store, you need to learn to keep your goddamned mouth shut. We decided that one person had to be in charge three years ago, and it sure as hell hasn't been you." He walked out.

My breath came in spurts. I slipped into the office chair and spun it around, mirroring the spin in my gut. After a few minutes I excused myself to the clerk working the sales floor and left for the house. After a soak in the hot tub, I wrote in my journal. My thoughts were jumbled, and my writing was hardly legible. I mixed up yeast dough for sweet rolls and kneaded out my frustration.

It became clear to me that my work at Joyce's Fabric was finished.

Before we retired, Andy reminded me to be at the store early the next day for a staff meeting. I complied. At the staff meeting, he introduced a strategic plan and detailed new titles and responsibilities for each clerk. He announced he had signed with a public relations company to handle all advertising.

I listened. Since day one, for 23 years, I had planned promotions, written copy and narrated radio and TV ads. Andy gave me only one assignment: Develop class outlines. He had to know that I already had teaching guides for each model of machine, as well as each sewing class. In that meeting it became clear to me that my work at Joyce's Fabric was finished. I consciously breathed deep and slow, inhaling the reality that I was no longer a significant part of the business I'd built.

Andy offered a perk to the employees. He would take them to Denver for a Zig Ziglar Success Seminar. He suggested they would probably need to close the store. I broke my silence and volunteered to keep the store open those two days. Later, we prepared school machines for Colorado accounts, so I could deliver them the next morning, on my way to Colorado Springs.

Andy thanked me at dinner that evening for offering to work so he could take the staff to Denver. Then he asked if I planned to spend most of my time here or in Colorado.

"I'm not ready to answer that question yet. Judging from the pain I've had this week; I may need time away to recover."

"What are you ready for, Joyce? What do you want for yourself, and what do you want for me?" The furrows on Andy's brow deepened, his countenance as gray as his hair.

"I'm ready to teach part-time."

"And what am I supposed to do, sit and wait?" he asked.

"On the drive back from Vegas, you said you didn't want to leave Colby or sell the store for at least three years. Our future should become apparent during the next three years."

"But I need to know if I'm supposed to change careers," he said.

"Don't push me to make decisions about your career, Andy."

The doorbell ended that discussion, Neighbors stopped on their walk to invite us for pie and coffee in about an hour.

I smiled at the neighbors. "Pie sounds good. We'll be there."

As the door closed behind our friends, Andy grabbed papers from the sofa. "I was going to take care of this first thing when we got back from Vegas, but I haven't had time." He adjourned to the basement to watch television. So much for the vow to sort mail.

We do not heal the past by dwelling there.
—MARIANNE WILLIAMSON

19

Why Am I?

*Give me clarity so I will be aware
of clues for my future.*

I stacked bills, junk mail, and personal letters before we went to the neighbors for pie. In the morning, I left home early so I could stop in Bethune and Burlington to deliver school sewing machines. Driving west, the midday sun sparkled on grain bins—the success pillars of dirt farmers, while cattle grazed on the short grass and I sang oldies along with the radio. Upon arriving in the Springs, I closed my eyes and breathed gratitude that I could look forward to a week alone. The next two days I journaled, drank nutritional shakes, and napped.

Though I dreaded having a root canal, I arrived at the dentist early the next morning and reminded his assistant that I might need to take a break to avoid a panic attack. Ignoring my request, they inserted a contraption to hold my mouth open, then ignored my gasps, and worked as if I were a cadaver.

Though I left the dentist trembling, I managed to drive to a café to meet Adele for lunch. She suggested a walk around the block to calm me. Walking, I shared with Adele how sick I felt when we arrived in Colby after our trip to Sedona and Las Vegas.

After we ordered lunch, I said, "On a happier note, I've been talking with my therapist about returning to work soon, maybe teaching classes for the Viking dealer here, and maybe some in Colby. Andy has reorganized the store, even asked the clerks to teach …." My friend's visible shudder stopped me, "Why? What does that look mean?"

Why are you holding on to this marriage?

Adele picked up a crouton. "I don't want to put any pictures into your head."

"This is so hard for me to see. You can be more objective. Be honest with me," I said.

Adele stabbed her lettuce. "Why are you holding on to this marriage? Every time you are with Andy, you come back with your energy drained, then you spend your time here recovering so you can go back again."

"That sounds like such a simple observation. I'd never thought of my energy cycling that way."

"The more I am with you, the more amazed I am that the universe is so gentle with you, allowing you so much time to make this decision." Adele stirred her salad.

"Whew! That's more honesty than I expected. Thanks."

"Life gives you little clues to nudge you along, and when you miss them, the clues get bigger. I wouldn't want something catastrophic to happen to my friend." She lowered her gaze.

"Andy has been pressing me to give him answers about the future, and I'm the one stalling. Many times, Andy has said I was just keeping him around until I was well. I hate to admit it but being alone would be less stressful."

"Perhaps I've been too outspoken today, but I feel a sense of urgency, like some decision is imminent. Do you have your ducks in a row, financially?" Adele poked at her Caesar salad.

"That's what frightens me the most. Andy has said so many times that I can't manage money. I'm afraid it may be true."

"Do you think you could put your hands on documents that would give an accurate summary of assets?" Adele lowered her voice.

"No, I'd be at Andy's mercy. He manipulates figures so much I get confused. I know what land we own, but I don't see the official farm papers to know the profit margin."

"Maybe the urgency is that you need to be finding that information, so you would know what to expect," Adele said.

I pushed aside my half-eaten salad. "Talking about finances sounds so drastic. I know I wouldn't be destitute if we split, but I'd have to find work." Adele didn't pick up the conversation when I paused and, in an instant, I realized this was a strange conversation. "It's unusual for me to feel at ease talking about ending my marriage. Truth is, I am calm."

Though I wanted to continue our discussion, I needed to be on my way to an appointment with my counselor. Summarizing the lunch conversation to my therapist led into a review of previous trips home that confirmed the cycle of healing and illness that Adele had observed. My therapist stopped suddenly and asked, "Tell me what you are feeling in your body right now."

> **I really don't feel anything.**

With my eyes closed I scanned my body the way massage therapists had taught me to do: my eyes didn't hurt; there were no tears; no chest tightness; no clenched fingers; no knots in the gut; and no curled toes. "Strange. I don't know if I'm numb or detached, but I really don't feel anything."

"Would you still feel that way if Andy walked through the door right now?" Sophia asked.

"Probably not," I confessed.

"Then it's not a good idea to rush into decisions. In the past, your body has led you; you can trust it now. Notice where you are and how your body changes. In this game of life, all you really need to do is this." With her arm on my shoulder, Sophia took a step. "Just put one foot forward, and when it's firmly planted, lift up the other foot and step it forward."

Somehow, I always came out of therapy feeling better about myself and more confident I could make it through the day. Back at my place, I sipped peppermint tea and began to write in my journal. After three pages, I took a break and put in the Enya tape "How

Can I Keep from Singing" and sang along. Panning the room, I realized it hadn't been dusted for weeks. Still, I didn't have the gumption for housework.

Instead I slid into the cherry red chair, still vibrant after thirty years. The overstuffed Master Craft swivel rocker with a lifetime guarantee had cradled me while rocking my babies—sons who had now celebrated nineteen and twenty-seven birthdays.

It seemed as if the energy of my Guardian Angel Elizabeth drew near. I acknowledged that she had earlier sent thoughts to calm me.

"Please," I asked of my angel, "give me clarity so I will be aware of clues for my future; I don't want to wait for an emergency to give me direction. I don't even want to wait for anger to emerge. Tell me what to say; show me what to do. I'm afraid if I give up on my marriage, I may later regret that choice."

> **I need some answers and I need them now.**

My gaze paused on the Footsteps poster beside the mantel. I reread the last line: "that was when I carried you."

I closed my eyes. "Dear God … You'll have to carry me the next step in my unhappy marriage. I don't know what to do next."

The phone startled me. Although I was tempted to ignore it, that wasn't my style. Rushing from my chair to the breakfast counter, I cleared my throat and answered.

"A penny for your thoughts." The cheerful lilt in Andy's tone shocked me.

An incomplete truth felt safe. "Uhh, I was listening to an Enya tape and ... kinda lost in space."

"I was hoping you'd do some talking. Now don't hang up the damn phone. I need some answers and I need them now."

"I've said many times, don't rush me into making decisions."

"I'm lonely, Joyce, and I'm beginning to get depressed again. I need to know what you want me to do."

"I've told you repeatedly, I will never tell you where to live." I looked at the Footsteps poster and thought: *Dear God, did You have to answer so quickly?*

"If you are going to be there and I'm going to be with you, we need to consider career changes. We can't go on draining our investments."

I thought, yes, let's bring the discussion back to dollars. I said, "I hear that you want answers, soon."

"I deserve some answers. What do you want, Joyce? I don't think you are being honest with yourself or with me. What makes you want to be in Colorado? Are you running from me? Or are you running from yourself?"

If this wasn't pressure, I'd hate to see the real stuff.

"What I believe we need to talk about is—how can we get out of this unhappy marriage with the least amount of pain?" The words flew out of my mouth.

"I don't know what you mean by that crazy statement."

"Yes, Andy, you do."

"You don't know what you're talking about. You spend so much time with crazy, new-age people, you make no sense."

"I'll come home again soon, and we can talk more." I hung up the phone and returned to the cherry red rocker. I thanked my Guardian Angel Elizabeth for carrying me through the phone conversation.

Guilt welled up inside me.

The next evening Andy called again, reporting on a good day at the store. Our conversation was brief. Andy asked no questions and didn't mention last night's conversation. I reflected on the tone of Andy's voice and wondered what prompted him to be meek. Then I wondered how long his gentleness would last. Guilt welled up inside me. Why must I look for ulterior motives in Andy's behavior? The book about passive-aggressive behavior says we look for aspects in others that we deny in ourselves. Were ulterior motives lurking in my mind?

I returned to Colby for Labor Day weekend. We busied ourselves painting the living room. When we did talk, it was stressful. It was clear that Andy thought that working together in our home would change my mind. When I was adamant that I was ready to divorce, he demanded that I be prepared to tell our boys, our friends, and his family that divorce was my choice, not his.

As promised, I covered the store while Andy and the staff attended a Zig Ziglar seminar in Denver. At a staff meeting after their return, Andy dallied over coffee and cinnamon rolls reviewing tedious seminar details of direct marketing. Then he stared at me so intently I had to remind myself to keep breathing and not crumble.

"In summary, a merchant should send out three newsletters, spaced two weeks apart. The second and third letters would only go to the non-respondents of the first letter." Andy cleared his throat. "The greeting on the third letter should be: Can This Marriage Be Saved?"

I sat motionless during the staff meeting and my gut remained soft. When Andy and the clerks returned from lunch, I said, "I'm going to talk to Pastor Schmidt. Would you like me to deposit these checks in the bank on my way?"

Andy threw the deposit across the desk. "Let them rot. Everything else is going to hell."

I walked out of the office empty-handed.

The pastor's smile was welcoming. He reported that there was a lot of love and hurt coming from Andy last Friday. It was news to me that Andy had been here first. Then the minister asked if I was cutting myself off from all my past because of my abuse. I assured him that was not the case, but rather as I developed a stronger sense of self and found a new normal for myself, our lives were going in different directions. Pastor said Andy was worried about my finances, but he wasn't.

When I rose to leave, Pastor spoke. "As an individual, I can't hide my feelings, Joyce. I am genuinely hurt at the thought of losing you as a coworker. You have been a strong influence in the leadership of our town. Andy Meier isn't the only person who will be hurt by your absence."

Hurt was a triggering word for me. I hesitated. How much did I dare say? I dropped back into the leather armchair and began. "My life hasn't been as easy as it appears."

Briefly, I described to the pastor my conversation with his predecessor, nine years earlier. He had no idea that I'd confided in the former minister my frustration—that I felt like nothing I ever did was good enough for Andy. I didn't make enough money, didn't listen to his wisdom, spent too much time at the store, had too many friends and didn't give him his dues. In general, I didn't meet what he saw as the Bible standards of a virtuous woman. Or a good wife.

After a prayer, the pastor said, "I must admit, I never suspected you were unhappy. This gives me more insight. My prayer has been and will continue to be for reconciliation. But be assured that I will also pray for God to guide you in your future."

I left the church feeling calm, reassured that our minister did not find it necessary to belittle or reproach me. Fast-forward to a few weeks later when I asked him for a letter to include with my résumé. I expected only a character reference and was surprised when I read his last comment: *Joyce looks around for the issue that isn't being addressed, develops a plan to meet that need, and then turns the program over to someone else.*

I've asked Andy to dissolve our marriage.

At home that evening, I served supper and then baked brownies. Andy had invited the Bauers down at nine for dessert, so we could tell them the news together. This time Andy offered to take the lead, so I held back as we stuffed our faces with walnut-laden bars.

Soon after ten, Kent yawned and said, "It's getting late; we need to be going home."

"Well, could we talk for a few minutes about some kinda serious stuff?" Andy asked.

Then he paused and motioned for me to carry on. Silence followed as the Bauers stared first at Andy and then at me. I couldn't believe that Andy really thought that his statement was taking the lead.

Finally, I spoke. "We wanted you to know, to hear from us and not on the street. I don't suppose this comes as a great surprise. I've asked Andy to dissolve our marriage. Our lives are going in different directions. I think this is best for both of us."

Kent's neck turned beet-red—the color crept up through his beard until it reached his grey hair. Froglike, his throat bulged in and out. He was barely breathing … short snorts broke the silence. He stared at me, then swiveled his chair to face the fireplace. He stood, looked around as if he'd never seen the room before and bolted out the back door. Andy followed.

Rita spoke first. "Are you going to be okay?"

"I don't fear for my physical safety."

"Good. There have been times when I worried about that. What about Andy?"

"He hasn't threatened suicide like when we were first married. I think he'll be all right. You and Kent know more about my life with Andy than anybody else. And you know that I'd never consider suicide."

"It doesn't seem like either you or Andy have had much of a life the past few years. Maybe you can both get on with your life now and find happiness."

Andy and Kent came back in the house.

"You know, it's hard. We are friends of both of you. But now, it can't go on that way. Because of geography, we'll be here for Andy. We won't be there for you in the same way, Joyce. That's the sad reality." Kent's words hung heavy between us.

"Sadly, I get it, Kent. Yet without malice." Tears welled up in my eyes.

"That's just the way it's falling," Kent sighed.

Rita added, "And Andy, I want you to know that there is no judgment coming from us that you will be a divorced man. I don't think the community will be judgmental either."

Kent said, "Over the past thirty years, we've shared a lot of shit. We won't be sharing shit anymore."

Rita hugged me. Her cheek brushed mine; our tears merged.

I pictured her at the Goodland Airport in 1971 when they were leaving to teach for the Department of Defense (DOD) in Nuremberg, Germany. We were both sobbing. I knew she didn't want to leave US soil. At that time, I whispered, *"Go Rita, just go and don't look back."*

Now it was my turn … to go and not look back.

Kent embraced me, his body still trembling. In silence, he turned, and they left.

I closed the door behind my dearest friends. A part of me wanted to run after them, but I'd agreed that Colby folks were Andy's support system, not mine.

I couldn't sleep yet. "I'm going to the hot tub for a while. Want to join me?"

In the hot tub, Andy offered financial advice, tips on house-buying and trivia, while I was thinking that our dearest Colby friends now knew of our impending divorce. And now I just wanted to return to Colorado and *my* support system. During the wee hours, I got up and wrote a note to Rita and Kent, thanking them for their friendship and love over the years, and especially for their kindness last night in a situation prone to enmity.

There were two other individuals in Colby I would tell without asking Andy's permission: Dr. Ted Fischer and my friend Neva. There were no appointments available at the clinic, so Ted told me to come in after hours. Between store customers, I gathered up personal teaching supplies and demo materials that I would need in Colorado.

You are not going to rot in Hell.

My doctor beamed. "Congratulations. I told you long ago you needed to do something for yourself and now you have. You look great."

"Yes, I finally have enough self-respect to know it's okay."

"As long as I've known you, you haven't had any self-worth. And, I don't care what anybody says, fibromyalgia, cystitis, back pain, numb limbs—all the illnesses we've been dealing with for twenty years—are exacerbated by the stuff you've been putting up with."

"It was difficult telling my mother-in-law last weekend."

"Is that your job? Come on, I thought you were giving up taking responsibility for everyone else." Ted frowned.

"Guess I slipped into the old pattern."

"That's okay. You'll get there. And I can assure you that you are going to be happier, and better off emotionally, spiritually, and especially physically because you are taking care of yourself. And you are not going to rot in Hell. The only guy who was perfect told us we couldn't be perfect. So, we admit that we're not perfect and go on with our lives. You are gonna be fine."

"Thanks for your time and care, Ted. I wouldn't feel right leaving Colby without telling you how much I've appreciated your help through the years. You believed in me when everyone else thought I was a hypochondriac with my strange afflictions. And when I lost myself trying so hard to please others, you said what no one else would say … that when I was sick and tired of being sick and tired, I'd do something about it."

Ted chuckled. "I remember that!"

"This is goodbye then, Ted. I'll always remember you and be grateful for your help."

I left the clinic to join Neva for coffee. With her usual sensitivity, she said, "You look like you've just been sneaking strawberry jam from the pantry."

"I've just told Ted that I asked Andy for a divorce. He was pleased to hear it. But I expect that a lot of people here, especially church friends, are going to see Andy as a saint and me as a really bad person."

Neva shook her head with gusto. "Oh, but I know better. I've watched Andy Meier for years. I'm convinced you've never had a marriage in the way that God intended it."

"Really? Why have I never heard this before?"

"Because it wasn't appropriate to tell you before. Now that you've taken this step, I want you to know … I fully support you. Andy never treated you with the respect you deserved."

> **Think for yourself and let others
> have the privilege of doing so too.**
> —VOLTAIRE

20

A Beginning

I will sign these when I have clear ownership of the stocks and bonds that balance these assets.

The next morning, I drove to the Springs for an afternoon therapy appointment. Sophia Fair's eyes softened; she took in a long slow breath. "I hope you are recording all that took place the past few days. You'll want to go back and read those affirmations." Sophia paused. "There are bound to be times you will grieve and feel the loss. Retrieving kind words from friends will be important."

"Yes, it's written down. I journaled a lot because I was surprised at what folks said."

"It makes sense that others are affirming your actions because you aren't seeking their advice. You are very clear about your decision to divorce."

"Is there something weird about me? I am in the midst of what is considered chaos—a major stressor—yet I feel calmer, lighter, taller … at ease."

Sophia looked at me so intently that I began to squirm. A grin started at her twinkling eyes, lifted her cheeks and crept up to her curly hairline. "Joyce, do you know what a great story you have to tell other women in their mid-fifties who are in unhappy, unhealthy relationships?"

I scrunched my forehead in disbelief. "You think they'd want to hear about my life?"

"Certainly!" When my hour was up, she walked me to the door and gave me a lingering farewell hug. I've never known anyone else whose hug felt so genuinely nurturing, I call it a Sophia Signature Hug. Not a quick squeeze, but a firm embrace that settles in and holds on long enough to dissolve tension.

The following day, Rita phoned me from Colby.

"After some time to digest the news, I have two suggestions. If this is the course of action you want, I highly recommend that you: One, do it as soon as possible; and Two, get your own attorney." Rita paused.

Joyce, are you still going ahead with this?

"We've been through a lot with you, Joyce, and I don't want this to drag out and get physical again. I know Andy Meier and I know how he operates. He's going to drag this out and make you miserable. I wouldn't rule out the possibility that he could get physical."

"Thanks, Rita, for sharing your insights. I'd have to admit that I've pushed details like that out of my mind. I'm taking your words seriously. I'll keep you informed."

More validation. I wept. Then I recorded my friend's advice in my journal.

I spent the rest of the day cleaning the apartment. Andy phoned early evening. "Joyce, are you still going ahead with this?" The lilt of his voice conveyed he expected me to crumble.

My friend's advice … get it over as soon as possible and get your own attorney … repeated in my head. I said, "Yes, Andy, I want a divorce."

"Then you need to be inquiring about rolling over capital gains from the investments you will get in the settlement. I'm close to finalizing the property division. I've documented your medical expenses at $75,000 for the past four years and subtracted that from your share."

That was more information than I could absorb at once.

"Let's talk about property when I have papers in front of me. I'm a visual person. I can't grasp figures over the phone."

Reflecting on my husband's call, I realized why—years ago—he started keeping accurate records of all my Colorado expenses. He insisted on having, in detail, all the health food store bills, gas bills, motel bills, rental and housing expenses—in addition to therapy. I knew some of those expenses weren't mine, but what could I do about that?

When I returned to Colby a few days later, I looked over the property settlement figures Andy had prepared and asked, "Wouldn't it be fair to give me credit for the $13,000 that AAL disability has already paid us for my medical expenses?"

Surprise registered in Andy's face. "I guess so."

"And is it fair for me to take all the tax hit for capital gains when you transfer stocks from your name to mine? And if I am to get the final balloon payments for the two parcels of farmland you sold on contract, that means I'd have to pay all the income taxes on that also."

"Okay! I'll refigure the whole damn thing." He threw the stack of papers on the table and left.

In just a few hours, Andy came back with a settlement that raised my portion by $40,000. I closed my eyes and thanked my Guardian Angel Elizabeth for directing my thoughts.

A few days later, Andy stunned me with another conciliatory move. He'd engaged out-of-town counsel to represent him. He admitted to me that his attorney said we had been married for more than thirty years. That, along with the fact that I'd been running Joyce's Fabric for decades and thus contributing to the family income, meant that I'd already paid half of my healing expenses. Instead of subtracting $75,000 from my share of our assets, Andy reduced the figure to $37,500. I kept to myself that the attorney Andy consulted had been on the Hays Mental Health Hospital Board with me for several years before the onset of incest memories. Again, I felt calmly assured that my angel and guides were taking care of me.

The arrival of Andy's sister and her husband from San Antonio in mid-September was a reality check for me. Andy came with them to Colorado Springs, on their way to spending a week in the mountains. Joining them for lunch, the conversation was inane and safe, far different than when Andy's mother learned of our impending divorce. My mother-in-law's response was that she'd come to love me, and she wouldn't give me up without a fight. In contrast, the Texans were anxious to get on their way when we finished our meal. Before the three left, Andy handed me an envelope with his proposed property settlement.

Our Saturday group therapy session focused on addictions. While others bemoaned giving up drugs or alcohol, I talked about letting go of working. The store would soon be totally Andy's. After the divorce, I could no longer turn to the fabric store for distraction from any unhappiness I felt. My identity as a successful storekeeper had evaporated. Truthfully, for the past three or four years, I couldn't focus on my store for solace. More recently, I learned that I needed to keep my goddamned mouth shut.

> **I had everything I needed to file for divorce.**

Back at the apartment, I studied the property settlement. It was detailed and specific. A part of me wondered how long he had been working on it. Preparing such a thorough division of property so quickly was unlikely. Then the reality hit me. I had everything I needed to file for divorce!

Andy even included a letter from the Colby Mental Health Center saying that he needed an emergency divorce. Apparently, he'd had at least one counseling session. In Kansas, there's a provision for emergency divorce. That is, you can finalize a divorce in two weeks for the mental health of one party. My therapist refused to write such a letter, saying that it would take more than two weeks to effectively end a thirty-five-year marriage.

Since Andy was vacationing in the Rockies with his sister for a few days, I had a perfect opportunity to drive to Colby and file for divorce. I phoned a Colby attorney for an appointment. Andy phoned that evening from Glenwood Springs where he was vacationing. He said he was wondering what I was up to. I talked about the weather.

Then he asked, "How am I supposed to go on living?"

I sensed his old patterns returning, but knew it was essential that I let him know I would not feel responsible if he decided to end his life. "You take it one step at a time, and you ask God to lead you. Let's talk about something practical. Is the property settlement the way you want it?"

"It's done as far as I am concerned."

After small talk about his visit to the hot springs, our conversation ended.

With Andy's assurance that the property settlement was complete, I proceeded with my plan to drive to Colby to file divorce papers.

The female lawyer I chose to represent me was stunned when I met with her. First, with the fact that I wanted to ask for a divorce. And second, how prepared I was. With Andy's property settlement and his letter from the Mental Health Center, she assured me that an emergency divorce should be no problem. I could come back tomorrow and sign official papers.

That evening I visited briefly with Neva before I began packing dishes and crystal. She invited me to spend the nights at her house when Andy returned. That was respite I appreciated. The following day I continued packing and stacking boxes in the garage until the divorce papers were finished.

Thursday, September 28, 1995, Andy was still in Colorado with his sister when I signed the papers that would make me single—in a mere fourteen days. Afterward, I drove west into the setting sun, anxious to return to Colorado so I could relax. My massage therapist had invited me to join her on a trip to the hot springs in southern Colorado. The pools where we spent a couple days were more tepid than hot and clothing optional was creepy. They were a poor substitute for where I wanted to be. Andy would never stop at Glenwood Hot Springs west of Denver for me, but he was there an entire week with his sister.

I'd been back only a few minutes when Andy called. "Where the hell have you been? I've been trying to call you for hours."

"I've spent a couple days with friends."

Silence followed … Andy's and mine.

I finally said, "I have to leave in a few minutes to introduce the Viking 9000 at a Colorado Springs dealership."

"Are you still planning to do that here in October?"

"Certainly. I have it on my calendar—October 13 through 16. I should have the demo down pat after doing it here a couple times."

Talking about sewing machines diffused the tension; I was relieved that Andy didn't find it necessary to degrade me after his initial greeting. The demo at the Colorado Springs dealership went well and shored up my confidence for returning to the work scene.

I drove to Colby, knowing that I would be a single woman when I returned to Colorado. Andy refused to go to the courthouse on October 12, 1995, for the divorce hearing. I went with my attorney to the courtroom and the judge quietly said, "Let's adjourn to my chambers. There is no reason this needs to be a public hearing."

> **I heard an inner voice say: *Don't do that.***

Only the judge, a court reporter, and my attorney were with me when the judge granted our divorce. Back at the attorney's office, my lawyer phoned Andy to join us in order to complete the paperwork for division of property. When Andy arrived, she handed me a pen and said that my signature on the quit claim deeds would transfer ownership of our properties to Andy.

With pen in hand, I heard an inner voice say: *Don't do that.*

Pen suspended midair, I silently asked of my guardian angel: *"Why not?"*

When I heard nothing, I began to stutter. "I, uhh, I don't know if I can uhh … do this."

Then the voice in my head spoke clearly: *You don't have clear title to your share of the property.*

I said, "I will sign these when I have clear ownership of the stocks and bonds that balance these assets."

Andy's face flushed. He stomped out, slamming the door behind him.

"Andy told me earlier that it could take weeks, maybe months to get the stocks and bonds transferred. I'm hoping he can find a way to make that happen sooner."

When I wasn't demonstrating the new Viking 9000 at Joyce's Fabric, I was sorting and packing household items. Andy avoided being at the house when I was packing. I retreated to Neva's house at night.

When I finished introducing the new model of sewing machine on Monday, Andy again handed me an envelope. Inside were papers transferring the stocks and bonds from his name to mine. Apparently, he'd managed to transfer the documents via fax much faster than the weeks or months that he had predicted. Before I left for Colorado, I signed the quit claim deeds that settled our division of property.

I drove the 230 miles back "home" and met up with Andy and Kent. They unloaded boxes of my household goods from the farm truck into my rented storage shed, and then I bid them farewell.

Back at my Colorado condo, I pulled out my journal. It fell open to a therapy session with Nora, a psychologist I consulted before I transferred to Sophia for individual therapy. Nora had given me a writing assignment that I had ignored at the time.

1. Think about chaos theory and apply it to my situation.

2. Tell what it would mean to live creatively.

3. Tell what it would mean to evolve as a wise woman and a model for healing.

4. Describe my spiritual growth as a result of my healing crises.

I remembered her saying that spiritual evolution comes out of choices—choices made from a clear sense of purpose, values, and beliefs. That word was nostalgic for me. Many of the ads for Joyce's Fabric used the slogan: Shop Joyce's for the Best Choices. Then I thought about writings of Caroline Myss. She proposed that it's the little choices we make in our daily living that move us toward our destiny.

At that moment, it felt right to do the assignments I'd avoided. Wisdom and guidance came to me at odd places the past five years. But my place didn't feel the proper setting to write on an esoteric topic. I drove to Cheyenne Cañon and sat beside the meandering stream to write about chaos theory, creativity, and what traits I envisioned in a wise woman.

> **One cannot consent to creep
> when one feels an impulse to soar.**
> —HELEN KELLER

21

Who Am I?

*Wisdom sometimes
comes from unexpected places.*

Chaos is commonly considered a state of disorder. The five years of my life within these pages could be described as a season of disorder—*My Season of Disorder!* Physics tells us that the strange attraction in chaos always acts out of integrity; that there is order even in what appears random. Now I was willing to look at how life events coalesced to organize my chaos, so that I could more effectively move through earth school. Looking at my place on earth through a wider lens, I was ready to apply lessons I'd learned in order to contribute to the recovery and resilience of others.

Though I didn't realize it when I attacked my son in 1989, the confused woman in the murky mirror asking *who am I?* entered chaos on the way to reclaiming her authentic Self. Choices during my walk-through chaos felt frantic and sporadic, nurtured and reviled, but always directed. When guidance was shrouded by conflict, trust in something bigger than my humanity was essential to reach integration.

The wisdom of the written and spoken word convinced me that personal empowerment and discovery of authentic Self comes from dancing with the dark side. By dancing with my occluded self in a way that released repressed experiences from my past, I was able to relinquish much of the judgment and anxiety that troubled my earlier years.

The Native Shaman sees man as Healer, Magician, and Warrior; American psychology views people as healthy parent, inner child, and adult. The Shaman believes that women in our culture suppress their warrior aspects, while men suppress their healer aspects. The two concepts have similarities and both mesh with my experience. Only after years of therapy could I embrace the warrior elements in my personality.

Looking at psychology, many fail to follow the ideal model that involves dealing effectively with the critical parent to allow it to evolve into a healthy inner parent or conscience guide. Until a crisis, I had allowed others to guide my conscience and my choices. The alien is the dark, disowned part of self, the things within us that we don't want to see. I did not see my inner child and her secrets for decades. Acknowledging Little Joyce and integrating her life with mine was excruciating, costly, and rewarding. Together, we looked at life more realistically.

> **I perverted my feminine being mostly by denying it.**

Although I had to travel far in order to approach becoming a wise woman, my healing journey led me to wise souls who modeled vital traits of a mentor.

A wise woman is totally present for others; she supports them in their process.

> *She:*
>
> *Affirms without judging their position as right or wrong, without accusing them of moving too slow or too fast.*
>
> *Is available for reality checks but not for assuming guilt for anyone else's process. Presents herself in loving support, but not as an all-knowing superior.*
>
> *Reserves time for her own growth and self-nurturing, steadfastly refusing to neglect her own spiritual sustenance.*
>
> *Emerges from her process aware that she can be available for others only to the degree she has taken care of her own needs.*
>
> *Can give to others only out of her abundance, not out of her scarcity.*

I perverted my feminine being mostly by denying it. I attempted to become calculating, scientific, and methodical. In doing that, I discounted the validity of my creative intuitive nature. In the past, any value in my creative self was acknowledged only if what I created had increased profit for Joyce's Fabric Store.

With great effort, I suppressed any urge to be spontaneous and impulsive; I snuffed out the spark in life that inspired me. Like a flame deprived of enough oxygen, the spark in me flickered. The winds of guilt and the floods of grief almost snuffed out the wick at my core. Through countless hours of bodywork and therapy, the strength buried deep within my being emerged. Like melted paraffin that solidified and regained its shape in a protected environment, the soul that had melted into a shapeless mass began to take form again. Like soft paraffin, the shapes were not always sustainable and had to be molded in painfully slow increments. Eventually the shape found equilibrium and evolved into a candle that carried the healthy flame of a renewed life.

Now, when I look in the mirror, my inner child is at peace. She looks at me with trust and I look back at her with the integrity of our shared walk through the fire—the walk that united us into the one person we were always meant to be.

I am convinced that trauma can ignite a loss of Self; and that the evidence of recovery is a reclaimed Self. In the future, I will continue to use the voice of my reclaimed Self and my personal story to raise consciousness to the greater issue of gender-based violence, its impact, and the resulting personal and cultural cost.

Frequently, I returned to the scripture that had been like a mantra for me:

> *I have learned, in whatever state I am, to be content.*
> —Philippians 4:11 RSV

It is interesting to note that prior to healing from incest memories, there was another scripture that I claimed as a favorite—although I couldn't explain why until after lots of therapy.

CHAPTER TWENTY-ONE: Who Am I?

> *We rejoice in our sufferings, knowing that suffering produces endurance, and endurance produces character, and character produces hope.*
> —Romans 5:3-4 RSV

It took years of therapy to realize that by embodying a scripture that rejoices in suffering, I'd chosen to live in a victim stance. I thought the angst I experienced and the frantic pace I chose was a normal lifestyle. I was so steeped in patriarchy and fundamental religious thinking that I believed a woman was on earth to serve others; that self-sacrifice was her duty, and self-denial made her a virtuous woman.

As my healing morphed from months into years, I mused about the decades that I worked long hours and kept constantly busy to avoid introspection. Would I ever have slowed down long enough for incest memories to surface if it hadn't been for the debilitating pain in my left leg? Numbness curtailed my activities enough to let flashbacks surface. The shock from recovering those memories neutralized my drive to succeed as a merchant. It's honest to acknowledge that for five years I spent more effort on healing than working. Before flashbacks, I worked feverishly at the store and was never satisfied with the level of success I achieved. Was my striving unique? Did others follow a compulsion to reach for some elusive, inexplicable, unattainable goal?

I've come to believe that we are in earth school in order to learn our lessons and to remember our True Self. We interact with scores of individuals over a lifetime, and we never know when we are in the presence of an angel who will spur us to evolve. Sometimes it is the people we have the most difficulty with that teach us our greatest lessons. Getting our ego out of the way in order to learn the challenging lessons we encounter in relationships is an invitation for our spirit to shine and our personality to grow.

I'm grateful to Caroline Myss for the wisdom she shared with the world in *Anatomy of the Spirit*. Through her words, I've been able to see the Divine with an open heart. When I read her explanation of "a place called knowing," it felt like an explanation of the intuition I'd attributed to my Guardian Angel Elizabeth.

Even in the most tumultuous moments of crisis, I had experiences of *knowing* with clarity and certainty that was beyond my ability to explain. It just was. I believe my knowingness developed as a result of paying attention to the nudges and glimpses of insight from my intuition or my internal compass. Knowingness is something we all possess, and it can be numbed away or activated depending on how alert we are to listening.

Go back with me to the Fishy Myth I wrote early in my healing. I considered the paragraph too brief to be a real myth and the words to be meaningless babbling. At that time, it didn't occur to me that "another time he (brother) dug his fins into her and shamed her" could be opening a door to remembering incest.

Following are a few of the times when I paid attention and took action so that knowingness helped me move forward. I *knew* something was ominous in my future when I said goodbye to my beloved father on my fiftieth birthday. I *knew* I needed to continue with Rolfing over the objection of those I loved. I *knew* when I needed to change to a different therapist. I *knew* when my marriage was over. I *knew* the moment my mother left this earth, although I was 500 miles away. I *knew* in 2003 that one of my brothers was terminally ill before I was told.

Rumi, a thirteenth century wisdom teacher I revere, gave me another jewel to carry in my heart:

> *Out beyond the place of right doing and wrong doing, there is a field. I'll meet you there.*

That simple statement helped me release judgment of myself and others.

Black-and-white thinking was all I knew growing up—and well into adulthood. It was a manner of thinking full of judgment that ushered in so much self-recrimination that I felt woefully inadequate. As a result, I could not accept leadership positions. In high school when I was to be nominated for president of an organization, I responded by saying I didn't plan to join my senior year. As a merchant, when I was voted in as president-elect of the Chamber of Commerce, I announced I was resigning from the board of directors. Those actions were not premeditated, rather spontaneous behaviors that I didn't really understand until years later.

> **Are you running away, Mother, or are you running toward something new?**

Some people say our hearts must break to let love in. I don't know if that applies to intimate love. In my experience, it aptly applies to self-love. Caroline Myss wrote that one must be betrayed by one's tribe in order to find one's True Self. Her wisdom informed my healing and supported my ability to find my Self and move to a new fulfilling and peaceful normal.

Wisdom sometimes comes from unexpected places. Speaking by phone with my elder son Sam at the time of my divorce, I shared that someone had accused me of running away.

He responded by asking: *Are you running away, Mother, or are you running toward something new?* With just those few words, my son lifted me out of self-judgment.

Life isn't more real when it is easy. It isn't more sacred when we pretend. I took many big leaps and a few great falls as I walked around earth school learning my lessons. The struggles and the triumphs coalesced to make up the amalgam called My Life. Within that amalgam and directing my future is my True Self.

> **To conquer fear is the beginning of wisdom.**
> —BERTRAND RUSSELL

22

Who Are We?

Choices I made before, during and after recovering from abuse memories have hurt others.

What will I take with me into the future after I've spoken my truth? It will not be anger, bitterness, or resentment; it will not be pride in airing what some consider dirty laundry. It will be personal empowerment from giving voice to what I endured and what has been endured by countless others who remain silenced. It will be the satisfaction that voicing my experience will inspire others and serve as a beacon for their healing journey.

There may be moments when I wonder what my life would be like if my childhood had been different. Truth is, those experiences shaped my future and set me up to be strong and resilient. What thoughts will I entertain about my birth family as I move forward in my life? I carry in my heart the following portraits of my primary earth school family.

Certainly, not all memories of my first family are negative. Mother's mantra "we only remember the good" may have contributed to my repression of violence. But it has also been a consistent reminder to look for the good in each individual and every event. When a crocus pops through snow and sun shines through rain, goodness glows. I appreciate beautiful elements in simple artwork, the streak of goodness in a villain, the sweetness in a developmentally challenged individual, and the gifts within suffering.

Mother was a pedophile who silenced her victim with threats. She was guilty of perpetuating intergenerational incest, and she refused to participate in healing my abuse wounds. She was guilty of being thoroughly steeped in the beliefs of her generation—that things like sex, suicide, incest, and family squabbles were to be endured. They were private and should never be spoken aloud.

Dad was a rough-hewn man who tilled the soil, successful in his humble vocation. He endured extremes of nature, from hot summers harvesting crops to frigid winters caring for livestock. He was strong and capable as a midwife in the birthing of calves, lambs and piglets. Father was a tender man who loved words. He could recite passages of Longfellow with the elocution of an actor, although he only achieved an eighth-grade education.

> **My father was a pedophile who seduced his victims with charm and silenced them with fear.**

But my father was a pedophile who seduced his victims with charm and silenced them with fear. He was guilty of self-indulgence at the expense of the powerless. Although he endured brutality during his childhood, he failed to grow from that experience.

My father lived without compassion for his victims, and he died without acknowledging he was a sexual predator.

Choices I made before, during, and after recovering from abuse memories have hurt others. My two sons carry inner scars from my unhealed trauma, my volatile temper, and my addiction to work. When my sons were young, I had not internalized the concept of unconditional love and they grew up thinking they had to perform. Although my therapists urged me to pass the blame for my sons' wounds on to my perpetrators, I believe I bear part of the blame; I always had a choice. I could have lived at a less frantic pace and given my sons more of the attention they deserved.

In the twilight of my life, I count my blessings. I have sensed Divine protection and guidance during painful as well as joyful times. Today my reality is a past rich in experience, infused with trauma and tempered with love. Because I chose to heal incest memories rather than deny them, I am more fully alive and more truly whole than ever before. My creativity expanded into surprising genres. I embrace the philosophy that relationships in earth school are for the purpose of nudging us toward our Higher True Self. I am at peace with myself, with my relationships, and with my God.

> **Man's [woman's] mind stretched to new ideas never goes back to its original dimensions.**
> —OLIVER WENDALL HOLMES, JR.

23

Who Do I Serve?

I carry with me many stories of survivor healing and transformation that I witnessed.

Years passed; I tested my footing on unfamiliar ground. For me, empty-nest syndrome was further complicated with newfound roles of divorcee, permanent resident of Colorado rather than Kansas, unemployed, and estranged from birth family, in-laws, and old friends.

I had a brief career as a sales representative for a fabric and notions wholesaler. The owner came to train me the first week of my employment. But after two days calling on customers, he said, "You know this business; just do what you do. I'm leaving early because you don't need training."

Traveling Colorado, Kansas, Texas and New Mexico was a delight and I enjoyed the work. Driving through the Rocky Mountains to

Gunnison or Leadville, I would pinch myself to remember that this was work. Work that I knew and loved. However, I wasn't firmly grounded enough to handle the interaction with coworkers and found myself hospitalized for a three-day hold after a visit from a mid-level manager. After I outsold my direct supervisor in the spring campaign, he traveled with me for a week criticizing every move I made and every word I said. I was crushed. In hindsight, it seems strange that I managed to deal with flashbacks without being hospitalized, but a coworker's criticism landed me in the psych ward.

After that failed attempt to return to work, I busied myself decorating my home, tending my yard, and creating my Colorado sanctuary. I scattered wildflower seed in my backyard and relished in the visual feast of the black-eyed Susans, yarrow, zinnias, bachelor buttons, marigolds, and cosmos.

I meditated regularly, took Yoga classes and participated in peer-led survivor groups. It was a time for percolating new ideas and integrating my experience with present reality of who I was becoming. Eventually I discovered the concept of Post Traumatic Growth and began to apply the principles to my life. Basically, that meant accept the reality of my experience, share my story in safe places, look for the lessons learned and develop a cohesive narrative.

I continued to seek healing beyond the five years of this story by attending therapist-facilitated support groups. Important extensions of therapist groups were informal gatherings of survivors where we shared our challenges and our coping strategies that worked.

My peer-to-peer experiences were key to my role in the establishment of Finding Our Voices, a nonprofit organization that has supported sexual abuse survivors in the Pikes Peak region for more than a decade. In April of 2007, I went to a small art exhibit in conjunction with Sexual Assault Awareness Month (SAAM) at a domestic violence center in Colorado Springs. There, I recalled the progress that I experienced through the Healing Images Artfests in the mid-1990s where I exhibited some of my paintings and spoke on a survivor panel. SAAM is a national movement each April to call attention to the issue of sexual violence. I volunteered to be a part of the leadership for the local 2008 SAAM exhibit with the theme: Finding Our Voices.

In 2009, I wrote the application for nonprofit status for Finding Our Voices (FOV) and have continued to be involved in the leadership of that organization. FOV has presented annual exhibits each April since, showcasing art of survivors and their allies. Those exhibits include performance as well as visual art and serve as a means of advocacy in the community. Additionally, FOV has sponsored weekend retreats for adult female survivors with sessions led by therapists and artists.

It has been a privilege to be at the helm of FOV since 2008. My experience of working beside other survivors as a peer has been empowering and rewarding—giving meaning to my abuse experience and purpose to my retirement.

I carry with me many stories of survivor healing and transformation that I witnessed through FOV activities. Mary came to us through a chance meeting with one of our participants at a garage sale. She was detail-oriented and had organizational skills that I lacked. She helped me prepare for a weekend retreat and shared that she had made self-destructive choices in the past but that she didn't think she was a survivor of sexual assault. Like so many others, she believed that she deserved assaults because of the choices she made. After a couple years of participating in FOV activities, Mary spoke of her transformation in a video where she credited FOV with healing not only herself, but the relationship with her children, grandchildren, and siblings.

Many survivors reported that FOV was the first and only place where they felt safe and believed when they spoke of their abuse. Ellen shared how she had no idea that she could do artwork until she came to our workshops. She told how proud she felt as an exhibitor at the FOV art show and how empowering it was to tell the audience what it meant to create her piece. JoAnne told how her husband reminded her when the second Saturday of the month rolled around. He wanted her to attend the art workshops because she was easier to live with after she'd been to an FOV workshop. Sarah shared how it took months before she had the courage to attend her first workshop. Once she attended, she rarely missed for several years, because expressing her feelings through the creative process relieved her tension in ways that nothing else ever had.

Finding Our Voices (FOV) is unique in that it is a survivor initiative and does not receive support from any government agency. It is governed by a volunteer board of directors that maintains financial viability through grants and individual donations and offers activities to survivors and their allies on a donation basis. The peer-to-peer relationships that survivors and their loved ones receive in FOV are an important part of their recovery to a new normal, so that they are better equipped to function in relationships and in community.

It was a pleasure to hand off the leadership of FOV to a passionate and dedicated board. They possess skills and talents far greater than I and their leadership is certain to result in expanded services for survivors in the Pikes Peak Region and beyond.

Most rape crisis centers are available to survivors on a time-restricted basis, usually six to eight weeks. Peer-led initiatives, like FOV, have the potential to be available to survivors over a longer time period. The survivor population can benefit from peer support in the same manner as alcoholics benefit from Alcoholics Anonymous. The upsurge of peer movements to support survivors and hold offenders accountable have the potential to change the current culture of tolerance that perpetuates sexual violence. The reality has been, and continues to be, that the prevalence of sexual abuse in our culture means that there will not be enough institutional or governmental programs to serve the long-term needs of the survivor population.

> The upsurge of peer movements to support survivors and hold offenders accountable have the potential to change the current culture of tolerance that perpetuates sexual violence.

On a broader scale, it is encouraging to see survivors coming together to support each other in the MeToo movement as well as TimesUp and NoMore. The MeToo movement started in 2006 by social activist Tarana Burke and took off in 2017 with a #MeToo post by Alyssa Milano on Twitter. The Harvey Weinstein saga sparked the TimesUp Movement led by high-profile entertainers including Gwyneth Paltrow, Ashley Judd, Jennifer Laurence, Oprah, and Reese Witherspoon. Personal revelations from famous women and men emboldened millions of survivors to give voice to their violation and to seek help in healing the aftereffects. A letter signed by 400 women expresses their commitment to holding the workplace accountable. TimesUp spurred the establishment of a legal fund to benefit those who couldn't afford counsel. Thousands of women and men have used the legal fund created by these celebrities.

Actress Mariska Hargitay turned her television role in *Law & Order: SUV* into a social advocacy group that seeks to unify and normalize the conversation around domestic violence and sexual assault. Hargitay started in 2004 with the Joyful Heart Foundation and eventually broadened the scope of her advocacy into the NoMore initiative.

In addition to leading the nonprofit Finding Our Voices, I've advocated in the community with a presentation called "Aftershocks." By sharing paintings that I created while I was in crisis, audience members learned of the long-term effects of sexual assault and became aware of how they could be involved in changing societal norms.

In addition to speaking to service organizations and faith groups, I have presented at annual conferences for: Colorado Coalition Against Sexual Assault (CCASA), Survivorship, and the Wings Foundation; at the Air Force Academy (USAFA), and at Buckley Military Base in Denver.

You have an opportunity to support the work of Finding Our Voices through the purchase of this memoir. Twenty percent of the profit from book sales will support survivor programs offered by the nonprofit Finding Our Voices.

> **The most common way people give up their power
> is by thinking they don't have any.**
> —ALICE WALKER

24

How Do I Evolve?

*The goal is not to be over incest
but to be able to cope effectively with daily life.*

When I walked away from the roles that had identified me for my first fifty-five years, I had no idea what to expect in the future. All I knew for sure was—I felt compelled to work through and beyond crisis. I'd had enough therapy to know that the goal was not to be over incest, but to be able to cope effectively in daily life. Additionally, I was aware that I'd entered a phase in my life where there would be no one else to blame if I didn't emerge from this transition healthy—in body, mind, and spirit.

I turned to my primary therapist to get feedback about my process. She said:

- that my trauma was not unusual
- the extent of my search was unique

- my quest to heal was greater than anyone she had ever known
- my desperate search for healing was fueled by a desire for wholeness, not by addiction
- my story differed from others because I was willing to be candid and open
- my years helping other survivors indicate how far I've come in my recovery

The prevalence of sexual abuse in our culture is revealed in statistics: at least one in four girls and one in six boys will experience sexual violation before the age of 18. And only one in ten of those youngsters will report their violation. The next alarming statistic is that those nine who do not report it will wait twenty-plus years before they seek help. During those intervening years, many will struggle with PTSD symptoms, eating disorders, addictions, relationship issues, career and employment problems, as well as mental health challenges.

Many authors supported the bridge to my transformation. Ascending the on-ramp, I encountered Wayne Dyer, Louise Hay, Marianne Williamson, Maya Angelou, and John Bradshaw. Crossing the bridge, I was supported by Peter Levine, Bessel Van der Kolk, Caroline Myss, and Sandra Felt. As I near the off-ramp, my journey has been affirmed by the research and writings of Lynn McTaggart, Bruce Lipton, Gregg Braden, Joe Dispenza, Donna Jackson Nakasawa, Kristen Neff, and Kelly McGonigal.

It is exciting to be living at a time when science and spirituality come together in the writings of dedicated individuals who support changing paradigms with peer-reviewed, solid science. There was a time when any departure from long-held beliefs was labeled New Age and discounted as speculation at best and heresy at worst. Louise Hay's little paperback, *You Can Heal Your Life*, was severely discounted when it came out in 1984.

Lynne McTaggart's work on intention helps us understand why peer group support is beneficial. She describes the mirror effect on individuals who meet to "intend" for healing of another. The mirror effect is the phenomenon that the intenders also reap positive rewards from their altruistic intentions. McTaggart's work is not speculative. She keeps accurate records to statistically support the intention work she has initiated both internationally and in small groups.

Caroline Myss in the 1990s wrote that our biography becomes our biology. That statement resonated with my experience. Today the reality of that statement is underscored by the scientific studies of Bruce Lipton and Gregg Braden. No longer do we need to take Myss's statement by faith, there is scientific evidence behind the concept. Bruce Lipton's *The Biology of Belief* cites research that shows how positive thoughts like gratitude and compassion release hormones that keep us well and content, while stressful thoughts like fear, anger, and resentment release hormones that lead to dis-ease and discontent.

Nakasawa's *Childhood Disrupted: how your biography becomes your biology and how you can heal*, presents clear evidence of the effect of childhood trauma on long-term health and well-being. Nakasawa shows trauma survivors a clear path for releasing angst and overcoming the complex physical, mental, and relational aftereffects of negative experience. For me, this book read like a sequel to the Adverse Childhood Experience (ACE) studies that confirmed the long-lasting negative effects of childhood abuse. The ACE study in the 1990s, conducted by the Centers for Disease Control (CDC) and Kaiser Permanente, has led to many organizations and communities integrating trauma-informed practices into their programs.

In the 1990s, many of my healers urged me to write affirmations and responses to affirmations that led to underlying beliefs. Today the words of many wise individuals coalesce to underscore the critical role of positive thoughts in creating the chemicals in our bodies that keep us well. Today, solid science shows that negative thoughts contribute to dis-ease.

Brain research from Dispenza, Braden, Lipton, and The Heartmath Institute all inform our current understanding of optimum health. These studies reveal that we can interrupt our ruminating thoughts and replace them with positive thoughts that help us maintain good health during our walk through earth school. It wasn't long ago when many of us embraced the belief that our thoughts just were—that we didn't have control over them. With current neuroscience, the idea of changing our thoughts in order to change our health is becoming mainstream understanding. The science of epigenetics assures us that internal and external factors have a great deal of influence on whether we develop conditions for which we have genetic predispositions.

Even entertainers recognize the value of positive thoughts and openly share their struggles. Josh Grobin talks about the "River of Change" in his mental health struggles. He composes songs and sings in order to lift all of us who know that walk through darkness. Comedian Jim Carrey, in a graduation address at Maharishi

University in 2014, shared the importance of using the "reset button" in our minds.

The writings of many, including Gregg Braden, help us understand the long-term consequences of Darwin's 'survival of the species' concept as it relates to competition throughout our culture and our world. Braden observes that competition pervades every aspect of our culture, whereas cooperation is the basis of survival in the natural world. From Braden's books that explain the coming together of science and spirituality, we have a vision of a sustainable future based on compassion and cooperation.

When I was in crisis, the concept of self-compassion was not in the literature or even in discussion. In 2000, there were only a handful of studies on the matter of self-compassion. Today we have a proliferation of research and writing on the subject, and it is widely recognized that the absence of self-care is self-neglect. Kristin Neff gives step-by-step guidance on developing healthy self-compassion. Similarly, Kelly McGonigal interprets the Neuroscience of Change in terms that are understandable and applicable to self-care in everyday living.

The decades-long research of Joe Dispenza illustrates that common people are doing uncommon things in terms of self-healing by becoming aware of their minds. Lynne McTaggart is one of many internet leaders in movements that connect individuals from all over the world to advocate for peace and unity. These movements stand as a beacon of hope amidst the chaos of our day.

In these times of uncertainty and upheaval in our country and world, I feel privileged to have at my disposal so many writers whose vision presents a counterbalance to a fear-based culture.

As individuals, we may not be able to do everything we would like to improve the world. Each of us can, however, become informed and do something to improve the circumstances in our circle of influence. In every interaction with another human, an exchange of value takes place. By intending that our every word and action creates a positive exchange, we can be a partner in improving the world.

In my earlier life, I didn't know I had a self to reclaim. I lived my life for others and thought that was what I was supposed to do.

Reclaiming my health came through changing my paradigms regarding effective healing modalities.

Reclaiming my inherent right to nurturing relationships instead of toxic came after I gained enough self-compassion and self-respect so that I had the courage to make the necessary changes.

Reclaiming my true self came at times through tiny, incremental steps and other times through quick flashes of insight and bold moves.

Reclaiming my inner compass came slowly and powerfully as I learned to trust my instincts and my guides.

Through focused effort, each one of us can reduce the aftershocks of our trauma by embracing healing modalities that really work, by participating in nurturing rather than toxic relationships, and by navigating earth school by way of an internal compass rather than by external pressures.

**One can have no smaller or
no greater mastery than mastery of oneself.**
—LEONARDO DAVINCI

25

Final Word

Denial of your personal truth is a dive into the river of self-deceit—a place where you can drown in regret.

Thank you for walking beside me through this slice of my life. I don't know why you've chosen to take this journey with me, but I welcome you. Perhaps you are curious about the MeToo Movement and the loosening of the taboo on talking about the subject of sexual abuse. If so, I hope you've a greater understanding of the depth of the wound and the difficult challenges of recovering a sense of self.

Perhaps you or someone you love has been wounded by incest or rape. If so, I hope you see that growth can come out of adversity and that reaching out to peers can be empowering in a profound and reciprocal manner.

You witnessed that my awakening came in small increments. Yours doesn't have to evolve at such a snails' pace because there's a wealth of resources to facilitate your growth, and your healing.

Surround yourself with like-minded individuals who support your recovery process.

Nay-sayers and cultural norms try to convince survivors of sexual trauma, as well as survivors of other severe traumas, that it's best to forget it—just move on with your life. That norm of ignorance has prevented survivors from seeking peer support and learning from the trials and triumphs of our fellow survivors. In the company of others, you learn that you are not alone in this challenge to survive and thrive.

I urge survivors of childhood sexual assault to join hands and hearts and voices. Let our communities and the world know that this pervasive and preventable crime that creates massive personal pain and community costs must be exposed and stopped.

What I believe with certainty is that you and I and everyone who tastes the bitter truth of sexual trauma has within us everything we need to face and overcome adversity. It starts with self-awareness … with being present as you live and breathe each moment.

Bring your thoughts into the NOW. Do you know that you have 65,000 thoughts every day? And neuroscience research proves, you have control over the thoughts you think. The challenge is to find the stop button and reset the thoughts you think. That, my friend, is a massive amount of control. Release the matters over which you have no control and concentrate on the thoughts you can control. Thoughts lead to feelings and feelings lead to action. Yes, action.

Take action…whether it is a faltering step or a giant leap. Action builds confidence and confidence fuels greater action. As you act toward what your heart desires…what your inner compass guides you toward…you will find that life is happening through you, not to you.

Note how your body reacts to what you experience, to what you see, and to what you hear. That is your internal guidance system, and it strengthens when you pay attention to it and make appropriate choices. Science tells us that it takes repetition to establish new neural connections that support new habits. It requires conscious effort to break old habits and repeatedly take new action, and we are all capable of making conscious changes.

Denial of your personal truth is a dive into the river of self-deceit —a place where you can drown in regret. Your truth, that is your story, is important to your resilience. Keeping your truth silenced within you serves to preserve the pain. You may not need to tell the world, but you need to tell someone safe and let them support you. Speaking it makes your experience real and opens the door to growth and support.

There's much talk today about tumultuous times. Times have always been uncertain and tumultuous. Bear in mind that feelings are as contagious as the common cold. Be aware of what feelings you spread. Fear breeds more fear. Balance engenders more balance. Gratitude and appreciation and compassion enliven love within community. Finding the reset button in your mind and switching from negative to positive thoughts will change not only your feelings, but the feelings of those in your company. That simple act of embracing positive thoughts is how each one of us can heal our SELF and in turn contribute to making our world a better place.

> **What I believe with certainty is that you and I and everyone who tastes the bitter truth of sexual trauma has within us everything we need to face and overcome adversity.**
> —MAVA JOYCE

How to Work with
MavaJoyce

MavaJoyce shares her awakening and journey of recovery from more than a decade of incest, not so that people will know more about her, but so that attendees will know more about themselves. Many survivors of sexual assault believe the pain will never end—that they are losing their mind and that they have no value; to themselves … and to others. MavaJoyce will reveal her pain; her awakening and how unconnected forces came together to make her whole. She is the first to remind us: the journey to recovery is not a solo act.

MavaJoyce empowers survivors and gives hope to support others in their journeys to recovery. Attendees will not be the same after hearing and experiencing her words; her wisdom; and her "Self." Book MavaJoyce for your next conference.

Her presentations include:
Beyond Aftershocks: Resilience after Trauma
Audience will learn:
- Two essential factors to release
- One essential factor to embrace
- One critical element for happiness

Let The Games Begin: Reset your Thoughts and Reclaim your Dignity
Audience will REAP the following benefits:
- Recognize learning styles of our two brains
- Engage learning style of unconscious brain
- Activate new habits in the unconscious brain
- Protect new habits by silencing the contrarian

Freak, Speak And Tweak: Navigating Post Traumatic Growth
Audience will:
- Learn the basic components of growth after trauma
- Play firsthand with the basic steps of post traumatic growth

Reboot To Suit Your Style: Self-compassion as a Doorway to Service
Audience will explore:
- Self-esteem vs Self-compassion
- Basic components of Self-compassion
- Proclivity of compassion to grow and expand with use

To check on her availability, contact her:
MJ@MavaJoyce.com
phone: 719-660-3125 | www.MavaJoyce.com

Follow MavaJoyce on:

 Twitter.com/MavaJoyce

 Facebook.com/mavajoyce

 Pinterest.com/mava-joyce/

Recommended Reading List

Braden, Gregg. *Resilience from the Heart: the power to thrive in life's extremes.* Carlsbad, CA: Hay House, 2014.

Ibid. *The Divine Matrix: bridging time, space, miracles, and belief.* Carlsbad, CA: Hay House, 2007.

Ibid. *The God Code: the secret of our past, the promise of our future.* Carlsbad, CA: Hay House, 2004.

Bradshaw, John. *Healing the Shame That Binds You.* Deerfield Beach, FL: Health Communications, 1988.

Briles, Dr. Judith. *When God Says No: Revealing the YES When Adversity and Loss Are Present.* Mile High Press, 2019.

Brown, Brené. *Daring Greatly. How the Courage to Be Vulnerable Transforms the Way We Live, Love, Parent, and Lead.* New York: Gotham Books, 2012.

Dispenza, Joe. *Becoming Supernatural: How common people are doing the uncommon.* Carlsbad, CA: Hay House, 2017.

Ibid. *You Are the Placebo: making your mind matter.* Carlsbad, CA: Hay House, 2014.

Dugard, Jaycee. *A Stolen Life. A memoir.* New York: Simon & Shuster, 2012.

Felt, Sandra. *Beyond the Good-Girl Jail: when you dare to live from your true self.* Deerfield Beach, FL: Health Communications, 2016.

Gilbert, Elizabeth. *Big Magic: living beyond fear.* NY: Riverhead Books, 2015.

Huffington, Arianna Stasinopoulos. *Thrive: third metric to redefining success and creating a life of well-being, wisdom, and wonder.* NY: Harmony Books, 2014.

Lerner, PhD, Harriett. *Dance of Anger.* NY: Harper & Row, 1985.

Levine, Peter. *Healing Trauma: a pioneering program for restoring the wisdom of your body.* Boulder, CO: Sounds True, 2008.

Levine, Stephen. *Unattended Sorrow: recovering from loss and reviving the heart.* U.S.: Rodale, 2005.

Lipton, Bruce. *The Biology of Belief: unleashing the power of consciousness, matter & miracles.* Carlsbad, CA: Hay House, 2015.

Merryn, Erin. *Living for Today: From Incest and Molestation to Fearlessness and Forgiveness.* Deerfield Beach, FL: Health Communications, 2009.

McGonigal, Kelly. *The Neuroscience of Change: a compassion-based program for personal transformation.* Boulder, CO: Sounds True, 2012. (audio)

McTaggart, Lynn. *The Power of Eight: harnessing the miraculous energies of a small group to heal others, your life, and the world.* NY: Atria, 2018.

Myss, Caroline: *Anatomy of the Spirit: the seven stages of power and healing.* NY: Harmony Books, 1996.

Ibid. *Energy Anatomy: the science of personal power, spirituality, and health.* Louisville, CO: Sounds True, 1997.

Nakazawa, Donna Jackson. *How Your Biography Becomes Your Biology, and How You Can Heal.* NY: Atria, 2015.

Neff, Kristin. *Self-Compassion Step by Step: the proven power of being kind to yourself.* Boulder, CO: Sounds True, 2018. (audio)

Northrup, Christine. *Dodging Energy Vampires: an empath's guide to evading relationships that drain you and restoring your health and power.* Carlsbad, CA: Hay House, 2018.

Oates, Joyce Carol. *We Were the Mulvaneys.* NY: Penguin Putnam, 1997.

Oliver, Mary. *Upstream.* NY: Penguin Press, 2016.

Raphael, Marty. *Spiritual Vampires: the use and misuse of spiritual power.* 1996.

Robbins, Mel. *The 5 Second Rule: Transform your Life, Work and Confidence with Everyday Courage.* US: A Savio Republic Book, 2017

Peck, MD, M. Scott. *People of the Lie: the hope for healing human evil.* NY: Simon & Schuster, 1983.

Sax, Robin. *It Happens Every Day: inside the world of sex crimes* D. A. Amherst, NY, 2010.

Siegel, Daniel J. *Mindsight: The New Science of Personal Transformation.* NY: Bantam Books. 2010

Seigel, Ronald. *The Mindfulness Solution: everyday practices for everyday problems.* NY: Guilford Press, 2010.

Smart, Elizabeth. *Where There's Hope: Healing, Moving Forward and Never Giving Up.* NY: St. Martin's Press, 2018.

Smiley, Jane. *One Thousand Acres: a novel.* NY: Anchor Books, 1991.

Tolle, Eckhart. *The Power of Now.* Vancouver, BC: New World Library, 1999.

Van der Kolk, Bessel. *The Body Keeps the Score: brain, mind, and body in the healing of trauma.* NY: Viking, 2014.

Williamson, Marianne. *A Return to Love: Reflections on a Course in Miracles.* NY: HareperCollins Publishers, 1996.

Resources on the Web

After Silence
www.AfterSilence.org
Extends assistance through online support groups, message boards and chat rooms.

The Blue Bench
(formerly RAAP: Rape Awareness & Assistance Program)
www.TheBlueBench.org
Prevention and support center offering advocacy, prevention programs, individual and group therapy, case management and low to no-cost client services.

California Coalition Against Sexual Assault
www.CALCASA.org
Note: most states have a coalition like California's
The California Coalition Against Sexual Assault (CALCASA) provides leadership, vision and resources to rape crisis centers, individuals and other entities committed to ending sexual violence.

Colorado Coalition Against Sexual Assault
www.CCASA.org
CCASA provides leadership, advocacy and support to address and prevent sexual violence. Formed in 1984, it is the collective voice of rape crisis advocates across the state.

COVA Colorado Organization for Victim Assistance
www.ColoradoCrimeVictims.org
The Colorado Organization for Victim Assistance (COVA) is committed to fairness and healing for crime victims, their families and communities through leadership, education, and advocacy.

Finding Our Voices
www.FindingOurVoicesCS.org.
Located in Colorado Springs, FOV empowers survivors of sexual assault to thrive by sponsoring creative healing activities and by advocating in the community.

Institute of HeartMath
www.HeartMath.org
This institute has dedicated 28 years of scientific research into the study of the physiology of learning, resilience and performance.

1 in 6
www.1in6.org
Assistance for male survivors of unwanted or abusive sexual experiences, on-line support groups, trainings and webinars.

MeToo Movement
www.MeTooMvmt.org
Movement founded to help survivors of sexual violence, particularly young women of color from low-wealth communities, find pathways to healing.

No More
www.NoMore.org
Committed to ending domestic violence and sexual assault; offers education and community engagement, grassroots activism and fundraising, outreach and technical assistance.

Prevent Connect
www.Learn.PreventConnect.org
A national project of CalCASA, aimed to enhance sexual assault prevention and relationship violence.

Pandora's Project
www.pandys.org
Offers assistance to survivors of sexual violence and their friends and family, on-line support community, and free sexual assault lending library

RAINN: Rape and Incest National Network
www.RAINN.org
Operates the National Sexual Assault Hotline and the Department of Defense Help Line, local Sexual Assault Service Provider database, provides public education, implements sexual and violence prevention programs.

Survivors Art Foundation
www.SurvivorsArtFoundation.org
Effective expressive outlets via on-line gallery, national exhibitions, outreach programs, publications and development of employment skills.

Survivors Can Thrive

www.SurvivorsCanThrive.blogspot.com

Sexual assault and abuse survivor support, resources, meditations, self-care, comfort tips and blog.

Surviving In Numbers

www.SurvivingInNumbers.org

Survivor stories, posters, High School curriculum, campus workshops, military workshops, how not to blame survivors and more.

Stop It Now

www.StopItNow.org

Helpline: 1-888-Prevent

Education and support for adults in providing safe and healthy environments for children. Provides child sexual assault prevention tools, resource library, online help center and training.

Survivorship

www.Survivorship.org

Educational information, webinars, community outreach, training, newsletters and on-line support forum for survivors of extreme child abuse, including sadistic sexual abuse, ritualistic abuse, mind control and torture.

Surviving Spirit

www.survivingspirit.com.

Offers creative arts, a speakers' bureau, newsletter, website and brochures to help those impacted by trauma, abuse or mental health concerns.

Time's Up

www.TimesUpNow.com

Platform addressing sexual assault, harassment and inequality in the workplace; pushing for improved laws, employment agreements and corporate policies.

WINGS Foundation

www.WingsFound.org

#HealingHappensInCommunity | #TogetherWeSoar

Offers therapist-facilitated support groups, training and education, therapist referrals, onsite resource lending library, workshops and presentations for adult survivors of childhood sexual abuse in the state of Colorado.

Acknowledgments

This book would not have been birthed without the expert direction of Dr. Judith Briles, The Book Shepherd, who came to me through a series of serendipitous connections. In turn, Judith connected me with the expertise of Kelly Johnson, virtual assistant; Rebecca Finkel, graphic designer; and Michelle Renee, website designer.

Earlier in my writing career, the wise counsel of Sandra Felt, Sonja Mehaffey, Rose Johnson, Therese Martin, as well as Cara Koch and Phyllis Sperber of the Colorado Springs AAUW Writing Group encouraged me to share my recovery story. When the task of publishing seemed daunting, a broad array of friends and sister-survivors spurred me on.

I am deeply grateful for the many in my 'chosen family' (too numerous to name) who have supported me on my journey into Self and then into sharing my story. I am truly blessed to have a strong circle of support within the Finding Our Voices organization and within my adopted state of Colorado. And I am blessed by every reader who gleans some morsel of truth within these pages and uses it to strengthen and uplift her/his experience of life.

www.ingramcontent.com/pod-product-compliance
Lightning Source LLC
Chambersburg PA
CBHW071148070526
44584CB00019B/2706